VIETNAM

OSPREY
PUBLISHING

VIETNAM

A VIEW FROM THE FRONT LINES

ANDREW WIEST

First published in Great Britain in 2012 by Osprey Publishing,
Midland House, West Way, Botley, Oxford, OX2 0PH, UK
43-01 21st Street, Suite 220B, Long Island City, NY 11101, USA
E-mail: info@ospreypublishing.com

Osprey Publishing is part of the Osprey Group

Front cover: American Airborne troops in Vietnam, 1965. (© Tim Page/Corbis)

A CIP catalogue record for this book is available from the British Library

ISBN: 978 1 84908 972 2
E-pub ISBN: 978 1 78200 323 6
PDF ISBN: 978 1 78200 321 2

Index by Angela Hall
Typeset in ITC Stone Serif and ITC Machine
Originated by PDQ Media, Bungay, UK
Printed in China through Worldprint Ltd.

13 14 15 16 17 18 10 9 8 7 6 5 4 3 2 1

Osprey Publishing is supporting the Woodland Trust, the UK's leading woodland
conservation charity, by funding the dedication of trees.

www.ospreypublishing.com

CONTENTS

This work is dedicated to my mother, Wanda Stegall,
who instilled in me a love of learning and a love of life.

INTRODUCTION

World War II and the Vietnam War are perhaps the events that best define America in the twentieth century. During World War II the United States strode onto the world stage, marking the dawn of a period of world dominance not seen since the Roman Empire. One can argue, though, that it was in Vietnam that the United States came of age. The newest world power failed in a war against a tiny, third-world nation. Certainly that third-world nation had superpower backers; certainly the Americans fought with strict, self-imposed limits due in part to roiling problems on the home front. The explanations for failure, some valid and some not, are legion, but the truth remains: the United States committed itself to defending the freedom of South Vietnam, a nation that is no more. America failed in its stated military mission; the colossus had stumbled.

Vietnam and its era very nearly pulled the United States to pieces. Protests ripped at the fabric of American society, pitting generation against generation, class against class, race against race. Assassins' bullets rang out; presidents fell from power; cities burned in great blazes of societal anguish. The United States that emerged at the end was still dominant, but it had changed. Perhaps it was all part of a great national maturation process. Perhaps it signaled the beginning of the end of America's international authority and greatness. Regardless of its perceived long-term impact on America's future, the Vietnam War is without doubt a part of what it means to be an American today.

As is to be expected of such an important period in American history, a plethora of books detail the Vietnam War. Generals, politicians, historians, journalists, novelists, and filmmakers have all turned their attentions to defining the conflict. Arguments, sometimes intriguing and sometimes dangerously ill-informed, abound on the thorny questions in the intellectual briar patch of the history of the Vietnam War. Did the United States enter the war for valid reasons? Could America have won the war, or was it an unwinnable exercise from the beginning? Who was to blame for the eventual American failure – the military? The media? Protestors? The South Vietnamese? How did the war affect the United States, and why does it remain a source of political angst after so many years? The historical fight for the soul of the Vietnam War remains in doubt.

Sometimes lost in the high-stakes academic struggles for ownership of the Vietnam War are the simple and eternal stories of the soldiers and Marines who fought it. All too often in academic, journalistic, or film attempts to seize the high ground of the Vietnam narrative, the fighting men – the frightened, dirty, bloody actors in battle – are either ignored or are treated as stock characters to make a larger point. The battlefield, the sharp end of war, is where doctrine becomes reality, where orders become action, where the narrative intersects with life and death. Battle is the true story of war, and those who fight battles are the scribes of conflict. Those who have never served can understand much about war – its leaders, its driving forces, its outcomes – but anybody who has not been there will never understand combat; its true nature will always hover just beyond our collective grasp.

It is not the purpose of this study to evaluate the causes, tactics, or societal impact of the Vietnam War. Instead of contributing to the enduring historical debates that surround the conflict, this study will center on the lives of the American combat soldiers during the Vietnam War. Each soldier was a young man with his own story, torn away from the most formative time of his life to spend a year in a violent and surreal world. Truly, to understand the Vietnam War we must understand the soldiers' lives. What was it like to receive a draft notice a week after you were married? What was it like to burn leeches off of your skin after slogging through the rice paddies? What was it like to feel your body lurch as bullets struck home? What was it like learning that you would never walk again? These are the deepest questions of war.

Although their hair is graying, the members of the Vietnam generation are still here. Their presence is a historian's dream come true. They are the living history of the war. All you have to do is talk to them. Oral history, interviews with the men themselves and their families – men who often have been waiting for decades for someone to ask them about their war – is perhaps the most efficient tool for understanding the beating heart of warfare. Like any other historical implement, oral history must be used with great care. Memories dim over time and details fade. But when leavened with corroboration from other sources, including unit histories and after-action reports, oral histories can serve as an important window on the past. For many, the memories of the most important events of the Vietnam War are seared onto their minds. The moment when they first met their bellowing drill instructor. The moment they first killed someone. The moment when they opened the door to learn that their husband was dead. These indelible memories allow us to experience, at least in part, the reality of war.

Soldiers, sailors, airmen, coast guardsmen, and Marines served in and around Vietnam in a variety of essential functions, ranging from driving trucks to piloting fighter aircraft. While those positions were all vital to the United States' war effort, this study will focus on the experience of members of the US Army and Marines who served in ground combat. Even with this limitation, no collection of oral histories can pretend truly to be representative of the overall experience of the over one million Americans who served in combat slots in Vietnam in a war that lasted for eight years. Since a sample of statistically meaningful size would fill an archive, not a book, this collection will instead use a dual focus in an attempt to bring the soldiers' experience of the Vietnam War to life in a meaningful way.

Wars are prosecuted in units, ranging in size from fire teams to armies. Especially at the sharp end of war, men function and live or die in groups. The military is well aware that it is not patriotism or love of the flag that makes men risk their lives in battle; it is small unit loyalty. It is devotion to one's comrades. Men who endure the rigors of training and the crucible of war together form the closest of bonds. Soldiers struggle past their own fear and charge a bunker line not because of tactics or orders, but because the very best friend they will ever have might die if they don't. Combat is a story of brotherly bonds, whether bonds of boozy fellowship at base camp between missions or bonds born of battle. It is often difficult, however, for oral histories, as singular stories, to reflect the intricate bonds formed by a group of men in wartime. To best understand how it felt to lose a friend in battle, you have to understand the depth of the shared friendship, its genesis and its nurturing as well as its violent end.

To illustrate the powerful group dynamic of war, one group of oral histories in this study is taken from men who all served in the same unit – Charlie Company, 4th Battalion, 47th Infantry. Charlie Company was the focus of my last book, *The Boys of '67: Charlie Company's War in Vietnam*, which had as its research foundation a series of over 60 interviews with survivors of Charlie Company and their families. During the interview and writing process for *The Boys of '67*, I became about as familiar with a military unit as an outsider can be. Because of that familiarity I knew how the unit functioned, how it hung together, and how its stories intertwined. In this study a few of those stories are revisited – stories that are interlocked pieces of the puzzle of how a unit of brothers comes to be and how that unit functions in war.

But Vietnam was more than 1967, the year of Charlie Company's service. Vietnam was more than the Mekong Delta, the place of Charlie Company's service. Vietnam was geographically and chronologically complex. If the collective testimony of Charlie Company serves to illustrate the depth of the group nature of the conflict, a second series of oral histories must stand for the war's breadth. The Oral History Project of the Vietnam Center and Archive at Texas Tech University has done a wonderful historic service by first gathering and then transcribing and digitizing hundreds of oral histories with Vietnam veterans. The collection represents the raw materials of history, a vast mother lode awaiting prospectors. The second group of interviews in this study is taken from the collection of the Oral History Project, and investigates different places, different experiences, different forms of combat, and different relationships in an attempt to hint at the vastness of the experience that was the Vietnam War for Americans in combat.

When conceptualizing this project I first envisioned arranging it chronologically. But it struck me that the chapters would get endlessly repetitive – here is combat in 1965; here is combat in 1966; here is combat in 1967. Jettisoning that idea I moved toward organizing the project around the "big events" of the war – the Ia Drang Valley in 1965, Tet 1968, Hamburger Hill. But that organizational scheme seemed so tired and worn – focusing on well-known stories and mega-events. Neither format lent itself to what I wanted to accomplish – to tell the soldiers' story of Vietnam, of the war in its infinite small-unit complexity. After internal debates and external discussions, I decided to arrange the book in the manner that the soldiers themselves experienced their war. Readers will be able to follow the soldiers and their families through the conflict, from before they were drafted, through training, through their first experiences of war, through combat, through hospitals, through funerals, to today. Although the stories contained in the study vary chronologically, they are eternal stories of civilians becoming soldiers, warriors, and veterans. In this manner readers will be afforded the clearest understanding not of individual events but rather of what it meant to be a soldier in Vietnam.

Each chapter is preceded by a short introduction intended to provide necessary context for the oral histories themselves. How many people were drafted and how? What was "Search and Destroy?" Where were soldiers trained? When were the major periods of combat in Vietnam? How did the soldiers come home? Providing insights on such basic questions is necessary to frame the stories, to tack them onto the bulletin board of history. While the introductions will often by necessity address points of contention – the draft, US tactics, the poor reception of returning soldiers – they will not descend into taking sides in the roiling historical debates on these issues. The introductions will serve only as the picture frames; the pictures themselves are the point of focus.

Oral history, in its raw form, does not always make for riveting reading. Interviews are often somewhat conversational in nature, full of asides, bantering between interviewer and interviewee, long pauses, ummms and hummms, yawns, sneezes, and potty breaks. What is contained in this collection are transcripts of interviews that are edited enough to make them readable. Most questions from the interviewers are redacted, but some are incorporated into the transcript when needed to help the answer make sense. Some colloquialisms, when not central to the story, are cleaned up. The oral histories will not include ellipses to indicate omissions – or the entire manuscript would be littered with endless dots. In the end, I had to strike a balance between readability and transcript accuracy. The editing attempted to adhere as closely as possible to the original transcript, with its original meaning left intact at all costs. Readers can access the original, raw transcripts themselves to see more of the stories. Those transcripts taken from the Oral History Collection of the Vietnam Center and Archive are digitized and available online at www.vietnam.ttu.edu/oralhistory/. The oral histories taken from Charlie Company are housed at the Center for Oral History and Cultural Heritage at the University of Southern Mississippi. Transcribing and digitizing the interviews is presently underway. Researchers can access the interviews as they become available at www.usm.edu/oral-history. While listed as a single-author book, this study has been a collaborative effort. Robert Thompson, a Ph.D. student who is working on pacification efforts in the Vietnam War at the University of Southern Mississippi, has played a major research and authorship role in the project since its inception. Rob helped to identify the interviews used in the study taken from the Texas Tech collection, he handled many of the transcriptions, and he authored chapters 3, 7, and 9. Without Rob's capable across-the-board help and his willingness to write three of the chapters, this project might never have seen the light of day.

1 WHO WE WERE

It was the 1960s, an era in American history that was already destined to be tumultuous. It was the time when the massive baby boom generation came of age – a generation collectively determined to do things differently than had their World War II-era parents. It was the era of Civil Rights – with the passage of the Civil Rights Act of 1964 and the Voting Rights Act of 1965, the legislative peak of the movement had passed. But militancy, assassinations, and cities on fire in the long, hot summers were still in the offing. It was the time of the counterculture, of rock-n-roll and Woodstock and Altamont, of the Stonewall Riots, and the beginnings of the Gay Rights Movement. The discord in America was palpable, almost a living thing. The final, and perhaps the most corrosive, element of this toxic mix was the Vietnam War – a war that would have been difficult at the best of times. A war made almost unwinnable by the buffeting storms and crashing seas of its historical era.

VIETNAM

What it was to be an American during the Vietnam War era is maddeningly complex. On one hand the country seemed somehow quaint. It was a much more rural nation then – a nation that for many seemed to be epitomized by one of its most popular television shows, *The Andy Griffith Show*. The America of Barney Fife and Mayberry. But it was also the America of bad acid trips and Charles Manson. It was the era of Doris Day singing "Que Sera Sera" on her variety show, but it was also the era of Dennis Hopper and the rebelliousness of *Easy Rider*. It was in this schizophrenic era, from 1964 to 1973, that over 50 million young Americans turned 18. This largest-ever US generation, while pulled in so many directions by myriad cultural and societal forces, was quintessentially American. They were city toughs in leather jackets; they were tanned and rugged farm boys; they were California surfers; they were factory laborers. In numbers greater than ever before they looked forward to a college education. They looked forward to marriage and raising families of their own. On one hand theirs is the story of an America between acts, of an America caught in a costume change. On the other hand, their story is eternally American, a story as true to the unchanging American soul as apple pie.

As the war in Vietnam gained momentum, it was up to the nearly 4,000 local draft boards to provide the military with much of the manpower necessary to transform first President Lyndon Johnson and then President Richard Nixon's strategic notions into violent battlefield reality. While common perception sees the rice paddies and highlands of Vietnam as populated by luckless draftees, the reality is somewhat more complex. There were roughly 1,800,000 draftees in the Vietnam era, making up 33 percent of the force committed to Vietnam. The remainder of the military was comprised of nearly equal numbers of volunteers and "forced volunteers," men who enlisted under the threat of the draft, usually in hopes of getting a better military assignment.

The draft – the perceived sword of Damocles hanging over the baby boom generation – became the natural focus of controversy and national division. To many male boomers it seemed that a nameless and faceless bureaucracy was hell-bent on sending them to Vietnam. As the war lingered, the fear and paranoia grew, resulting in a well-coordinated anti-draft movement that roiled across college campuses nationwide. In reality, though, the draft was shot through with loopholes, leaving over 57 percent of the male boomers deferred or disqualified from military service. Enrollment in college, physical infirmity (which often only required a note from a friendly doctor), joining the National Guard (which boomers knew was not going to get called up for service in Vietnam), and marriage status were all well-known, and quite legal, ways to avoid being drafted. Despite the perceived voraciousness of its appetite, for the vast majority of males the Vietnam-era draft was a toothless tiger. Service in Vietnam, for draftees and volunteers alike, was very much the exception for the baby boom generation. Whereas nearly every male of military age had served in some meaningful capacity during World War II, and 70 percent of draft-age males served in the military during the Korean War, only 40 percent of draft-age males had served in the military during the Vietnam era, with only 10 percent of draft-age males seeing direct service in the Vietnam War itself. It fell to this 10 percent of the male baby boom generation to do the fighting and dying in a country half-way around the world.

The US military personnel who went to Vietnam hailed from across the nation – from the streets of Harlem to the plains of the Midwest, and from the cotton fields of the South to the urban sprawl of California. Although geographically diverse, the Vietnam era military shared some defining traits. The military was slightly more African-American and Hispanic than the population as a whole, with blacks suffering 12.5 percent of the casualties in Vietnam, being only 11 percent of the overall American population. The military in Vietnam was overwhelmingly made up of the sons of working class America – sons of factory workers, farm laborers, and sharecroppers – with over 80 percent of the soldiers having no more than a high school education. Perhaps most importantly, though, the Vietnam era soldier was young, with the most common age being 19, as opposed to the average soldier of World War II, who had been 26.

VIETNAM

The dominant story of Vietnam, then, is of young Americans just out of high school – hard-working young men with World War II veteran fathers and uncles. These were young men who were planning for their futures, planning marriages, planning careers – planning lives. This is the story of a minority within America's largest-ever generation. A minority that did not want war, a minority that desperately wanted to live – but a minority destined for war. For many, the journey from civilian life to Vietnam began with the receipt of a simple letter:

Selective Service System
ORDER TO REPORT FOR INDUCTION

The President of the United States,	Local Board No. 67
To Timothy D. Fischer	Lake County
	Rm. 115, WACO Bldg
	125 East Earle Street
	Painesville, Ohio 44077

Greeting:
You are hereby ordered for induction into the Armed Forces of the United States, and to report at Painesville Post Office Lobby on May 18, 1966 at 6:45 AM DST for forwarding to an Armed Forces Induction Station.

M. J. Nolan
(Member or Clerk of Local Board)

BARBARA HILL

Barbara Hill was born in South Dakota, but her family soon moved to California. In Canoga Park High School she met Fred Kenney, whom she married soon after graduation. Fred was drafted in the spring of 1966 just before Barbara learned that she was pregnant. Fred served in the 3rd Platoon of Charlie Company, 4th of the 47th Infantry, where he was universally known as "Cool Wig" because of his wavy hair. Fred Kenney was killed in action on July 11, 1967. Barbara remarried to Don Hill and had four more children before their divorce. Barbara worked for a First American Title Company for 22 years before retirement. She and her son Freddie do their best to honor Fred's memory.

I was born in South Dakota on the Pine Ridge reservation. When I was one we moved to Santa Monica and later up to the Valley. Freddie [Fred Kenney] lived with his family in a ranch house on 5 acres back then. His father died when he was only 34. They had eight children and lived in Chatsworth. During high school I got to know Freddie's sister, Ruthie. We just hit it off, and we started hanging out. Freddie had gone to Europe, and I was at their house when he came home. And we just like met, and that was it. It really was one of those things. Freddie and I just hit it off, so we just started hanging out from that moment. He was very good looking. He was the nicest guy. We were so young, but he was just so nice to me. He was just crazy about me. And that made me feel the same way about him. He was just so nice. I knew of him in high school, but I didn't really hang out with him. One of my friends, Bonnie Hood, she was kind of dating him. But she'd gone back to North Dakota, in the summer while he was gone. And she had a boyfriend back there. So it kind of just worked out [when] Freddie came home, and that was just it. I still remember that night, and we were inseparable after that. He came home, and he walked in. All the kids were around. It was always Ruthie, his sister, and his twin, Suzy, and a couple of his friends that he went motorcycle riding with. They were all really good friends. We all just hung out. We were young. We would drink some beer and just have fun.

Freddie was in the Checkers motorcycle club. And that's what we used to do on the weekends. They'd have a ride out in the desert, and we'd just pile in the cars and go out there the night before, party it up. And then he would ride. He was really good at it. He was very athletic. And he was just really strong. And riding those bikes out in the desert was really hard. And when I met him that's what he was doing. And we hung out at the house a lot. My mom loved him. She didn't care if I was there. I was 18. And I was working and hanging out up there. That's what I did. Freddie was not quite a year older than me.

We got married December 10 of '65. I never even knew his name was Elmer. When we got married, when they said, "Do I take Elmer?" I couldn't believe that they were saying that 'cause we didn't call him that. The only Elmer I knew back then was Elmer Fudd or something. Then Freddie worked as a carpenter for a few years, with the union. And he made pretty good money too. We got this little brand-new, one-bedroom little house kind of on stilts looking over Chatsworth Lake. And it was really nice. My sister gave us a dog, and he ruined the carpet. The guy came to fix something, and he saw that. There were no animals allowed. So we got kicked outta there. And we went to another apartment in Chatsworth. And that's when he got drafted. It wasn't a very long time. It just all happened so fast. We were all scared, and we didn't want it to happen. I know there were a lot of people that thought of ways to get out of it. But I don't recall anything like that. It just seemed like horrible timing. And we'd got this new apartment, and we were kind of like starting fresh. It was like everything was going to be perfect, and then he got the draft notice.

I lived with my mom after Freddie left for training. It was April when they got drafted. A month later, I found out I was pregnant. So, I just stayed with my mom, and I still hung out with Ruthie and everybody. Then my mom decided they were moving to Cottonwood, California, up north. So I was kind of stuck in limbo. That's when I was sleeping on Mary Lou's [Fred's sister's] couch, waiting for this baby to come. Freddie was very excited, and then when he came home on leave in December, we were all at the Kenney house. They all were having their same parties and stuff. I don't even remember how long he was home. It was a couple of weeks, and then he had to go. It was very sad. Somebody took our picture. I have it. It was December, and the baby was due in January. It was very sad. And then when he was on the boat to Vietnam, in January, our son was born. His name is Frederick, Freddie. We didn't do the Elmer thing: Frederick Anthony Kenney.

JAMES NALL

James Nall was from Fairfield, Alabama, where he wanted to grow up and be the next Willie Mays. After graduating from high school, Nall moved to Los Angeles to live with his sister and went to work for the US Post Office before being drafted in the spring of 1966. He served in the 1st Platoon of Charlie Company, 4th of the 47th Infantry, with Steve Huntsman, Carl Cortright, Ernie Hartman, and John Young. During his service in Vietnam, Nall was transferred to the 5th Battalion of the 60th Infantry and was later wounded in action. After returning from Vietnam, Nall went back to the Post Office in Los Angeles, where he worked for another 34 years.

I'm from Fairfield, Alabama, in Jefferson Country about 7 miles out of Birmingham, Alabama. I'm from a family of 12 – number seven. My dad's name was Sidney, and my mother was Mabel. My mother used to tell me that she worked cleaning up for people, maybe would get 60 cents a day to clean up. My daddy worked in a steel mill for 30 years. We lived in a three-room house, which had a front room, a middle room, and a kitchen. It had a little old bathroom on the end. We had a houseful; used every room. A lot of the boys slept in the kitchen. We had a roll-away bed. We had a little garden in the backyard; raised a little corn and beans. Fairfield was 13,000; half and half. Black people, basically they lived on the hill, and the white people lived below. We had two movie theaters in Fairfield, one for the whites and one for the blacks. 51st Street separated the whites from the blacks. Over behind some woods was a part of Fairfield, but we didn't know that it existed. It was where most of the well-to-do whites lived. We didn't know what was behind them trees.

We had separate schools. On 54th Street was a white school in kind of a zone. Black people lived around it and could look into the white elementary school, but couldn't go to it. In Fairfield we didn't have any [race] problems. I guess you could say you had your space, and you had your place. You knew what to do. We could go to downtown Fairfield to shop, but there wasn't no blacks working in downtown Fairfield. Didn't own no businesses. When I was a kid I went to school, but I picked up bottles: cokes and RC bottles. We would get a penny a bottle. In Fairfield we had corner stores owned by Italians. They lived on the hill next to their stores with the blacks. Their kids went to the white schools. There were about ten Italian stores up on the hill. If people didn't have no money, they would write up in a little book, and they would pay them later.

VIETNAM

My daddy used to drink a lot of moonshine. He didn't do his money like he should have. With 12 kids, he really probably had to take a drink. But he loved his moonshine. People had little houses and sold moonshine. Even the police department knew about these liquor houses. They used to go in 'em. Some people were on the take. They had some good cops, and some low-down, dirty cops too.

Daddy was the type of guy – mama would go down to meet him at the plant to get the money. 'Cause if daddy had any money in his pocket, he would go in them liquor houses. You know that moonshine? You get hot. You can go to sleep in there when you drink that moonshine. They'd clip you. Some lady called my mama one time and said that she had daddy's money, but she knew that he needed it with all them kids. Some people never worked. They just had them liquor houses and made money on the men coming out of the plant.

When I was a kid, on the weekend we worked. Old Mr Brown, who lived a couple of houses down, had a mule named Frank and a wagon. He used to drive that wagon through town, and the kids in the neighborhood would get on the back. And he had a field down there, and we would go and we were picking cotton, potatoes – you know, to make a little extra money. He would pay us two cents a pound for cotton. Some of them people could pick cotton. But every time they brought that croaker sack full of cotton, he would mash it down like there ain't nothin' in there. The most I ever made? I don't think I made a good three dollars picking cotton.

I graduated high school in 1962 and went to Wynona Trade School in the Birmingham area. I took cement finishing and plastering for two years. I got a certificate, and we did a lot of work in Birmingham, back when they used to plaster the inside of houses. That's hard work. I made a little bit of money, but I wound up having to get a regular job working in a cafeteria. The black people who worked there couldn't eat on the floor; we had to go back upstairs. But the white kids could eat on the floor. Like when they took a lunch break they could sit out there [with the customers]. But we couldn't sit out there and eat. We had to go back up by the locker room. It was separate. I lived at home until I was 21. Mom and I went downtown a lot. And I remember all those signs. We used to have to go back to the back of the bus. There would always be a lot of seats up front, but you couldn't sit past that sign. You couldn't move the white sign up, but white people could get on and move that sign all the way back. You might only have six rows of seats in the bus, and the rest of them is white. You can't go and sit there, even if it is empty. You can't go past a white person and sit in front of them. It was the law. When we would go to stores there would be white water fountains. You had the colored water and the white water. I never tasted any of that white water. For all them years, I obeyed. I didn't never know how white water tasted.

After I finished trade school in 1964 and I worked for the cafeteria for a year, then my sister, who was in California, said, "Why don't you leave?" So I went out to California in 1965, and I got drafted in 1966. I was in California about a month before the Watts Riots. I finally got a job in the post office in February 1966. And in May of 1966 I got drafted for the Vietnam War. But I never really gave it [being drafted] much thought. I never looked at it from that point of view; I never did think that it was a race thing. I just looked at it like, "Okay, I've been drafted for two years."

PAULINE LAURENT

Originally from southern Illinois, Pauline Laurent was working in a bank after her freshman year of college when she met Howard Querry, who she married two years later. Querry left for Vietnam in March 1968 and served in the 2nd Platoon of Alpha Company, 3rd of the 39th Infantry. Howard was killed in action in a battle on May 10, 1968 in the Mekong Delta near Saigon. Two months after learning of her husband's death, Pauline gave birth to the couple's child, Michelle. Pauline had great difficulty adjusting to life after the loss of her husband, but has now written about her experiences in Grief Denied: A Vietnam Widow's Story *and serves as a life coach to help others.*

I went to high school in Red Bud, Illinois a few miles away from where I lived. I graduated in 1963. It was after my freshman year in college that I went to Chicago. I had met a woman who invited me to go to Chicago for the summer, which was just so exciting to me because I had never really been out of southern Illinois. So she said, "Why don't you come to Chicago and live with me and my family, and you can work up there and then you can come back in the fall," which is what I did. It was so exciting. When I went to work out of high school, I was making $220 a month as this stenographer, and now in Chicago I was making $400 a month. I mean, I was on my way to the moon.

It was in Chicago that I met Howard Querry. He was very dynamic and very good-looking, kind of like Frank Sinatra. I worked at the same bank where he worked, and it was really a small bank. We were all in this great big room together. So he would look at me and smile and, you know, I would try to work and of course, you know, he got my attention. Once he started paying attention to me, I started paying attention back.

We met in the summer of '65 and started dating. But what happened was I went back to Carbondale at the end of the summer. But Howard was persistent, would not let go. He started coming down to Carbondale like once a month to see me. "What're you doing this weekend? I want to come down." I'm like, "Well, I got studying to do." Howard somehow got enrolled in St Louis University. So, he was going to St Louis University then and coming down to Carbondale to see me on weekends, and sometimes he'd take me up to St Louis, and I'd stay in the girls dorm and he'd show me St Louis. [But soon Howard left school and] moved to Carbondale where I was in school and got a job as a retail clerk in a grocery store. So here's Howard, working in a grocery store, and for him, it was like he couldn't give a damn what he did; he just wanted to be near me.

He was only in Carbondale a couple of months until he got his draft notice. And so the recruiter told Howard, "You know, if you're willing to give us an extra year, you can go to Officer Candidate School [OCS], you know, you'll have an administrative job. If you are married your wife can go with you, you know, wherever you're stationed. You won't be in a combat zone." I mean, just one thing after another. Painted a glorious picture of how we could avoid the whole Vietnam fear that was building and escalating.

So, instead of getting drafted Howard enlisted, planning to go to OCS. And it was from Carbondale that he left and went to basic training at Fort Leonard Wood, Missouri. In many ways, the military was perfect for him. He always had a really lighthearted attitude about it. You know, what he showed to me was that he never took anything too seriously. He'd always joke about everything. He was very comical and had a great sense of humor, and everything was funny. I mean, even in Vietnam, in the letters he wrote home, he would say: "I'm too skinny to get shot. They'll never shoot me, I'm just too skinny."

Later, when Howard was at OCS he called me one night and he was really, really depressed, and I said, "What is wrong?" And he said, "I got kicked out of OCS. I'm not going to finish OCS." And I said, "Why?" And he said, "They told me I wasn't forceful enough to be an infantry officer." And I said, "Well, then we can't get married. We cannot live on an enlisted man's salary, so we can't get married." And he got really depressed then. He said, "You can't do this. Please marry me." So, I went to Georgia for the weekend; he took me out for a drive to this hillside, and we got out of the car and we walked over the hillside and there was, you know, a thousand stars and a big moon and he said, "Will you marry me, even though I'm not going to finish OCS?" He said, "I want to take those stars and put those stars in your pocket" or something like that. He was very romantic. You know, he was going to put all the stars in my pocket, and of course, I fell for it. "Oh yes, I'll marry you. Absolutely."

He came home when he was in the NCO training, and we got married on a Saturday, and we had to report back within a couple of days, and I was able to go with him for a while to Fort Benning and then Fort Jackson. He'd have nightmares in the middle of the night, and he'd start wrestling with me and fighting with me and I would say, "Wake up, what's going on with you?" He was having nightmares about being in Vietnam, and he wasn't even there yet.

And so that's how I kind of intuitively figured out that this guy is more stressed out than he's telling me. It just became a bigger inferno. The closer he got to leaving, the more fearful I became. And it was like this hell that was engulfing us and there really was no way out now. It was just a walk through the fire basically and that we were going to walk through this fire together.

TERRY MCBRIDE

Terry McBride was from Greenfield, California, where he had a rural upbringing and loved boxing. Drafted in the spring of 1966, McBride served in the 3rd Platoon of Charlie Company, 4th of the 47th Infantry, alongside Fred Kenney, Larry Lukes, Elijah Taylor, Steve Hopper, Richard Rubio, Don Trcka, and Ron Vidovic. As a machine gunner, McBride was heavily involved in most of Charlie Company's major battles. After the war, Greenfield, California just didn't seem quite the same, so McBride picked up and moved to Alaska, where he worked in several "tough" jobs, including as a bouncer at a topless bar. McBride enjoys riding motorcycles and fishing, even though he has serious Vietnam-related health problems.

[I am from] Greenfield, California. My dad was on the USS *Intrepid*. In World War II in Okinawa they took three kamikazes. One of them went directly into anchor deck, because the anchor was up, and it went straight through and into the lower space. And it wreaked havoc on the main deck. That was close to the end of the war, Okinawa. I was born October 11, '46, and he died in April of '48. So, I was a year and a half old when he died. He was also a boxer. My grandpa used to box bare knuckles, and all the kids that were in the family all grew up open-hand slap boxing.

My mom moved back with my grandparents. Until I was eight years old we lived on a farm, and it had hay and cattle and pigs. At nine, we moved back into town. But I still hauled hay every summer. And we had horses. We had domestic hogs. You didn't want hogs comin' at you, I'll tell you right now, if you don't know what to do. Their eyes are on the side of their head. They don't look straight at 'ya. They have to turn to see where they're going.

You've got to stand still right in front of them and make a step at the last second. And you've got to lean forward, hit them on their nose and just knock them on their ass. At the same time, you don't really wanna be doing that with the wild ones because he might just be a little stouter than the domestic little slugger you're used to slugging.

I went to a Catholic school until I got into high school. For the first six years that I went to school, the teacher I had, every time I graduated so did she. So I had the same teacher all the way through. I could be sittin' in the back room thinking of something and I'd get in trouble for it. She knew me like a clock. I was a history buff [in high school]. I loved history. The guy that taught me history was a logger when he worked at the school. Every summer month, he logged, and he was a great big breather too. Mr Zeller was his name. I played football all four years, and I played basketball too. I hauled hay all summer too. So, I was in pretty good shape. Everybody else had to get in shape for football or basketball, and I went to school buff already.

Me and my buddies fought a lot. Most of the people we usually got into it with were migrant workers, or whatever they were. They were kind of seasonal, come in the area and kinda' try to take over. Every Halloween, we used to have a big deal at the end of the tomato season, when the tomato harvest was over. People gather up tomatoes, load up in pickups and go to the runway and pick tomato fights. And that usually ended up in a big scrap. I just didn't take a lot of shit from people. My [older] brother, I'll tell you what. I'm surprised he didn't get killed because he used to fuckin' harass me, and I would never fuckin' put a hand up to him. He scared me. He went in the military, in the Navy in '61, and took off and went to boot camp. Later he went on the maiden voyage on the *Constellation* and came back to San Diego. It was summertime, and I was sleeping in my Grandma's back porch. I heard somebody in the room, and I was trying to figure out who the hell it was. I thought it was my Uncle Walt at first. But I'd never known him to be drunk, and I thought this guy was drunk. I just kind of rolled over and went back to sleep, and he came in the back room there on the porch and grabbed me. That was the worst thing he ever did 'cause I didn't see him for like three years before that. When he left he was my older big brother, and when he came back he was my older little brother. And I jacked him up and kind of beat his ass up on a dresser and wacked him one time in the solar plexus, and he said, "Hey, you know I've been meaning to tell you it's time for me and you to become friends." So that kind of tells you where we were at.

That sounded like a perk, the military. After I started thinking about it, the war had started, I was iffy about it. I talked to one of my uncles, and he went through Okinawa, Saipan, Truk. He was badass, and I never understood why he was so shut down. He never talked. He always seemed like he was in a pissed-off mood, angry. He said it's your decision, you have to make up your own mind. He said if you don't go in on your own, they're gonna draft you. And I said then they're gonna draft me I guess. And that's what happened.

I worked for Pacific Gas and Electric, working on towers [after high school, before the draft notice]. We stayed in camps, but I went home on the weekends and shit. [The draft notice came on] May 1, and they gave me two weeks to get ready to go. And then May 16 we were there.

ANTHONY GOODRICH

Anthony Goodrich was originally from Ogden, Utah, but his family moved several times following his Air Force enlisted-man father from post to post. In May 1968, after the Tet Offensive, Goodrich enlisted in the Marines. In the summer of 1969 Goodrich joined his unit, Mike Company, 3rd Battalion, 5th Marines in the An Hoa area in I Corps in northern South Vietnam. Goodrich was involved in several major operations that year, including Operation Durham Peak. After returning from his service in Vietnam Goodrich took classes at the University of New Mexico and eventually went to graduate school and got married. But Vietnam remained a constant presence in his life.

I was born December 8, 1949 in Ogden, Utah. My father was a career Air Force enlisted man. After the Korean War we went to Greenville, South Carolina, Donaldson Air Force Base, and that's where I started school. I went through one year of Catholic school, then, did not do well with the nuns. My father, he had to come and get me quite often there because the nuns and I just didn't get along well. In 1956, my father got stationed in France. We stayed there until '59, when we came back to Biloxi, Mississippi, Keesler Air Force Base. My dad was the first sergeant of a training squadron there. In 1962, went back to Europe, back to France.

I remember one day my dad came home, and we were listening to Armed Forces Radio and the President talked about photos of missile sites in Cuba. And he gave them so much time to get out of there. I remember the blockade, they put a blockade on, and I remember my mom was scared to death. My dad was his usual stoic self, and we got to stay out of school for a couple of weeks. I mean, that was fine with me. But I remember listening to the radio quite often to see what was going on, and since we were in Europe, they thought that we would be the first ones to have to go to war, because the Russians might come across the German border. I remember my dad telling us that we had to be prepared to go to where they had shelters, because we used to have nuclear drills, you know, the duck and cover. A couple of times they took us to these places on the base that had food and water stored. We did that a couple of times; I always thought that was fun.

I knew I was going to go into the military as I was growing up. I just knew it was a matter of time. It was just something that was there; I never questioned it. Both my brothers went into the military. My older brother Sam was a pilot in the Navy, and my younger brother Kevin was an F-4 mechanic, and they went in after I came back from Vietnam. It was just something we knew was going to happen, and it was a way for me to give back to the country, and it was just that honor and duty ethic that my father had. It was just part of the family, part of growing up.

[After high school I went to the University of New Mexico.] Well, starting I guess in '67, there was some protest on campus against the war. I guess I was for or on the side of the war. I'm not exactly sure how to put it, but I started to become aware of my feelings about why are these guys against the country. I guess I believed that they were wrong to protest the war. I just didn't understand that, but I think that's mostly because I was pretty naïve about things then, but naïve in the respect that I just didn't understand why they were doing this. And my opinion said that these people aren't being the loyal Americans that they ought to be. But I think that was just my youth coming through or something. I didn't quite understand things yet.

I think my dad started getting disillusioned after the 1968 Tet Offensive. After Westmoreland got on TV and said, "The light's at the end of tunnel," my dad said, "I remember when he got up there and said, 'We can win this war in six months; we have them right where we want them,'" and then all of a sudden Tet happened. It was a big, huge surprise, and my dad said, "Is the government lying?" My dad's saying this stuff. I think that's where his disenchantment started; that he didn't think that we were being told the truth, and that right there amazed me. My dad never ever questioned anything the government did. You know that was the same year that LBJ resigned. Martin Luther King was killed that April; Bobby Kennedy was killed in June, and my mom thought the country was falling apart. Tet; I remember watching Tet and seeing the embassy in Saigon on TV being attacked, and I didn't really know what was going on. I knew there was a real war going on there, but I guess it wasn't till then that I saw scenes of what was really going on there. I joined, I guess in the first week of May is when we went down to join up.

FRANK LINSTER

Frank Linster was originally from Hardin, Montana, but his family eventually moved to Sacramento, California, where he was drafted in 1961. After serving several years as an enlisted man Linster went first to Officer Candidate School and then to flight school for training as a helicopter pilot. In 1967 and 1968 Linster flew helicopters for the 188th Assault Helicopter Company, supporting operations of American troops in the field in several different areas of the war zone in South Vietnam.

I was born in a little place, Hardin, Montana, right across the highway from Custer's last stand. When I was three, my parents moved to North Dakota from Montana. We lived on a farm until I was six and then moved to town and had a restaurant and a hotel where I spent [much of my childhood]. I went to St Mary's school system through my 11th year, and played all four sports in school. At 17 my dad decided to sell his hotel and business and move to Sacramento, California. We went out there and went to a public school for the first time. The high school had 4,300 kids in three grades. I went out for football and I found out that they had about 600 guys out there trying out for three football squads, and we must have played pretty good football in North Dakota because I ended up making the varsity my senior year as a walk-on. That's just before school started. I ended up being fourth in the city in rushing that year and one of the other guys in the backfield with me was number two in the city in rushing. Needless to say, we went 10-0. We had a pretty good season. We had a graduating class with 1,106 students. After school I went to work on the freight docks working for an outfit and teamsters. When I was 21 I got a draft notice.

ALAN RICHARDS

Alan Richards was from Mequon, Wisconsin, where he was raised as part of a family of nine. His father passed away when he was too young to remember. Drafted in the spring of 1966, Richards served in the 4th Platoon of Charlie Company, 4th of the 47th Infantry. Richards was wounded in action on June 1, 1967, and again on October 6, 1967. After the war Richards worked in management in a machine shop in Wisconsin prior to opening his own business, from which he retired in 2007. He also served as state commander for the American Legion.

I'm originally from Mequon, Wisconsin, immediately north of Milwaukee, right along the Michigan coastline. It's a small town. My father had passed way, so my mother took care of us. And she just did odds and ends, things to help ends meet. I come from a fairly large family, a family of nine. Mom would go and take care of elderly people and cook for them and maybe take care of their kids while they were gone, kind of a live-in thing for awhile. As we [the children] got old enough, we all got jobs. I probably started working around 12, cutting grass. I caddied at a golf course one year and ended up getting summer work for the greens keeper, which fit in good with my school. My older brothers and sisters would work at like the local grocery store and that type of thing. During winter if they needed help shoveling out the barn or something, my brothers and I would do that on occasion, helping with the harvest sometimes. I was a country boy.

I went to a one-room schoolroom for grade school, where it was 1st – 4th and then 5th – 8th. I think my graduating class was like five or six kids. When I graduated, they had just built the brand new high school in Mequon. And that's where I went. By that time, that area had started getting more subdivisions, people moving out of Milwaukee wanting to get out of the big city. It started being a little more influential. After high school, I did go on to a technical college for a year. Because we were poor, I was trying to work and go to school at the same time, and I just started getting so far behind that I dropped out of school. Of course, going to school at that time was your deferment from the draft. So as soon as I dropped out of school, after a year, I got drafted. I was studying electronics. Back in that time it was just radios and TVs. I worked in gas stations while I was going to school. Once I got out of school I got into factory work in a machine shop and worked there for almost a year before I got drafted, or actually went in. I started getting my notices before that. At that time, it was pretty scary because Vietnam was pretty much in swing by then. I knew the odds were probably pretty good I'd end up over in Vietnam. Some of them [my older brothers] were in wars. By then I had a nice red convertible and was dating and having fun. So, it was kind of a shock to give that up.

I went down to Fort Leonard Wood to be inducted, and I remember pulling a fire watch at night in those old wooden barracks. Those things would burn down in a couple minutes, so they would always have shifts of guys up at night walking around making sure everything was all right. I remember pulling my shift the first night

I was down there. There were guys in their racks. There were guys scared and some crying. And I'm wondering to myself, "What am I doing here?" and "How can I get out of this?" Then I remembered something one of my older brothers told me about attitude, that that's the only thing you ever really have control of. Kind of just from that point on [I] went, "Yeah, you know I'm here. I'm just gonna do the best I can while I'm here and do my thing for two years and go back home." That night walking around just kind of struck me and changed my whole attitude about it.

MIKE LETHCOE

Mike Lethcoe was born in Virginia, but his family soon moved to Houston where he survived polio at the age of eight and was abandoned by his father at the age of 14. Drafted in the spring of 1966, Lethcoe served in the 2nd Platoon of Alpha Company, 4th of the 47th Infantry. He was walking point at the outbreak of Alpha Company's major battle on June 19, 1967, and was one of the few men in the company who was not killed or wounded that day. After the war Lethcoe worked as a truck driver before becoming a commercial deep sea diver.

I was born in Abingdon, Virginia and moved to Houston [Texas] with my mother and my little sister. My father left. It was tough for me. He left when I was 14, so I knew him well. We were close. He had an alcohol problem. And he and my mother divorced, and he was gone. I haven't seen him since. My mother's sister lived there, so we moved to Houston.

We were poor. My mama was a seamstress all her life, and we weren't middle class at all. I lived on farms most of my life until I moved to Texas, into the middle of a big city. I was milking cows and feeding animals. I had polio when I was eight. I wasn't hurt too bad about it. I got it from the Salk vaccine evidently. I was down for about a year or so over it, then back up. And I couldn't play a lot of sports and stuff because it did make my legs a little weak at first. But I got over it. I was in the band. Because I was in the band, I learned how to march. Because I knew how to march I was a sergeant the whole time I was in Vietnam.

It was tough in Houston. I had done the 9th grade in Virginia where I was in the band, and I was taking Algebra, Biology, and Latin. College prep courses. But when I came to Texas, I had to do the 9th over again. In Virginia, I played sousaphone in marching season. It was just beautiful. I loved that. When I went to Houston, though, they only had a beginning band. The people couldn't do anything. I could only take general science, general math, and things like that. And I was just bored to death. And I was sort of an outcast because I was a hillbilly.

I quit school the day after I turned 15 and went to work to help my mother pay bills so my little sister could go to school. I worked as a machinist's apprentice in a machine shop for a little over three years, never missed a day, and helped my mama out. Then I went to work on a tugboat as a deckhand. While I was on the tugboat, they put a notice on the bulletin board for someone to train as their yard diver to take lines and stuff out of the wheels of the boats. And I was trained as a diver by an old Navy diver who didn't want to do it anymore.

I got married when I was working on the tugboat, when I started diving. Divers made a humongous amount of money back then. I'd had a girlfriend for about nine months or a year. So I decided we'd get married. She was 17. I was 19. Her parents didn't like me at all because I had built a motorcycle. We got along just fine until I rode up on my new chopper, and boy her mother went berserk. "You deceived us. You didn't tell us you was one of those kinds of boys." Just because I was ridin' a bike. I was mild-mannered actually, and I've always cared a lot about people and tried to do the right thing. And it just blew me away and I rode up on that bike, and she just did a 180-degree turn and hated my guts from then on. They didn't want her seeing me, and I kept seeing her anyhow. And one night I took the doornails out of her back door and took her out. We went to Mexico and got married.

Instantly regretted, but I did it. More or less because they told me I couldn't see her I think, more than anything else. That didn't last long. We were together a couple years. I was working on the boat. I'd be gone three days, and I'd be home three days. And of course the first day I got back I was sleeping because you pretty well worked all three days you were out. And she was out running around. And when I got drafted, I went to Vietnam. I wasn't out of sight before she was with somebody else. That didn't last. So we divorced while I was in Vietnam, so I just decided to stay in Vietnam.

I loved getting my draft notice. All my family had been in the military. My daddy hadn't, but all of my uncles had. I figured this was something you do. It was part of your responsibilities. And they had told me about all of these foreign places and foreign people and all that. And to me it was a grand adventure. I was at work one day, and I heard on the radio, "This month the Army is drafting married men for service in Vietnam." And I thought well, good, maybe I can get drafted, and a few months later I did. I loved it. I faced it as a big adventure, and I thought it was a good deal all the way around. Excited about the military, I really didn't know I was going to go to Vietnam. I'm mechanically inclined. I was a machinist. I figured my skills would be needed. I'd be a truck driver or mechanic or something, so I wasn't really worried about going to Vietnam.

BARBARA JOHNS

Barbara Johns was originally from Indianapolis, Indiana but grew up in Haddon Heights, New Jersey. After high school she attended Beaver College outside of Philadelphia, where she met Jack Geoghegan, who was attending nearby Pennsylvania Military College. The couple wed a week after Barbara's graduation from college. Jack had a two-year deferment before entering the military after graduation, some time of which was spent working in Africa. After attending officer training and the birth of his daughter Cammie, Jack went to Vietnam and served as a lieutenant in Charlie Company, 1st Battalion, 7th Cavalry. Jack was killed in action in the battle of the Ia Drang Valley on November 15, 1965, while tending the wounds of fellow soldier Willie Godbolt. In 1969 Barbara married John Johns, who eventually rose to the rank of brigadier general. In 1990 Barbara received word that Joseph Galloway and Hal Moore were working on a book about the Ia Drang Valley, entitled We Were Soldiers Once … And Young. *Barbara assisted with the book, and also later with the movie* We Were Soldiers.

It was in my junior year in college. Jack called me on the telephone because I had been at what was then Pennsylvania Military College two years before that. I had gone there for a mixer. And I remember meeting a couple of PMC cadets, and they remembered me. I never dated any of them, but a couple of them remembered me and told Jack Geoghegan about me and dared him to call me. I'm really amazed that anybody would remember after two years. I remember being in the phone booth and I was just shocked. He was very, very polite and very gentlemanly and apologetic for calling me out of the blue. We talked for a little while. I can't remember what we talked about, but I remember that I liked him over the phone and I thought "Gee, I'd like to get to know him better, but I don't want him to think I would just go out with anybody who would call me on the phone like that." But he said he would call again and he did. And he called and asked me to go to a dress parade at PMC on a Sunday afternoon. I thought "Well, that's harmless enough. It's in the middle of the day in daylight, I can sit there in the stands and that's it." It sounded good to me. So I accepted and he came and picked me up in his uniform. I remember noticing the big stripes on the side of his uniform and we went to PMC. He put me in the stands next to some of his friends, and I was talking with some of the girls and I remember one of them saying, "Well, there's your fella out there leading the parade." They all looked alike. The cadets are all dressed alike and marching alike, and that was when I found out that he was the brigade commander.

I remember he was very handsome and very, very gentlemanly and very, very polite and made sure that I was taken care of while he was out there on the field. He was just a very, very nice person. I liked him very, very much when I met him and wanted to continue dating him.

During my senior year he was at the University of Pennsylvania. He graduated in '63 from PMC. Then he wanted to get his master's degree in international relations, and he went to the University of Pennsylvania so he was still close by. Otherwise he would have gone right into the Army. He got a two-year deferment in order to get his master's degree. His long-range plan was hopefully someday to become an ambassador, and I think he would have been a very good one. I graduated from college in '64 and we married a week later.

When we married we had a year left on his deferment. So he wanted to use that year to help somebody else, is the way he put it. And so he started to look for opportunities to go to a third-world country, and he was researching various organizations and ultimately found the Catholic Relief Services. And we went with the Catholic Relief Services to Tanzania. I was looking upon it as a great big adventure, which it was. He was in charge of the school lunch program that fed 120,000 children a day, and after a month or so, I thought, "I'd like to find something to do myself," so I walked to the nearby elementary school, and they were very happy to see me, and they showed me a typewriter sitting there and said, "There isn't anybody here to use it. Would you be willing to be our secretary?" I was very happy to be their secretary and I also did some substitute teaching while I was there.

Jack was a very, very good person. He was always doing for other people and it just seemed to be the focus of his life, to devote his life to helping others. Even in college, when he was in PMC, when he learned one time that one of the cadets couldn't afford tuition for the next semester Jack formed a committee, and they went around throughout the night and collected enough money from the whole corps of cadets to pay this one person's tuition.

Of course that was our first – and only – year of marriage. We used to feel – when I got over my terrible homesickness which was unlike anything I had ever experienced before – when I got over that, we used to look upon it then as a great adventure that the two of us were away from family and friends that we had known all our lives, in a whole other part of the world, just the two of us. And it was a wonderful feeling to be part of this big adventure and at the same time to feel that we were doing something for someone else.

We came back from Africa knowing he had to go into the military. And that was just the beginning of Vietnam. We came back in April of '65 and then we visited with our families.

Jack was an only child, and he had a cousin who was two years older than he was, and he was more like a brother. They lived in Pelham, New York, and they were a very close family. I adored his parents. They were very, very loving and very non-judgmental and just very easy to get along with. My mother-in-law and I used to sit and talk for hours. She was just an incredible person, a wonderful person.

After visiting with our families we went to Fort Benning in May of '65. Actually, I ended up in the hospital for six weeks. By that time I was pregnant with Cammie. I had severe toxemia, and I was very, very ill. In fact I even had the last rites of the church. They kept me in the hospital because I had extremely high blood pressure, and they were waiting until Cammie was far enough along that she would survive. I was only seven and a half months pregnant when she was born. For the last month, I was in the hospital. She was only four pounds when she was born.

After she was born, I'm still in the hospital for another two weeks and then came home, and she had to stay in the hospital until she was a month old. Cammie, I used to say, was granted her independence on the Fourth of July. It was the day she came home from the hospital.

Jack was ecstatic to be a father. And even early on, she looked like him. She had his features. Jack went to the infantry officers' basic course in June of '65 and it was after that – I think it was well into July before he knew for certain that he was going to Vietnam – that he was going to be assigned to the 1st Cavalry Division.

Jack and I went back to Connecticut when we knew that he was going to Vietnam. We made a quick trip to Connecticut and also visited my parents in that time. That was very, very difficult – when we were with his parents and they were just devastated that he had to go to Vietnam. I remember my mother-in-law saying when we got back from Africa in April, she said, "I thought we would never see you again." I remember her saying that. And then only a matter of a few months later, Jack was going to Vietnam and that was just horrible for her and terrible for his father. And my mother-in-law was a very strong person, I think. She had to be strong. Jack's father enabled her to be the stronger one of the two and I'll always remember Jack's father looking out the dining room window, just shaking his head and saying, "I'll never see him again."

But Jack didn't ever think that he would die in the war. The only even slight hint was when the night he left and he said to me, "If anything happens to me – nothing's going to happen to me – but if it does, I want you to marry again. Cammie needs a father." Of course she was only two months old. He would hold her a lot and he would tell her to take care of me and take care of her grandparents and to be a good girl and to grow up and do good things and be a good person.

2 DROP AND GIVE ME 20

After receiving a draft notice or enlisting, the civilians who were about to become soldiers journeyed to the local military induction center for their physicals, where they also received rough haircuts, their new uniforms, and a few rudimentary military instructions. Most importantly the new inductees received their training assignments, which sometimes meant life or death, and were then sent to one of the many main training centers in the country, including Fort Riley, Kansas; Fort Polk, Louisiana (home of the famed "Tigerland" training area); and Fort Ord, California, while Marines trained at Parris Island, South Carolina or the Marine Corps Recruit Depot in San Diego, California. At these training sites, harried recruits met the bane of their young existences – the drill instructor.

For roughly eight weeks of basic training, the recruits – often confined to the dubious comforts of their barracks complete with pipe-frame cot and footlocker – marched, ran, negotiated obstacle and bayonet courses, were sworn at on a seemingly constant basis, and generally got into the best shape of their lives. Even though Americans somehow mustered the ability to poke fun at basic training while watching *Gomer Pyle USMC* every Friday night from 1964 to 1969 – the very height of the Vietnam War – the training was deadly serious. The regimen was often harsh, and was designed to lessen a civilian's sense of individuality and to make him into a soldier – part of a lethal killing machine. As had generations of young men before them, Vietnam-era trainees griped, fought, formed friendships, negotiated ends to their virginity at local bars, did endless rounds of pushups as punishments for gaffes, and loathed military life in general. But, as had their World War II-era fathers, like it or not, the young men of the Vietnam era left basic training as soldiers.

After the conclusion of basic, the newly minted soldiers moved on to Advanced Individual Training, or AIT, where they learned their new Military Occupational Specialty, or MOS. For most this meant working long hours training with the M14 rifle, working toward an MOS of 11 Bravo – or rifleman – the standard rifle-carrying infantryman of the Vietnam War. Other infantry specialties included machine gunner, mortarman, radiotelephone operator, and – perhaps the most specialized area of training of all – medic. Beyond individual training in their weapons specialty area, AIT also involved the basics of navigating and functioning as a unit (sometimes including assaults on mock Vietnamese villages, even in the dead of winter) and being held in simulated prisoner of war camps. In many ways AIT was even more pressure-packed than basic – because this time it was for real. Instructors and students alike understood that learning the lessons of AIT, and learning them well, could mean the difference between life and death in Vietnam. There was no luxury of a real break-in period in Vietnam; soldiers knew that they could be out on operations within days or even hours of arriving in country. Learning in training about punji traps, tripwires, snipers, firefights, ambush patrols, and cloverleafing could be the lesson that meant returning home to civilian life once their part in the war was done.

After AIT many soldiers received a final home leave before making their way to Vietnam. For most it was a powerful moment – a final party with friends while trying to act like Vietnam wasn't looming so close; a final meal at the table with parents who tried not to cry; a final goodbye to children and wives fearful of the future. To this point the training regimen in preparation for service in Vietnam was much like that experienced by any American soldier preparing for war. But, after the final goodbyes, everything changed dramatically. Soldiers in previous conflicts deployed to the war zone in coherent units that had trained together and would then serve together. In Vietnam, though, everything was profoundly different. In Vietnam the United States military generally sent soldiers to the combat zone for a one-year tour of duty. Instead of rotating entire units in and out of Vietnam, the unit would remain in country while individual members of that unit rotated home at the end of their year tour. For most men in Vietnam, then, the war meant arriving in country as an individual replacement for someone who had been killed, wounded, or who had reached the end of his tour. American soldiers of the Vietnam era, then, trained in units and flew to Saigon on crowded aircraft – but the soldiers on that aircraft were all individuals. Upon arrival in country most had no idea with whom they would serve, where, or even in what capacity. American soldiers boarding the aircraft in the US for their year deployment were embarking on a military experience unparalleled in its individualism. They went to war alone.

Charlie Company, 4th of the 47th Infantry, 9th Infantry Division, though, was different. As part of the only division raised, trained, and sent to Vietnam as a coherent unit, Charlie Company was special, hearkening back to America's military past. Training and serving together as a band of brothers, the experience of Charlie Company stood in stark contrast to that of most Vietnam veterans, a contrast that helps to define and understand the American soldier in combat.

JAMES NALL
Member of 1st Platoon of Charlie Company

When we got to Fort Riley, Kansas, they always said, "kill or be killed." Being around all the white guys was new. Some were cool, and some weren't. Some would mix with you, and some were, you know, separate. Some when we went places would sit with each other, and we would do the same. It was like an ordinary thing. I was used to being around black people; it felt comfortable, because that is what I was around all my life. And then we get into a war, and we train together. They told us we were going to fight communism, that's what they told us. I had already had people in my home town that had been killed. But I was most comfortable hanging around black people. Because we understood each other, what we went through. And the race thing. We figured that nobody had gone through what we had gone through. But with all that we ALL trained together. We ALL were going to protect each other. They always told us, "You have to look out for each other."

Basic training was like the first day, they come in yelling to get you up. And if you hesitate at all they would just dump out the whole bunk and dump you on the floor. If you looked at them wrong they would make you drop down and do pushups. "Drop down and give me 20! What you lookin' at?" You would answer, "I was lookin' at you, sir!" They would answer, "Do you like me? Do you like men?" But if you said you don't like him, he was going to make you drop again and do more pushups. It was all part of the training. You had to run before you eat breakfast and do those [monkey] bars. Then you would go to classes. You would get sleepy in there. One time I got a little too sleepy after rifle training, and one of the sergeants saw me in the bleachers and said, "Let him sleep. He's going to get killed in Vietnam anyway." That woke me up quick!

During our time off of training I went to Junction City to meet the women and then went back home to the base. I didn't miss no meals in training. I would get back in time to eat. In fact I often did KP [Kitchen Police] for guys who would pay me, because they wanted to go into town. I didn't know a whole lot about that town; I didn't want to go down there at night and get mugged. I didn't drink, and I still don't drink. Folks ask me, "How did you go through what you did in that war and not come out drinking?" Some guys spent their money eating in Junction City, saying they didn't like the slop at Fort Riley. I didn't waste any money. I ate on base. I sent my money home to my mother and didn't waste it.

Sometimes when we were in formation they would tell you to drop and do the cockroach. Lie down on your back and carry your legs up in the air and your hands up in the air. They called it the dying cockroach. You had to kick your legs. Shake your hands and your legs the way a roach does when it's on its back. Sometimes if you messed up they would tell you about your mind. "Where's your mind?" Then they would tell you, "Go out and find your mind. Go over and talk to that tree and find your mind. Go and find out if that tree has your mind, and then bring it back in your hands." Then, when the guy would come back with their minds in their hands, they would yell, "Now dig a hole, and put your mind down in the hole." They had all kinds of ways of getting you. Sometimes you would be wanting to laugh, you know? But then they would have you jump down and do some pushups. Some of the things they did didn't bother me, because I came out of a large family. But some of them kids couldn't take it. Some would go over the wall. They couldn't take them guys hollering at them. It didn't bother me; I was used to getting hollered at. But if you were spoiled and wasn't used to getting hollered at, some started crying. We had guys that would cry because they couldn't handle it.

Some guys were real heavy when they got in there, but after training they had slimmed down. It was like we were competing against each other. Who's going to get into the best shape? That's back when they had us running in boots. You had to qualify on a 2-mile run. We trained hard, and we were ready. When we got through in December we went on leave before we went to Vietnam. I went to see my parents in Alabama. My mom was probably scared, but I never thought about anything like that. When I got on the train to go back to Fort Riley after leave I saw another guy from my unit who was coming back from Montgomery, Alabama, Don Peterson. He was from Glendale, California, but his wife was from

Alabama. I just happened to get on the train and saw him sitting there. He said, "Man, my wife just had a baby boy." I just saw that glint in his eyes, how happy he was. We rode all the way to Kansas together on that train. Peterson [who was white] was a down-home guy. I always got along with Peterson, he was a happy-go-lucky guy. Always joking. That's why I took it so hard when he got killed. When he got killed it just changed my whole life. Turned it around. You know, I didn't realize until we started getting shot at that the targets were going to shoot back at us. They just taught us how to shoot and hit that target. They said we were combat ready, and that we were going into Vietnam to destroy them guys. And the whole thing blew up on us when Peterson died.

ALAN RICHARDS
Member of 4th Platoon of Charlie Company

In training you kind of remember the good times and forget the bad times. But there are quite a few things that I remember. At Custer Hill, there were smaller rooms in between the two big [platoon] bays on each side [where the men had their quarters]. One of our guys from Tennessee just opened the door [to the quarters where the NCOs had their offices] and screamed like a woman and then ducked back into the platoon bay. The sergeant came out screaming to high heaven about "Who did that? Tell me who screamed into my office!" Of course nobody would say; we were just sitting there laughing about it. When we did get to go off the base sometimes we went to Junction City [Kansas], going to 9th Street [the seedier side of town that "catered" to soldiers] and having some fun. One time we were on Custer Hill, and there was a club down there in Junction City where they brought in some entertainment, a stripper. Through basic training we were dry, quarantined. So when they finally started letting you out, guys would start drinking beer. These were guys from all over Fort Riley, not just our company. All it took was a couple of guys shoving each other or trying to get a better view or something, and one night the whole place, it was like an old western bar brawl that you would see on television. I remember that a couple of us who were down there from my platoon kind of grabbing each other and making sure that we got the heck out of there. We all ended up in the girls' bathroom and ended up jumping out the windows of the bathroom. One of the girls who was there to perform was there too, and we helped her get out. By then all the MPs [Military Police] were showing up. I remember turning around and looking at the building, and it was like a cartoon. Every window had guys jumping out of it trying to get out of there.

There were times in training when we got into better shape. I remember one time my platoon was out marching somewhere and the sergeant stopped us so he could relieve himself. We didn't stop, though, and as a platoon decided to pick up the pace and he had to run to catch up. Boy, he wasn't happy. Mostly in training everybody got along with everybody else pretty well. Especially once you got to Vietnam, any personality conflicts that might have been there pretty much dissolved. Especially when you started losing guys; that just made the bonds stronger. Our platoon sergeant, Pedro Blas, was hard, but everyone respected him because he was fair. I remember him saying, "Either we are going to make you, or we are going to break you. And we are NOT going to break you. You are going to make it." He would push us, but, if you did something good, he would recognize it and say, "Hey, you did a good job." Once we got to know him a little bit better, especially if you were one of his squad leaders like I was, sometimes we would sit down for a meeting, and he would actually start talking about when he was younger. He was from Guam and would talk about back when the Japanese were on Guam. That was interesting, and we gained a little bit of respect for what he had been through.

Around Christmastime we had a leave after training before going to Vietnam. By then we all knew where we were going to go. It was a little scary to think about it. My friends back home [in Wisconsin] were very encouraging and told me, "You are going to make it. You'll be all right." But it was kind of strange, because for some reason I always had a thought that I would get wounded. As a matter of fact the first time I got wounded I remember saying to somebody, "I didn't think that it was going to be this soon." But I always thought that I would be wounded, but that I would make it back. I don't know why I had that feeling; I just always did. My mom would cry when I came home, telling me that I didn't write that much. We were actually told in training not to talk much about where we were going, but, of course, it was in the papers. I don't remember her being too emotional, though. Most of my friends were pretty good. Lots of the guys I had gone to high school with or who I had worked with in the factory were very supportive.

GARY FRANKLIN

Gary Franklin was from Hale Center, Texas. After graduating from high school Franklin first attended South Plains College and then Texas Tech University. However, everyone was getting drafted, so Franklin decided to drop out of college and get military service behind him. He was drafted in December 1967 and served as a rifleman, RTO, squad leader, and acting platoon leader with the 198th Light Infantry Brigade as part of the American (23rd Infantry) Division in Quang Ngai province from June 1968 to June 6, 1969. Franklin was wounded in action in an attack on Firebase Buff.

Well, I was inducted and went straight to Fort Polk, Louisiana for basic training. That lasted eight weeks, then everyone got some kind of assignment for advanced training, and it turned out that me and about three-quarters of the company were assigned to advanced infantry training, so we didn't really go anywhere except they put us on a bus and sent us over to North Fort Polk which they call Tigerland. There's a big gate there at Tigerland and a sign over it that said, "Training ground for the infantry soldier of Vietnam." It was very true, and everybody told us, "If you're in Tigerland, your next destination is going to be Vietnam."

Once we got over to Tigerland, most of those instructors were returnees from Vietnam and they were real knowledgeable about what was going on, and they trained us and taught us about a lot of things that had been overlooked before because it was such an unusual type of war, guerilla war. We had a lot of training on modified squad tactics and platoon tactics and what would work because you got ambushed so much over there, and a lot of training on things like booby traps and tripwires and detecting that and watching out for it. That was a big thing. They had just started a new training, which turned out to be beneficial, and it was quick fire with BB guns. They had small, outlined targets set up that probably wasn't 3 or 4 inches large, and they were about 6 feet away, and they gave you a little automatic BB gun, and targets would pop up and they would just quick fire. They taped a wooden stick over the sights of the BB gun so you couldn't just aim; it was a point and shoot thing. We did a lot of practice like that and that turned out to be one of the most beneficial things, too. That was really good because in the ambushes in Vietnam, you most often didn't have time to aim the rifle. It was just all quick fire.

In basic training we trained on the M14. Once we got over to advanced infantry training we trained on the M16 and the M60 machine gun and did some training on the M79 grenade launcher, and all the weapons we'd probably be using over there.

TERRY MCBRIDE
Member of 3rd Platoon of Charlie Company

After induction at Fort Bliss, I got on the plane and flew to Kansas. After training, when we got on the train to go to Oakland and get on the boat [to Vietnam], I told the guys in my platoon that if I ever come back to this fucking place [Fort Riley] again I'm gonna burn the whole fucking state down. It is the only place I've ever been in my life where you can walk all day, all night, and all the next day and still see the light on the tower at the barracks. Kansas was not pleasant in the winter; that wind would take you to pieces.

It was late at night when we got there, and everybody was kind of groggy and sleepy. I had a little attitude when I got there, so consequently I did a lot of pushups, a lot of running. We had a tough platoon leader. Every other platoon was asleep at 0400, and we were out running 4 miles before breakfast. I loved that guy

[John Hoskins]; he was a boxer and was tough like me. The deal was that they couldn't get a rise out of me. I would just stone cold face them. I had been through Catholic school with the nuns, and these guys had nothing on them. Sunday mornings everybody else would be sleeping in, and me and two other guys would always be out there with this asshole sergeant who just *loved* me. He would run us through the mud and get us all sweaty and lathered up, making us haul hay bales, which to me wasn't shit. I used to do that every summer. But I never complained; maybe I gave him the stinkeye every once in a while, but that was it. I tried not to let my ass overload my mouth. The sergeant had used to be in the Navy but had gotten seasick all the time, so he transferred to the Army. I used to call him butterball all the time, and that really got him.

On weekends off we tried to go to Manhattan, Kansas to meet girls, but there were MPs all over that place. I could always spot an ambush, though, so they never got me. So we went to 9th Street in Junction City instead, where there were hookers. I figured what trouble could we get in? Would they send us to Vietnam? Would they make us do KP? Hell, I liked KP. Sometimes when there was going to be an inspection they would put me on KP so I wouldn't be there in the barracks. But guess what? I caused so much shit on KP that they put me outside hosing out the barrels and the grease traps and all that. Once I took that big old hose and turned around and shot a guy from B Company, and he turned around and squirted me. And I said "You son-of-a-bitch!" And he said "Let's get it on, dude!" Instead of squirting him with the hose again I took a trashcan lid and a mop handle and charged. Then I hear my platoon leader hollering at me out of the window, "McBride! Knock that shit off!" So I got in trouble a couple of times. Even though I was a handful sometimes, I knew my job, and the platoon leader trusted me. I knew that this was serious.

After training we had a two-week leave before shipping out to Vietnam. My uncle had been in the Pacific in World War II and had it tough. I never saw him eat rice or look at a Japanese person straight on either. You could just see the hate in his eyes. I had worked with him nearly every summer, hauling hay and helping with the pigs and cattle. My uncle told me to shut the fuck up about that little war I was going to. It wasn't nothing like World War II, so he had better not catch me whining. I just looked at him and said, "You know what? Fuck you. I'll be back." That's when I was walking out the door.

MIKE LETHCOE

Member of 2nd Platoon of Alpha Company

We rode a train to Kansas. We got off the train in Kansas [at Fort Riley], and we all lined up out there. We had a DI [drill instructor] called Sergeant Hill. He was a little short, wide dude from Brooklyn. Man, when he got mad you couldn't understand a word he said. It was like he has his mouth full of marbles. And he got mad a lot. We got in a lot of trouble, because he wanted things done a certain way, and you couldn't understand him when he was yelling. When we got off the train we lined up out there, and he yelled, "Any of you mother fuckers know how to march?" I held up my hand and he growled, "Come over here!" He lined us up in platoons and put me up front and handed me an armband with sergeant's stripes on it. He then said, "You mother fuckers line up behind him and do what he does!" So I became a sergeant. He said, "You're an acting jack sergeant, and you will address your envelopes as sergeant, you'll be called sergeant, and you'll have all the privileges of a sergeant. Just not the pay."

I thought, "Well, that's cool." I was squad leader of 2nd Squad for about two weeks. They had this big, tall dude that was platoon guide, but he was a mess-up, so they made me platoon guide, like an assistant platoon sergeant. So I was a sergeant the whole time I was in the infantry – all because I knew how to march from having been in the marching band. I stayed platoon guide throughout basic training. I was the outstanding trainee for our platoon in basic training, and I was the second-best rifle shot in the company.

We had big, three-story concrete barracks. Central air and all the hot water in the world. They were really nice. Food was good. They ran us all the time; we ran everywhere. The training was tough, but they trained us as a unit. The platoons started out over 50 people, but then people started getting weeded out during training. Some out of the platoon were sent for specialized training like medic training or heavy weapons and then came back to us. We trained as a unit the whole time, so we were really quite an effective fighting force when we got to Vietnam. We were well trained, and when it hit the fan people did what they were supposed to do. Since I was platoon guide during all of our training it was kind of lonely at the top. I had to ride hard on some people. They tried to give me a blanket party once when I walked into the barracks. One of the guys was missing his entrenching tool. Somebody had stolen it, or he had hocked it or something. And we were about to have an inspection. I had my own room; squad leaders and platoon guides had their own rooms. I had gone to my room to get an entrenching tool and was taking it to this guy, and when I walked in the door the lights were off, which sort of bothered me. As I walked in the door they tried to throw a blanket over my head so they could beat me up. I just whooped everything in sight with that entrenching tool and that didn't happen again.

Nobody likes someone who tells them what to do. I was just a little bit older than everybody else. Most of these guys were like 18 or 19 and I was like 21. Nobody likes to be told. If they dropped their weapon I made them do pushups and things like that. A lot of these people were draftees who didn't want to be there. "I will not conform" was the password. They'd just make trouble and buck the system. I tried to tell them, "Look. These people are trying to teach you how to stay alive. We are going to combat. We are going to be fighting people, and people will be trying to kill you. You need to pay attention." And I tried to ride them hard because I knew that I was gonna be over there with them. I wanted people to learn their lessons so that we could all stay alive. And I took it seriously. I played the game. I was a soldier. I'd wanted to be a solder all my life. I was a soldier, and I worked hard at being a soldier. And a lot of people resented that. But that's the way it was with all the platoon guides and squad leaders. When you come in the same as everybody else, and you are put in charge, you are going to have people that buck the system. I didn't hurt anybody bad with that entrenching tool. I didn't put anyone in the brig. I didn't even report it. I just let it go. They learned their lesson. The people who were trying to do it got whooped pretty good, but nobody was seriously injured. I just let it be seen that I wouldn't lie down for something like that. If you are going to whoop me, you are going to have to do it. They didn't mess with me anymore.

We went through all of our training: we had basic infantry training, advanced infantry training, basic unit training, advanced unit training, jungle warfare, and then off to Vietnam. I went over with the advance party, before the whole unit went over to Vietnam. We spent two or three weeks with the Big Red One [1st Infantry Division] up there and went on patrols with the Big Red One and then came back and told the troops all about it. Then we all went by train to Oakland and got on a ship and went to Vietnam together. Getting to Vietnam was a big adventure. I just dug the hell out of it. It was the heat that knocked me down. It was the winter when I left Fort Riley, Kansas, and it was below zero most of the time. We were doing jungle training out there on the plains in the snow. The Green Berets [Special Forces] had put up a Viet Cong village that we were training in. But there was snow everywhere while we were training. Then when we got to Vietnam I could hardly breathe with the heat and the humidity. I had a tough time for the first couple of weeks there.

FRANK LINSTER
Member of the 188th Assault Helicopter Company

One thing about basic training and AIT in the 1960s still, the drill sergeants, you know, they didn't wear the smoky hats in those times. They would do the drills. I mean, they ruled the roost. When they said something, it was law. One thing about the 1960s, on payday you could leave your money lying on your bed and go down and shower, and when you came back somebody had put it in your locker and locked your locker for you. I mean, you didn't steal from each other. That was just a rule. If you did, you got thrown down the steps or you got a blanket party in the middle of the night, and the first sergeant would write up an accident report type of thing. I mean, you watched after your own people. You steal from the company next door – you know, their mops, their brooms, their whatever you needed to keep your stuff. But, you wouldn't steal from each other. There was a lot of camaraderie, which later on in my military career I didn't find that.

When I came out of basic training and AIT, I was convinced that I was a good infantryman. I was a good rifleman. I could shoot the weapons the Army gave me. I was a qualified expert on anything they ever gave me. I had a knack; I had an uncle who was with the Big Red One for five years that started teaching me to shoot pistols and rifles and shotguns when I was knee high to a grasshopper, I guess eight or nine years old. He started teaching me about weapons, and he did a good job. Everything the Army ever gave me I could shoot, and then when I got to flying gunships in Vietnam I could find I could shoot them, too. I could put a rock in your back pocket from 1,100 yards if that's where you wanted it. I never had a problem.

The military discipline actually wasn't as tough as the discipline that I grew up with. The nuns in that Catholic school? Whew, they were tough, and they ruled the roost. When they said that you did wrong, you did wrong. Nobody questioned their authority. If you got in trouble at school, you probably were in trouble at home, too. We had guys go AWOL because the basic training was too tough. I thought I could have done basic training standing on my ear. I thought it was easy. If you do what you're told to do when you're told to do it, it's simple, and when you start fighting the system is when you run into a lot of problems and life becomes very difficult, and that's the same thing in real life. But yeah, I felt very confident that I could handle whatever situation I got put into after I finished my 20 weeks of training. We got eight weeks of basic, we got eight weeks of AIT – advanced individual training – and then we went into small-unit tactics for a month. So yeah, we eventually ended up with 20 weeks of training before you ever went to your unit, and then when you went to your unit you were integrated into a squad, and then you start going out and practicing with that squad so that you got to know all the members of the squad so you knew what everybody would do under any given circumstance. You would know under this situation, this is how they're going to react, and so in the infantry we spent a lot of time in the field. I mean, normally on pay days and stuff like that we were back at base camp and got passes, but the rest of the time, Monday through Friday, if you weren't on post detail – clean up – you were out in the woods practicing your training, and you spent a lot of time out in the dunes, or on the range keeping your weapons qualification up because marksmanship is a skill that deteriorates. If you don't practice it, the real good marksman is going to lose his fine touch. The Army training is super.

[After rising to the rank of E5 while stationed in Okinawa, Linster turned down an opportunity to attend Officer Candidate School (OCS), and found himself called before his commander.] I went and got my coat and put it on, checked my brass and made sure it was shined, my boots were polished, went in there, and he just jumped on my case about me going to turn down my appointment at OCS. He said, "Listen, you dummy, you go to OCS, you get your commission. If you don't like what you're doing in two years you can transfer to another branch. Sign this paperwork, here!" "Yes sir." I signed the paperwork and in March I had orders to leave. As I was leaving, Sergeant Cullison told me, "If you get a chance to go to flight school, go to flight school. You'll enjoy that as a career, as a great career."

OCS is a higher level of intensity. You're all volunteers, higher level of motivation. The trainers, their job was to run you off, out of school, because they only want the best and the ones that really want to be lieutenants to survive. Our class started out 169 guys at noon on Saturday. By Monday night at eight o'clock we had 39 guys resign from the program. I mean, the first thing I did was I walked in – I had my stripes on – and this middleclassman, looked like he still had peach fuzz on his chin, told me I was out of uniform because I had stripes on my sleeves and he tore one of my sergeant stripes off my shirt sleeve, my coat. I wanted to deck him. I came real close to knocking him on his butt, but I bit my tongue and just took my time and understood this is what it's going to be like, and then the next 200 yards we duck-walked, with our duffel bags on our shoulders, to our barracks. That was my introduction to OCS. The PT [physical training] was a lot more difficult. They'd wake you up, and you had five minutes to get out of bed, get in your PT uniform, and be standing in formation outside the barracks. The first few weeks I was tying my shoes as I was hopping down the stairs, my tennis shoes. By the time I was an upperclassman, having done this for six months, I could make my bed, walk downstairs, and be there at least a minute ahead of time.

OCS was chicken-shit. Because what they're trying to do, they're trying to demonstrate combat stress without anybody shooting at you, so they were really nit-picking; I mean, the least little thing. At the end, after you got so many demerits you got restricted or grounded as you would your teenagers on Saturday where you couldn't go anyplace Saturday night; you had to stay in the barracks. If you got more demerits you got to do that Saturday and Sunday, but if you got more you had to run up the MB-4, which was a mountain round trip of 5 miles, to work off the demerits. If you got a few more, you got to run up there Saturday and Sunday; Saturday afternoon and Sunday morning, without stopping. The mountain was pretty steep at the end. After you'd gone out about 2 miles you had a tree, and you could break out of formation. You go up to the top, come back down, they give you salt tablets, you form back up, and come back in, and you had to run it in 60 minutes or less. The key was you could run it in 58 minutes, but if you fell out of your formation, it didn't count. You had to finish it with your formation, and we were running that thing at the end in 36–35 minutes, 5 miles. We had guys we were literally carrying; their feet were running on the ground but all the weight was being carried by other guys because they weren't in as good a shape.

Having been an NCO, I knew what it took to keep me straight. So, I didn't go up the hill until I became an upperclassman, and what happened was that I was what they called a middle-class cadet leader or CATO; I went down as a middleclassman to the lower-class group, and my job was to harass those kids and try to see how many guys would quit. Well, the upperclassman that was in charge of us came back and became my platoon leader. Well, he had made 13 trips up and back when he was in OCS, so he went and checked the chalkboard, and we had a great big board that showed how many trips everybody had made, and he found a bunch of us that had been CATOs had never gone, so we all had 13 trips before we graduated. We had eight weeks left and I got my 13 trips. I mean, he'd come in Monday morning and give me six demerits for rust on my plastic canteen, and you had the right to rebutt it in writing. So, I sat down and wrote an explanation that you can't get rust on a plastic canteen, and he'd give me six demerits for improper spelling, corrections, and grammar, because I found out he had his master's degree in English, so that didn't work either. What he was doing, he was just making sure – it wasn't harassment – keeping the pressure up, making sure I got my 13 trips, so by the time I finished my 26 weeks of OCS I had gotten my 13 trips all in the last eight weeks. So, I was in pretty good shape by the time I got done.

I once got caught by an officer walking when I was supposed to be running. My buddy had a buck-slip [a medical excuse] because he had a sprained ankle, and we were walking to the PX to get a haircut, and we were about ready to graduate, right, and he caught us, posted us up to his office, and Jerguson, he asked Jerguson, "How come you're walking?" "Well, I got a buck-slip." "Well Linster, how come you're walking?" "Well, I'm just walking with my buddy." "Well, let's see your buck-slip," and he showed him the excuse, you know, no running and he said, "Where's yours?" and I said, "I don't have one, sir," and he said, "Hit the brakes, we're going to do push-ups." He said, "How many can you do?" and I said, "I can do 100," and he said, "Fine, let's start." So, I'm counting them to myself and he says, "Stop cadet! Number one, I can't hear you. Number two, I don't hear your belt buckle hitting the floor. Start all over." I'd done like 20 already, so I start all over and then when I get up after finishing 100 he gives me six demerits for having an insufficiently shined belt buckle because I'd beat it up hitting the floor. It was just, again, another method of pressure. Well, at that time seven demerits ground you for

Saturday, and I'd already had some from my training officer from my inspections. So I got the write-up and I had to turn it in to my lieutenant; so the lieutenant gave me five more demerits for being stupid because I was walking when I should have been running. "Twenty-five weeks in OCS and you don't understand the rules?"

So, about halfway through OCS they came in wanting to know what you want to do after you graduate from OCS, and he had representatives from the ranger team, the airborne guys, special forces, they had guys from aviation who were there talking about the different careers, so I put down aviation as my number one choice.

Well, up to that point in my life I'd had like three commercial flights. I'd never seen the cockpit of an aircraft, and all of a sudden one day I get notice that a bunch of us, about 30 of us, are going to take the test. They pile us into this building and give us this written test, an aviation test, and I'm looking at all these gauges and stuff and I have no idea what the heck they are. I'm just guessing, and lo and behold, I passed the test. The next thing I know, before we graduate OCS I'm in taking a flight physical, passed it, and when I get graduated it wasn't very long and I went to Fort Walters, Texas and started learning how to fly helicopters. I graduated from flight school in November '67 on my way to Nam. So, next up was Travis Air Force Base to catch an airplane.

ANTHONY GOODRICH
Member of Mike Company, 3rd Battalion, 5th Marines

[My boot camp was in] San Diego. We left Albuquerque, and when we got to San Diego it was dark, and they had us wait. There was a Marine there, he must have been a drill instructor because he had his campaign hat, Smoky the Bear we called them. He had us stand in line; then we got on buses. The driver turned around and said, "You guys just made the worst mistake of your lives." We drive into a Marine Corps recruit depot, probably around midnight, and the drill instructor starts to get on our bus, and then he starts screaming at us to get off the bus, get off the bus.

We had to get out and stand on the yellow footprints. Of course the drill instructor's in front of us, and above him was the UCMJ [Uniform Code of Military Justice]. He pointed to it: "You're now in the United States Marines, but you're not Marines. The UCMJ is now your law and me. So forget everything you've learned; forget all your past life; forget your girlfriend, your mother. I am your mother, your father, your professor, everything."

We went to get haircuts right away; they shaved our heads. They gave us sweatshirts, utility trousers, tennis shoes, and covers, and then we had to pack up all of our civilian stuff, put it in boxes. We went and took showers, came back, and they marched us to our Quonset huts. It was probably two or three in the morning, and of course an hour later they came in there and started "get up and get out." The first week there was mostly processing. It was a lot of paperwork, a lot of inoculations, getting all our gear on, you know our web belt and our rifle, all that crap that we had to carry with us, our sea bag, and it was just a blur.

I was in pretty good physical shape because I ran track when I was in Albuquerque in high school. I was in real good shape. The physical part was easy for me; I could run 3 miles no problem, but it was the mental thing. They were trying to break us down. I learned quickly to not stand out. I tried to get to the middle of the formation. I didn't even want him [the sergeant] to know what I was, because I saw what happened to people. They would smack people; they wouldn't beat people, but they would smack you and hurt you with just one little blow. So I didn't want that to happen to me. I did not want that. They were very loud; they were very profane. "You're maggots; you're not Marines yet until I say you are." It was just very disciplined, learning how to think as a team. My dad was pretty loud, so even that didn't bother me; I knew how to polish boots. I was pretty good at doing all that stuff because my father was usually on my case.

The Marines had cut back quite drastically on their training regimen because they needed bodies, so it was eight weeks of boot camp. I guess the most fun thing in boot camp for me was going to the rifle range. I never shot a rifle, and I ended up being a sharpshooter. I was really good at 500 meters; I could hit a bull's-eye. [The drill instructors were] good at their jobs; they were really good at their jobs. It's funny, I remember their names – Collins, Soto, and Ross, staff sergeants, all staff sergeants – and I could still see their faces and hear their voices. They're definitely high on my list of what I expected in the Marine Corps. They were very disciplined; they looked good all the time; they cared about us, even though at the time I didn't realize they did, but they cared highly about us and getting trained the right way. All of them had been to Vietnam, all of them. It's funny; they didn't really talk about it till the end. When we're getting ready to graduate, they told us, "We've trained you the best we can. You just need to listen to your leaders in Vietnam. You're going to go to the infantry training now, just listen to those people. You guys are fine, you're Marines now, so just hold high the banner. This is the first step for you guys staying alive there, and you just need to listen, listen to your leaders and remember your training."

I loved running the obstacle course and pugil sticks [a heavily padded pole-like training weapon]. I think that was fun; I thought the bayonet training was fun. They had hand-to-hand combat where you had to choke a guy until he passed out then you let him go, and if the drill instructor or the instructor saw you weren't doing it right, he'd go down there and show you. They actually got us behind the eyes; you would pull up until he went limp and then you'd let him go, very realistic stuff, realistic as hell. They said when you go to Vietnam you might have this opportunity to be in hand-to-hand combat. You're going to have to learn how to kill that person, and they showed us how to kill people with cartridge belts. He says anything that's lying around, you better be able to pick it up and use it. Knives, they taught us judo, that kind of stuff, the choking drill. Matter of fact I still remember exactly what you do: tuck your head, and make sure they don't even grab you. And that was an eye opener when they were teaching us that, and these guys, if you weren't doing the position or the move right, they would get off the stand and come down – this is how you do it. "Do not fuck with me, private, because this is what you need to do; you're going to have to want to kill these people if they come into your position and you don't have anything to pick up."

I remember Staff Sergeant Soto used to get us out and he would ask us individually, "Why do you want to kill gooks?" And you would have to say, "I want to kill gooks because they're Communists or because they're killing Marines," and he'd say – he would look for a certain answer – "Why do you want to kill gooks?" I realized then, even at 18, that they were trying to dehumanize the enemy; I've heard that before. I didn't realize until he was saying that, "Why do you want to kill gooks?" and go down the line. I want to kill them because they killed a Marine, because they're Communist, because they're godless, all the propaganda we were taught, and I think that was a way for us to dehumanize them for us to be able to kill them, although somebody asked me once if I had to hate the Vietnamese to kill them. I don't think it had anything to do with it. With me it was staying alive. I never thought about hate. It wasn't a big hate thing; it was just a matter of staying alive and seeing a target out there.

We had two guys go over the fence [attempt to desert] the first day. You know, in San Diego [the training area] is right next to the airport, and they went through the fence. Believe it or not, when we were graduating, they were coming in in shackles. They had them cuffed up, and we were laughing at them: "you dumbasses!" But I guess we had some disciplinary problems. Then they had a thing called motivation platoon they would go to. These guys would basically go down to the beach and dig holes in the day and fill them up at night. I had no idea how long they would do this, but they would get motivated, and then they'd get sent back to the platoon. There was the fat farm. These guys would usually do PT all day and eat lettuce and skim milk at night. One of the things about Marine boot camp, if you got sent back you would have to go through the whole thing again. That's one of the things that motivated me to get whatever it takes to get through this, so I don't have to do this again. We had guys that were second and third time. We had a guy in our platoon that came in about halfway through, this was like his third attempt to try to get through boot camp. It was hard to get out of the Corps. You could not fake. I mean we had guys saying they were crazy.

Boot camp was good in the respect that it taught me teamwork. I think that's where they started instilling it in me. You had to trust the guy next to you. I remember we'd go on runs. If one guy dropped out, we would run around the guys until he got up and joined us. One man would fuck up, and everybody would get punished. I was confused until I got to Vietnam and realized you had to watch out for the weakest man in your platoon or your squad, because you've got to count on each other. Marines were real heavy on that - that you've got to trust the guys next to you, or you're going to die. I didn't really realize that until I got to Vietnam and saw it played out over and over again. You've got to be very aware of your strengths and weaknesses of the people on your team – and your own – and the whole teamwork thing, the whole thing about pulling together.

LARRY LUKES

Larry Lukes was from Sioux Falls, South Dakota. After high school his family moved to Fairmont, Nebraska where he worked on farms. Drafted in the spring of 1966, Larry married Kay in December prior to his departure for Vietnam. Lukes served in the 3rd Platoon of Charlie Company, 4th of the 47th Infantry, alongside Fred Kenney, Terry McBride, Steve Hopper, Elijah Taylor, Richard Rubio, Don Trcka, and Ron Vidovic. After the war Lukes returned to Nebraska and worked in a factory before taking a position as a truck driver. Lukes is now retired and owns 9 acres in the country where his grandchildren can come and play.

Sergeant Marr was our platoon sergeant, Sergeant Crockett was our company first sergeant, Captain Larson was our CO, and Lieutenant Black was our executive officer. I mean I was scared shitless of those guys. They were screaming and hollering and looked like they were 10 feet tall. I mean they were bigger than life, and when they spoke, you listened. Somebody was always screwing up or doing something goofy, and then I would start laughing. Then they would yell, "What are you laughing at, Lukes? Get down and give me pushups!" I think that I did more pushups that anybody in that whole outfit.

The maddest I ever got was when they had a simulated Viet Cong prison camp. We had to do everything: crawl through the mud, stand on your head. They would lock you up in footlockers and bury you in the ground and beat on them with sticks. So I got mad. I looked around and noticed that there was kind of a hole in the concertina wire. So I worked to make a hole in the wire big enough, and three of us crawled right through the wire and escaped from the prison camp. There was a guy pretending to be a Viet Cong officer; well, we messed him up pretty good and stole his jeep. We drove back to our barracks, took showers, and headed down to the mess hall. Next thing you know the MPs are there looking to arrest us. They took us in front of Lieutenant Colonel Tutwiler. He looked at them and said, "You ain't going to do nothing to these boys. I've been waiting for someone to escape from that place. That is what we are training them for! They are the only three who had gumption enough to try it." So he patted us on the backs and said good job, and that was the end of that deal. I told Lieutenant Colonel Tutwiler that if anybody ever captured me in Vietnam they had better kill me, 'cause I ain't never being locked up again.

One day Henry Burleson threw a cigarette on the ground, and Lieutenant Black saw him. He said, "Burleson, did you field strip that cigarette and put it out?" Burleson said, "No." Black said, "Well, then you are going to bury it." So they made Burleson dig a hole 2 feet wide, 3 feet long, and as deep as he could dig it. He put the cigarette in it, and of course we are all standing around and watching there at parade rest. He gets it all buried and done, and there was sweat running off of him everywhere. He is standing there, leaning on his shovel, and the lieutenant says, "Nice job. But was that cigarette out when you buried it? Dig it back up and see whether it was out." So I started laughing and Black turns around and asks me, "Lukes, what are you laughing at?" "Nothing, sir. Nothing." "Well come over here; I think that you can help Burleson dig." Boy we would get in trouble a lot, especially when we were out marching. There was this one big old boy from Tennessee. He didn't know his right foot from his left foot, so he always had to carry a rock in one hand to tell them apart.

VIETNAM

On a short leave after basic training I had gone home and proposed to my girlfriend, Kay. We had been dating three years. I told her if we get married now, I'm gonna get paid more. We're going to get married anyway; it may as well be now. Then I'll make more money while I am in the Army, and you can put that in the bank, and we will have some money to buy a house or do something when I get home. Her dad was a World War II vet and had married her mom before he left for Germany. So that's the way it went. We planned it for about six months, with her coming to Fort Riley on many weekends from Nebraska. We were married on December 17, 1966 on my leave before we shipped out to Vietnam. Kay came back to Fort Riley for the last few days and stayed in a hotel. My mom and dad, her parents, and my older sister and brother-in-law all came down for the big departure. We were supposed to all get together, but we never did. They loaded us all on a train. I saw them driving down the highway in a car waving at everyone on the train. I was waving at them too, but they couldn't see me. There must have been thousands of GIs hanging out of the windows and waving. They never did see me, but I saw them. That brought tears to my eyes, that I couldn't give her a big kiss goodbye.

3 WELCOME TO VIETNAM

During the Vietnam War roughly 3,403,100 United States Army, Air Force, Marine, Coast Guard, and Navy personnel served in the wider theater of war, while some 2,500,000 of them saw service within the borders of the Republic of Vietnam. The first American ground forces to arrive in South Vietnam were 3,500 US Marines, who splashed ashore on a beach outside Da Nang in March 1965. As the tempo of war quickened, though, more and more young Americans poured into South Vietnam at ports and airbases across the nation, from Vung Tau to Long Binh, with the troop total in country reaching a high of 543,000 in the spring of 1969. The new arrivals usually traveled by jet – sometimes on US military flights, but often on commercial Boeing 707s – and landed at one of the major air bases in the tiny country. The new soldiers next reported to replacement depots where military officials randomly assigned them to a parent unit usually as a machine gunner, mortarman, or rifleman.

VIETNAM

Before United States troops arrived in large numbers in 1965, few Americans knew anything about the geography and culture of Vietnam. For those who were even aware of Vietnam's existence, the country remained only a spot on a map where a communist North threatened a democratic South. As the war dragged on, American attitudes and knowledge of Vietnam changed dramatically, but Vietnam remained a forbidding and alien land of dense jungles, meandering waterways, steaming rice paddies, and people who had little in common with Americans. All too often ill-prepared for service in a country where most inhabitants maintained a rural lifestyle that Americans had long forgotten, US military personnel faced a host of geographic and cultural challenges shortly after their arrival in Vietnam.

For many young Americans, Vietnam was an unforgiving, if starkly beautiful, land. From the mighty Mekong to the rolling hills of the Central Highlands, the Republic of Vietnam's natural beauty took many Americans by surprise. But no amount of training could adequately prepare US troops for the climate awaiting them in Vietnam. The searing heat and relentless humidity packed a combined and physically draining punch. Monsoon downpours brought a torrent of rainfall that few Americans had ever endured, leaving soldiers perpetually soaked to the bone. For many, though, the smell of Vietnam was their first memory of the country – a pervading smell of rotting jungle growth, city squalor, cooking odors, and natural fertilizer.

Much like the environment, the people of Vietnam perplexed newly arrived American personnel, who marveled at the throngs of tiny Vietnamese civilians traveling on foot or by bicycles and wearing their traditional garb. The lifestyle of the Vietnamese surprised many Americans. While South Vietnam had growing urban areas such as the capital city of Saigon and the imperial city of Hue, approximately 90 percent of the Vietnamese population lived in the countryside. Most Vietnamese peasants farmed rice and raised domesticated animals, living much as their ancestors had for millennia. Village life, without modern conveniences of electricity and public sanitation, meant inhabitants conducted themselves far differently than people in the United States.

Public urination, although accepted by the Vietnamese, startled many Americans. Perhaps it was Vietnamese cuisine, though, that shocked Americans the most, with dogs and rats on display for sale in villages as ingredients for evening meals.

On their first operations in South Vietnam, US troops faced a bewildering array of threats, both manmade and natural. While tigers and a vast assortment of poisonous snakes were the most fearsome threats, a variety of smaller creatures were the bane of a soldier's daily existence. After slogging through rice paddies or hacking through dense jungle with machetes, soldiers often found themselves covered with leeches or ticks. Careless machete chops that struck one of the huge hives of red ants, constructed of leaves and almost invisible in the undergrowth, would result in an immediate offensive by thousands of stinging, biting attackers – leaving the victim no recourse but to strip and jump into the nearest body of water. Chief among the natural perils, though, were the mosquitoes; clouds of thousands upon thousands tormented patrols for days on end, with soldiers claiming that the vile insects would lick off their government-issue mosquito repellant before biting them.

Worst, though, for the incoming soldier was the seemingly ever-present threat posed by the Viet Cong and the North Vietnamese Army. For some of the new arrivals their first brush with death came with a rough landing on arrival due to enemy anti-aircraft fire or by sniper fire on long bus rides to a replacement depot. Once they received their permanent assignments, soldiers often found themselves on their first combat patrols within days or hours of arriving with their new unit. Alone among a group of tested veterans, the newbies faced the daunting task of operating in a countryside strewn with Viet Cong booby traps where an ambush might lurk around every corner. New soldiers in Vietnam had to learn their craft quickly or die.

DARRYL NELSON

Darryl Nelson was from the Yakima Valley of Washington and grew up with his uncles, aunts, and grandparents. At the age of 24, when he was already married with two children, Nelson received his draft notice in January 1965. Trying to have some control over his military fate, Nelson enlisted and went into the military police, serving in the 1st MP Company in Vietnam in 1966 and 1967. In 1970 and 1971 Nelson served a second tour as an advisor to the South Vietnamese Military Police. After 20 years of military service, Nelson became a correctional officer in Alaska before retiring and moving to Arizona.

Well, the reason I got picked to go to Vietnam is that I had doubts about the Army then. I went in and I told this lady in Assignments. I said, "I'm supposed to be going to Bremerhaven, Germany, I believe," and she looked at me and she said, "You're a damn MP; you're going to Vietnam," and I said, "Excuse me?" That wasn't a good phrase in those days, but that's what I said, and she said, "One of your damn white hats just gave me a ticket! All MPs go to Vietnam." So I looked at her and I said, "Where we'll be, we'll be. Let's get it on."

I got a welcome to Vietnam that most people don't get; I was on a 707, and we were coming in for a landing. Gear was down, flaps and everything, and we just were ready to set her on the airport when all of a sudden the throttles went to the firewall, and the 707 climbed out steeper than I thought it could climb. We came from probably about 40 feet off the ground and we went to 10,000 feet, and the pilot never said why. We just went up, and we orbited Tan Son Nhut for about five or ten minutes. We came back, and he started down again and somebody said, "Hey, we going to set it down this time?" And we landed and the gentleman came on the plane and he said, "You carry your own baggage. You're not to give these Vietnamese any American money," and the usual threats. We got on the tarmac, and oh my God, what have we got into? It was 100 degrees out there. The people looked a little different. They were yellow complexioned, and they were small. Just everybody was trying to tell me they wanted to carry my bag and I was scared to death to let anybody even touch my bag.

CARL CORTRIGHT

Carl Cortright was from Mission Hills, California where hoped to break into broadcasting. Drafted in October 1966, Cortright was one of the first replacements to serve in the 1st Platoon of Charlie Company, 4th of the 47th Infantry, where he served with James Nall, John Young, and Steve Huntsman. Cortright was wounded in action and paralyzed in a battle fought on May 15, 1967. After recuperation and learning how to function in society in a wheelchair Cortright worked in photography and with stained glass. Cortright also became a champion athlete in the National Veterans Wheelchair Games.

You know, I am not actually sure where I was when I first got to Vietnam. I was there for about four or five days. They put you in the Army depot and place you in a division. They just tell you what to do and that is it. I was waiting around for several days, and they gave me the orders, and I was assigned to the 9th Division, Charlie Company. I was bussed up there to the 9th and waited there for another three or four days. In the middle of nowhere Vietnam. It was hot and muggy, always the smell of the jungle. You are not prepared. We were being bussed and looking out the windows and everything was third world. You are never totally prepared for wherever you go. There would be girls in black pajamas along the road who would go along the ditch, raise up their black robes, pee, and walk right along again. After seeing that I thought, "Well, we are in Vietnam now." Another thing I noticed was how small they were. Vietnamese women were about the size of 12-year-olds to us.

I was finally in the 9th and assigned to Charlie Company. I went into a building and said I was trained a mortarman and had spent six weeks on it. He said let me talk to the colonel or whoever he was. He said, "I don't need another mortarman; I need a rifleman." That was kind of a blow for me. They put me on a helicopter and did not tell me where Charlie Company was. We were over the bay area and landed on a ship. The pilot didn't say anything, just landed. We are on a ship, but we were in the Army, so we knew this could not be the place. We were thinking we were headed to another dusty, dirty place. Ten minutes goes by, then 20, then the pilot says, "Get off; you are here!" I said, "We are here?" I still figured he was wrong, but I got off. We did finally start seeing evidence of Charlie guys who were on patrol.

We figured that we had it good on a ship and were housed the third or fourth level down, and then we heard some steps coming down. They must have left shortly after we arrived on the helicopter and they were gone for a couple days. They were tired and did not see us right away. We talked to Sergeant so-and-so and were treated pretty good being replacements. It was a good five days or so before we got geared up. They were really young, 20 years or so, but they looked old, worn, and haggard. So they came down and introduced a few people. Before [Don] Peterson was killed, he was my squad leader. He treated me pretty well. The day before he was killed he was trying to tell me what to expect. This was after three or four patrols. Pete was telling me that the North Vietnamese would rather wound you than kill you, because to save you they [the US forces] would have to send more people out to retrieve you. That was one thing I can remember him telling me that day. I thought that was a good thing to know; not sure if it was meant to make me feel better. I figured something was going to happen. It definitely sounded like we were going to be in some kind of an action.

On our first patrol, of course I was told right away I was making a couple of mistakes. One guy told me I was following too close to the guys ahead of me and to stay back another 10 feet. If he stepped on a mine, or if I did, then only one guy would be blown up instead of two or three. Later we did see a tripwire; they knew right away and took it apart.

In another incident, we were towards the back of the platoon and there was this replacement, a real nice big guy, and were trying to cross this river but it was like a big swamp, all full of water. I told this guy not to go this way. He got deeper in the water; his head was under the water. I went over there, with water up to my neck, and tried getting a hold of him. It was slippery and I was lighter. I was yelling and kept sliding down with him, and thought, "Well, great, I am going down with him." Another squad leader reached out his rife to me, and I grabbed a hold it and grabbed the guy's shoulder. I do not know how he held his breath that long. He was under water for like 45 seconds. Those guys in Charlie Company sure knew what they were doing.

ANTHONY GOODRICH
Member of Mike Company, 3rd Battalion, 5th Marines

I left about mid-June of 1969. I got on a flight at Travis Air Force Base up by San Francisco. We flew from there to Hawaii where we refueled. I stopped in Okinawa, where they checked my shot records. I was there for three days doing preliminary checking in for Vietnam. After three days I got on a flight. I flew into Da Nang Air Force Base. It was the middle of the night when we came in, must have been nine, ten, maybe eleven o'clock at night. And I think it's the first time that I started getting scared because I looked down as we were coming for our approach to land at Da Nang where I could see tracers and I could see flares being dropped, and I really started questioning what I had just done. I landed in Da Nang, got off the aircraft. First thing I remember is how hot it was there, hot and humid. I mean just it was like a furnace, and it was the middle of the night, and I wasn't looking forward to seeing the day and how hot it was there. Me – a young man from New Mexico where the humidity never gets above 10 percent – it was just like stepping into an oven.

The Marines were taken to a bus and taken up to the in-processing center. They gave us a rack to sleep in that night, in the barracks they had there, and the next day, we went and talked to an office administrative type that had our name on a roster, and they told us where we were going. I was assigned to go to the 5th Marine regiment. I had no idea where they were, who or what they were. All I knew was I going to go there as a machine gunner, and I was going to be in the infantry. I remember the guy telling me that the rear area for the 5th Marines was an area called An Hoa.

So they took us out to the LZ [Landing Zone], where I got on a helicopter, and they flew me out to An Hoa. I checked in to some administrative place there. I got assigned to Mike Company,

3rd Battalion, 5th Marines. If I remember there were probably eight or ten of us that went down to the company together. We went down there, we checked in with the first sergeant. He gave us a chit to go get our jungle utilities; we were still wearing our stateside utilities. So I went down and got my jungle utilities, helmet, flak jacket, backpack, and an M16. I came back to the company area; we slept in these canvas tents. The company was out in the bush, and they were going to wait for the company to come into the rear. They weren't going to chopper us out into the bush.

You could tell I was new because I still had polish on my boots and my utilities were clean. My helmet was clean. I remember sitting in the tent that we were sleeping in. There were some Marines in there from the company that came in and started telling us these scary war stories about getting ambushed and taking casualties, and how much we were going to hate it there. We were real stupid for going there and all kinds of things that scared the hell out of us.

We actually got to go to some kind of in-country processing where we went and sat in a group. They got an officer up there with a map that showed us where we were at on the map. Showed us where they thought the enemy was; what regiments, what divisions were around us. We were basically surrounded, he said. They also had demonstrations. They had demonstrations of AK47 fire. They showed us what RPGs [rocket-propelled grenades] looked like. They talked about booby traps. They actually had a demonstration of looking for tripwires for booby traps. They showed us different kinds of booby traps. Grenades inside of C-ration cans. They showed us where they could take an artillery shell or a bomb dropped from an aircraft that hadn't gone off, how they could set those up as booby traps. They talked about daisy-chain booby traps, which is more than one or closely set up in a line. They told us to basically keep your wits about you. Make sure you're very aware of everything that's around. Anything that's out of place, don't get near it or step in it or anything like that. Then they had a demonstration by a sapper. They had this guy come through the wire. Cutting the wire; he would tie it up. He was only in a loincloth with a satchel charge bag.

Came through, I forget, 50 meters of wire in about five or ten minutes. You couldn't hear the guy. You could not hear him. That was scary. I didn't get any of this training in the States before I got there. That was like a two- or three-day orientation.

I remember I got to go out on my first duty to go on a road sweep. They used to do road sweeps between An Hoa and a place called Liberty Bridge. Road sweep was actually a mine-clearing patrol so the convoys could come from Da Nang to us. What we would do was we would go from An Hoa to the Liberty Bridge and then another mine-sweep patrol would go from Da Nang to Liberty Bridge. When we got out there we reported to a staff sergeant. They gave me the mine-sweeping equipment. It was one of these, you put headphones on and you've got this little metal plate that you swing in front of you on the road. I remember being so damn scared. The guys said just listen for a beep. If you hear a beep then stop. I remember getting out in front of this column of Marines and then behind us were trucks. It took me probably an hour to go about 100 feet. Every beep I heard on the ground I would stop. They'd go up and they'd check. Nothing. I remember the lieutenant that came running up and started screaming at me, "What the fuck is taking so long here?" He looked at me, saw my brand-new uniform, my brand-new boots and said, "What the fuck are you doing here?" I said, "Well, the sergeant sent me up here." The lieutenant called the sergeant up and said, "You get this man to the rear of the column and get somebody that knows what we're doing or we're going to take all day to get this damn sweep done." I was grateful to that lieutenant. I got to the back of the column, drenched in sweat. Probably giggling a little bit because I knew that lieutenant saw me for what I was, which was a new green Marine who had no clue what was going on. That was my first introduction to being out in the bush, I guess you could say.

The company came in out of the bush about a week or two after; I'm not real sure about the timeline here. They were choppered in. The first thing that struck me was how dirty they were. They hadn't shaved. They just looked filthy. The uniforms looked filthy. The weapons, of course, looked clean, that's the thing that you had to have to stay alive. Just the filth and the look in their eyes too. These guys had the 1,000-yard stare they used to tell us about. These guys had seen things that I was going to see. That was quite frightening also. They had a pallet of beer on ice, and they were cooking steaks for these guys when they came in out of the bush. I got assigned to the 1st Platoon. I met my squad leader. He welcomed me to Vietnam. He'd been there eight or nine months. He said keep my eyes open to look at the guys that have been there for a while, just to follow their lead. Said he would try to show me everything I needed to know to survive. He immediately told us new guys that they had lost a whole gun team and some others. They had taken eight or nine casualties. We were actually taking the places of these. It was tough for me because I was afraid that these guys were killed. I was going to be replacing guys' friends or buddies. That scared me too. I was really afraid I might do something wrong, I guess is what it comes down to.

I did some stupid things. About the stupidest thing I did [was] in an ambush. My first ambush there. We were at our ambush site. I was on watch, and I don't think I slept the first month I was in country. I was so damn scared. I didn't eat much either. My stomach was kind of shrunken. I drank a lot of water; I remember that. Lots of water. Anyway we were on this ambush; I was on watch. They used to drop these gigantic flares out of the aircraft. Huge flares with huge parachutes. They would just light up the whole area. I remember watching this parachute come down with the flare burning. The flare burned out and this parachute and the flare, which was still glowing, fell 30 or 40 feet away from where our position was. Me in my infinite wisdom decided I'd like to have a parachute. I walked out there. I picked up the parachute with the glowing end of the illumination round and walked right back into the ambush site. As I stepped into the ambush site, my squad leader decked me. Knocked me silly. I could see stars. He said, "We're not in Camp Pendleton anymore, you stupid fuck. You could have got us all killed. If they would have been out there with a sniper, they could have picked us all off." He said, "We've got to move. We've got to move the position now, because of your stupidity. Don't ever let this happen again, or I'll kill you." It was a learning experience for me, to say the least. I look back on it now, and go, "What the fuck was I thinking?" Anyway, that was one of the few times I fucked up. You have a short learning curve there otherwise. You do that more often than once, you're going to get wasted.

ERNIE HARTMAN

Ernie Hartman was from Sugar Grove, Pennsylvania. His parents divorced when he was young, and by the age of ten, Ernie took odd jobs with local farmers to help pay the bills. After high school Ernie worked as a precision grinder and married his sweetheart, Jeannie. While on his honeymoon in the fall of 1966 Ernie received his draft notice. After training Hartman arrived as a replacement and served in the 1st Platoon of Charlie Company, 4th of the 47th with James Nall and John Young. He arrived just after the battle of June 19, 1967. Hartman was wounded in action on July 29, 1967. After the war Hartman went back to work as a precision grinder for 37 years until the company he worked for was sold.

I was worried, but I was the top man in my company with the M16. When I was training for a machine gun I was doing KP at the time and I got no training. When I got to Vietnam the Army put me up at Long Binh for a week to get used to the area for a little bit. Once at Long Binh they tell you where you are going. I could have gone up north or anyplace, but they assigned me to the 9th Infantry. I am one of the first replacements for my unit. They had all trained together, went over together, and did everything together. Then they told me I got a machine gun slot; now I'm worried. I was supposed to be in Long Binh for seven days, ended up being nine. They had a paperwork problem. I got to know a few of the guys going to the 9th while at Long Binh. The 18th comes and they ship out and an officer tells me there is something wrong with some paperwork and that I am not going. [Because of the twist of fate, Hartman missed a major battle on June 19.] That has crushed me over the years. Buddies who I just met went to battle, one got hit. I did not go until the 20th of June. That bothered me. I shipped out to the unit and first saw a pile of flak gear, helmets, guns, and all kinds of shit [taken from the guys who had died in the battle] piled 5 or 6 feet high. I wondered what the hell I had gotten into.

First I got assigned to a platoon, and John Young, the squad leader, took me under his wing. He taught me; he knew that I was there to help protect him, too. It took a while for the guys to warm up to me. They had just lost a bunch of friends. You can't really replace them. It was kind of a lonely place to be, but I still had the buddies that I had made in Long Binh. The new guys kind of hung together, and the other guys hung together.

STEVE HUNTSMAN

Steve Huntsman was from St George, Utah. After graduating from high school, Huntsman attended Brigham Young University before dropping out to get married to his sweetheart, Karen. Having lost his college deferment, Huntsman was drafted in the spring of 1966, and served in the 1st Platoon of Charlie Company, 4th of the 47th Infantry where he served with James Nall, Carl Cortright, Kirby Spain, and John Young. Huntsman was wounded in action on May 15, 1967. While recuperating in the hospital, Huntsman reenlisted. After the war, Huntsman worked as a truck driver for 27 years.

My first impression of Vietnam was how backward the people were, how dirty it was, and how third world it was. Hot and miserable; very smelly. We did not get off at Vung Tau; we stayed in the harbor for a couple days. At first our base camp was just dirt. The Army had just took caterpillars and made a berm and knocked down trees. When we got there they were still working. The first day we got there, a guy got shot in the head. Made me want to get down on my belly and crawl around. I remember thinking, "Boy, this is the real stuff."

I was still scared pretty shitless about going on patrols at first; I did not know what was going on. I really do not think they did either. I was a squad leader. We were hacking our way through the jungle; James Nall was running point with a machete, hacking along, and he hit a tree with red ants in it. Red ants showered down on him. I have never seen a man get naked that fast. It was so funny; in a heartbeat he was naked and trying to get the ants out of his clothes. They just rained down him; and he had hundreds on him. We helped as much as we could, but you had to laugh at it. We grabbed his clothes and shook the ants off.

We used to have to take our shirtsleeves down and button them real tight to fight the mosquitoes at night. Button up around your neck and cover your exposed areas with repellent. In the daytime we had our sleeves rolled up because it was so hot. There was also this bird or lizard that said "fuck you" all the time. I remember everyone talking about it. It was exactly like "fuck you." It was funnier than hell. It was not a legend; I heard it.

Operating in the Rung Sat [a mangrove swamp] was hell on earth. When the water came in, everything was covered in water except maybe for 1 or 2 percent of it. When it went out, nothing but mud. When you went through the mud, you would have to pull your legs out of it. When we would set for the night, for our ambushes, this one night I felt something on my lower leg and I reached down. I thought it was a lizard or something, but it was water coming in. It was about waist deep when it came in. Stayed up all night in water. We had hammocks and tied them to trees. We used to take our C rations and take out the best parts and stuff them into a sock and tie them on our belts. We stopped carrying all that heavy equipment. It was hard enough to live in there and walk without all that other crap on you. Just laid there down on the ground, used your steel pot [helmet] and put it on the back of your head and used it as a pillow, and just slept. I took a poncho sometimes so you would not have to lie down in the mud.

Every morning we would take off our shirts and count the ticks that had their heads buried into our skin. Whoever did would say, "I have the most; I am the champion!" We used a match to get them off. Light it up and put it close to them and pull them out. If you just pulled them off, their head was still buried.

FRANK LINSTER
Member of the 188th Assault Helicopter Company

Well, the first thing when the airplane landed and they opened the door: the heat. God, you know? This is December. In California it's in the 40s. I walk in there and it must have been 120 in the shade and no shade. But, by the time we got off the tarmac into the Air Force terminal, our uniforms were all wringing wet. That, and the odor from where they were burning all the human waste, the odor of that was a big shock. You could see the smoke all over the place where the base camps were burning the human waste. Got in the 90th Replacement Battalion, and within three days we had our assignments, and the 188th came down and they were only about 40 miles from Long Binh. They came down, picked us up, and took us right home, took us right in. Got processed in one day; the next day we were taking our check rides [on our helicopters] and the following day we were operational. We were doing missions. You barely had time to unpack your bag. They put you right to work. The intensity of the company, you picked it up real fast that this unit did a lot. The amount of hours they flew; there was a number of months consecutively we were the highest flying aviation company in Vietnam as far as how many hours we put in per bird. We had really good maintenance. We had different maintenance officers but always had really outstanding maintenance, and those guys were working 12-hour shifts, seven days a week minimum. And when we went out and got them shot up really bad, they even worked more hours to get them back in the air. It wasn't very often that battalion would stand us down. A couple of times they had to stand us down because we got like 18 or 19 birds shot up in nothing flat.

MIKE LETHCOE
Member of 2nd Platoon of Alpha Company

We spent the first two or three weeks filling sandbags. The temperatures were 95 and 100 degrees, and 80 to 90 percent humidity. We spent some time around the Michelin [rubber] plantation and patrolling around the plantation. At that time the worst contact we had was when we were out on patrol and a point element went into the jungle and brushed by a hornets' nest in the trees. The column was moving single file. By the time we got there these hornets were all pissed off. They attacked the entire unit, people were screaming and hollering. There were clusters of hornets on everybody. People were running through the woods, taking off gear, and heading back towards the river. I had an uncle who kept bees, so I knew they didn't like smoke. So I threw smoke and told everybody to start throwing smoke. So people starting throwing their smoke, and we had different colors of smoke drifting through the plantation. We had a couple of guys in the platoon who were allergic to bee stings. They just sat down by a tree and said they were going to die. So we called in a dust off. We had to blow down a couple rubber trees so the chopper could come in and drop a hook to take the two guys out who were allergic to bee stings. They were starting to swell up, but when the medics got there they shot them up with atropine, benadryl, and it started helping them.

You kept an extra pair of socks around your neck – your body heat would dry them – and you wore a pair. We would take our C rations out of the box and put the can in a sock and tie it onto our gear. We would use those socks as a replacement pair of socks. We would use a roll of C-4 [plastic explosive] about the size of your little finger – and later they gave us little heating tablets – to heat our water for coffee and hot chocolate at night. You fired it off with a cigarette; it would not explode unless it has a high velocity detonation on it, but the stuff burns really hot. Once you got it fired up, you put your steel pot over your can and then your socks on the steel pot to dry. I saw people take their boots off and their whole heel would come off. All the skin would come off with the boot because their feet were not dry.

When we were on patrol, the Viet Cong generally knew we were coming and were guarding their rear. They would fire on us just to slow us up, so everybody else could get away. They were mostly Viet Cong down there that were not equipped to sustain a heavy battle. It was normally sniper fire, booby traps everywhere. Any time you got around where they were, there were tripwires and punji pits to slow you up.

My first contact was on one day when we took a small base camp. We came in on the edge of it and started taking fire. We were coming through a tree line and you could hear the rounds popping in the air. There were punji pits around everywhere and tripwires. I remember those rounds popping in the air as they went by. They were firing indiscriminately, trying to slow us down.

We had this big open field to cross. Being a squad leader I had to be the one to say, "Come on guys, let's go," and get up and walk off so the guys would follow me across this field. I was so scared I would piss on myself every time I stopped walking. My knees were jumping so bad I could hardly stand up. I was hoping no one could see that. But still I am saying, "Guys, let's go; O'Ryan let's go."

We walked out into this open field with these rounds popping in the air. Obviously the VC were bad shots; nobody was aiming or something. We got into the place, and I was walking on top of a dike when I saw a tall bush move at the intersection of the dike about 25 yards away or so. So I jumped down into the mud alongside the dike, and there was a Viet Cong in a bunker at the intersection of the dike who opened up with a Thompson submachine gun. I had an M16 with a grenade launcher under it. So I started putting grenades on the bunker, while guys on the other side of the dike started maneuvering to it. As they got close, I stopped firing grenades on it and kept firing rounds in it. It got so hot on this little bunker that the Viet Cong jumped up and ran across in front of the whole platoon. The whole platoon stood up and opened fire on this man. He made it about 20 yards and was just shot full of holes. You could see blood flying out of him when he was still running. He had these little black pills on him, which I think were opium, which these guys would eat to give them energy to keep going. He must have been hit half a dozen times before he actually went down. Sergeant Hill grabbed an M79 grenade launcher from a grenadier, when this guy was running across, and fired on him. That was what actually brought the man down. So I went and recovered his Thompson from his bunker. Sergeant Hill said, "You killed the man," and I took it back in and cleaned it up and got new magazines for it.

KIRBY SPAIN

Kirby Spain was from Danville, Arkansas where he was brought up on a farm. After his father passed away when he was 18, Kirby worked for International Harvester in East Moline, Illinois. Spain was drafted in the spring of 1966 and served in the 1st Platoon of Charlie Company, 4th of the 47th Infantry, alongside James Nall, John Young, and Steve Huntsman. Spain was wounded in action by a booby trap on April 8, 1967. Later in the war Spain reenlisted. Returning home after Vietnam, Spain worked at several jobs including as a crop duster before becoming a long-haul trucker.

Those little ants, they were hostile. There is a plant over there with broad leaves that they liked to live on. I have stood there and watched them run to the back of that leaf and take off when someone is coming under it to get a running start. There was a saying going around there: "To hell with Charlie, just deliver us from the red ants."

They sent us out to pull security for an engineering company. They were right outside base camp on these big Caterpillars with the long plows on them. This one kid ran a bulldozer down into the jungle, and he went nearly out of sight. He backed up and kept pushing at all that jungle. He ran down in there and hit this one tree. I could see this tree shake, and a big old python came out of that tree and hit the hood of that dozer. When it did it wrapped itself around the muffler. Of course that killed the snake, but while it was doing that, the boy running that dozer, he done decided he had spent enough time there. He ran off the back and left the dozer down there in gear. Then finally the dozer ran off down the jungle and got to where it could not go anymore. It was sitting there just spinning. I think that they ate that snake.

GARY FRANKLIN
Member of the 198th Light Infantry Brigade

They flew us from Fort Lewis, Washington to Yokota Air Force Base in Japan and then on to Vietnam. I think it was a 21-hour flight. We arrived into Cam Ranh Bay. We got there about eight o'clock in the morning and my first thought was, "This is killing heat!" I looked over at one of the buildings there and you had the reflection off the white sand, too, so that made it even worse, and the building was a wooden structure with a metal roof and it had a thermometer underneath it, and it was 139 in the shade and high humidity. I thought, "This is going to be terrible!" It seemed like on every mission someone would fall out due to heat exhaustion, or they would pass out and we had to get them dusted off.

[When all of us aboard our aircraft arrived in Vietnam] we had no idea where we were going. They made a decision at Cam Ranh Bay, and sent us to the Americal, and it was basically who had the heaviest losses got the new people. That's why I ended up at Charlie Company in the 198th Light Infantry Brigade, because Charlie Company had pretty heavy losses about three weeks before I got there. [I arrived with two other guys.] I think of the guys who went out to Charlie Company that Bruce lasted two months and got hurt, and the other guy I think lasted two months and got killed. I was the only one that lasted the full year and came home.

Every once in a while the division would lose somebody due to heat stroke. It was just too hot for carrying a backpack and not being used to it in that 120-degree heat in that 100-percent humidity. Because of that they had started something new about four or five months before I got there, and they flew us from Cam Ranh Bay up to Chu Lai, where they had established a reception center. It was right on the South China Sea on the southeast corner of the perimeter of Chu Lai, and everyone coming in the country there that was going to the Americal Division spent a week there at the little reception center. They had some people that were veterans from the field and they kind of went over a review of your training a little bit about booby traps and the local people, and it gave you a week to get used to the heat and humidity.

Well, at first it was really scary [walking point] but after a while you got used to everything. Somebody said one time that the loneliest thing in the world was a point man in Vietnam, because everyone tried to stay about 10 to 15 meters apart, just for sniper reasons and booby traps. As a point man, they wanted you out there about 50 to 75 meters. It's kind of a lonely feeling out there, but after being there for a while I realized that the point man wasn't usually the one getting ambushed. They let the point man go by and then when they'd bust an ambush, they'd bust it on the guys behind you, especially if they could hit the guy next to the radio, then they'd try to get the squad leader and the RTO [radiotelephone operator] and then everybody was in a mess. The loneliest thing in the world was being the point man in Vietnam at night. Daytime wasn't near as spooky as at night. At night you'd often lose visibility of the other guys. We tried not to do that but sometimes it would start to really worry you if you couldn't see the guys behind you or you lose sight of somebody for a while.

We lost most of our casualties to mines and booby traps. They were real sneaky about it, I guess you would say. They were real slick as to ways to set up mines and booby traps. When I got over there they had taught us about punji pits, and they had these little ankle crushers. What they would do, they just built a wooden box, mostly out of teakwood, but they would put two planks in it and the planks would have nails driven from the back side, usually double wood so that the nails couldn't push back out. They'd drive the nails in one piece of wood, nail another piece of wood behind it to hold the nails, and then would put it on big nail hinges. You'd step in the center and your own weight would turn it in and your own weight would also drive the nails right through your ankle. By the time I got there in the middle of '68, they had discovered explosives. The Russians were giving them a bunch of Bouncing Betties, I guess, and anti-tank mines. They had a lot of that to play with. We were giving them a lot of dud artillery and bombs. I think they had an almost unlimited cache of explosives to mess with.

Well, one thing we ran into a lot [of mines] there south of Chu Lai. When I first got there, there were a lot of villagers, a lot of Viet Cong, and a lot of that area the French had mined it and there were little French minefields everywhere, and the French didn't record anything. They didn't have any records. So, we found them the hard way. We found a lot of them at night. We'd be in the middle of a French minefield, and somebody would get a foot blown off and we wouldn't know how to get out. It was usually just blind luck. We slowly were getting all those minefields recorded just from people having feet and legs blown off.

The Viet Cong were getting fairly sophisticated with their mines and stuff, and their booby traps. We had several times when squads would have a small mine or booby trap that would blow half of somebody's foot off or something and then there would be a delayed fuse for a minute later and they might have a 105 howitzer round or even a 250- or 500-pound bomb buried, and so they knew as soon as somebody got half a foot blown off all their buddies was going to rush up there to help them, and about a minute later the big one would go off and take everybody. We got to where if somebody would step on a booby trap, we'd wait a minute or so. We figured they probably wouldn't bleed to death, anyway within a minute or two, so we'd wait. I think one of the nastiest tricks, almost totally impossible to detect, was at Chu Lai; there were I think 6,000 Vietnamese that worked there, and they cleaned hooches for the officers and filled sandbags and did whatever they could be hired to do. The military trucks had a big 3½-inch gas cap, and they would pick up one of our grenades, because at the mess halls or whatever there was always ammunition belts or stuff laying around with grenades attached to them, and some Vietnamese would pick up a grenade and put a rubber band around the spoon, pull the pin, and drop it in the gas tank, and put the cap back on. It would take about a day and a half for the gasoline to eat the rubber band up, and then they had not only the grenade, but in the jeep the gas tank is right underneath the seat and it would usually have a half a tank or a full tank of gasoline. That thing would go up and it would blow the jeep nearly in half.

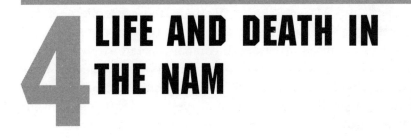

4 LIFE AND DEATH IN THE NAM

In large part it was up to the infantry combat soldiers and Marines to transform American military strategy into violent reality. The strategic decisions, in the main, fell first to General William Westmoreland and then to General Creighton Abrams, who served as commanders of US Military Assistance Command, Vietnam (MACV). The Vietnam War for which MACV planned was immensely complex. It comprised varied geographies. It was at once a civil war and a regional war. It was a war for the hearts and minds of the people while it was also a war of big unit combat. It was a war about rice harvests and a war about destroying enemy divisions. It was a war against Viet Cong insurgents and a war against regular units of the North Vietnamese Army (NVA). Considering the varied nature of the conflict there was no single, generic military experience for infantrymen and Marines in Vietnam. Soldiers on the front lines of the war sometimes served as advisors to the South Vietnamese; sometimes they worked as part of small long-range patrols; sometimes they worked with local civilians in rural security operations; sometimes they took part in major operations to hunt down and destroy major enemy units; sometimes they manned static artillery firebases.

While MACV's planning reflected the complexity of the war and involved major efforts aimed at rural pacification and working with the South Vietnamese military, for most American soldiers and Marines during Vietnam the centerpiece of the US strategic scheme revolved around the concept of "search and destroy." Limited to ground combat operations within the geographic confines of South Vietnam, Westmoreland in large part devised a plan in which US and South Vietnamese units, large and small, scoured the countryside of South Vietnam for enemy units, hoping to lock those units into battle and destroy them. Once battle was joined, Westmoreland and Abrams understood that a massive edge in firepower would allow US and South Vietnamese units to inflict terrible casualties on their Viet Cong and North Vietnamese foes – losses that MACV hoped would be so severe that the enemy would choose not to continue the conflict.

In general, US forces were housed in base areas large and small dotted around the South Vietnamese countryside – base areas that ranged from remote and vulnerable hilltops along the Demilitarized Zone that separated North Vietnam from South Vietnam to bustling and relatively safe divisional and corps base areas such as Da Nang and Chu Lai that had all the comforts of home. Operating from these base areas, units would often station one of their elements at the base for recuperation and the training of replacements while their other elements were on operations in the field. Sometimes a unit's assignment to the base area resulted in an extended rest period, with access to all of the standard wartime recreational opportunities pursued by soldiers down through the ages – from women to booze. On other occasions, units returned to their rear areas only to rearm and dry out their sodden clothing for a single day before heading out into the "boonies" again in search of the elusive Viet Cong and NVA.

LIFE AND DEATH IN THE NAM

The Viet Cong and NVA used their local knowledge of the countryside very much to their advantage. For much of the conflict communist forces utilized the tactics of insurgency and guerilla warfare, hitting US forces and then melting back into the hills, jungles, and villages of South Vietnam or slipping across the border into Cambodia or Laos where US forces could not follow. While there were major infantry clashes during the American period of the Vietnam War, most notably the Tet Offensive of 1968, generally the Viet Cong and NVA relied on elusiveness to offset the marked American firepower edge. But the US and South Vietnamese also enjoyed a substantial technological advantage. Along the rivers and streams of the Mekong Delta US forces employed converted landing craft to pursue the Viet Cong around the watery landscape, while in much of the remainder of the country it was the helicopter that provided US forces with a distinct advantage in tactical mobility. From their ships and helicopters the Americans seemingly could materialize almost anywhere in South Vietnam to dog the footsteps of the Viet Cong and NVA. In strategic terms it was rather simple – MACV relied on technology and firepower to offset the enemy's elusiveness. For the soldiers on the ground, though, search and destroy meant something quite different. Helicopters or landing craft could carry an American unit to where intelligence suggested a concentration of enemy soldiers was lurking. But the intelligence was rarely accurate. After reaching the landing zone or the beachhead, the slogging began. In human terms search and destroy meant slogging the countryside – up hillsides, through villages, into swamps, hacking through jungle – searching for an enemy force that usually did not want to be found.

In some areas, such as the Central Highlands or the Rung Sat mangrove swamps, the patrols navigated almost unpopulated countryside, where the chief enemy seemed to be Vietnam itself – the stifling heat, the tangles of elephant grass, the morass of mud. In other areas, though, like the populous Mekong Delta or the coastal littoral, patrols swept through densely populated areas – past farmers tending to their rice paddies and through the ubiquitous small hamlets that dotted the countryside. Often patrols were only what the soldiers termed "long walks in the hot sun." There was no contact. Perhaps men would find and destroy disused bunkers, Viet Cong base camps, or even tunnel complexes. In villages and hamlets the soldiers would check IDs, search for contraband, and detain any suspected Viet Cong. But then it was gear up and time to slog on to the next village, or through the next tree line.

For many the war played out as a seemingly unending game of cat and mouse. The enemy was out there, everyone knew it, and they were lethal professionals. In many areas the Viet Cong had been preparing the battlefield for decades. They knew every fold in the land, every prepared field of fire. Each and every tree line could conceal a bunker and a deadly ambush. The jungle, where your visibility was cut to mere feet, might be alive with eyes – with Viet Cong lashed to trees peering down at you ready to trigger a deadly blaze of small-arms fire. Every village could contain Viet Cong hiding in plain sight among the people – Viet Cong who were ready to kill you as soon as your guard was down. For the Americans patrolling Vietnam the enemy could be anywhere; a violent firefight might loom around every bend. Vietnam was alive with death. Patrols – even ones that made no contact – were, thus, always tense affairs. The Americans could never afford to let their guard down, especially at night, because any lapse in alertness – any slight sign missed – could result in death. Sure, chances were 90 percent sure that there were no Viet Cong lurking in that next tree line. But if your guard was down, and they were there, your lives were forfeit.

Most commonly patrols would make contact with a single enemy sniper or perhaps three or four Viet Cong unlucky enough to get caught unaware in one of their many bunkers or tunnels. As often as not any incoming sniper fire was poorly aimed, being fired by an enemy soldier bent on disrupting the American march and then getting away as quickly as possible. Sometimes, though, the sniper was deadly accurate and usually made a medic, a radioman, or an officer his target, often firing one round, followed by a short burst of automatic fire, before fleeing. Contact with small groups of enemy soldiers was often quite similar. The day would be silent and hot, then would be split by a few seconds of nearly deafening fire from both sides, before lapsing into silence once again. By the CRACK of the bullet flying past, followed by the report of the enemy weapon, experienced soldiers could tell what type of weapon was doing the firing (and thus what type of unit was doing the firing – AK47 or automatic weapon fire meant a sizable, professional unit), the direction of the firing, and even its approximate distance. If a small unit or a single sniper, US forces tended to move toward the fire, sometimes resulting in short, sharp firefights with the small enemy unit. More often than not, though, any return fire and pursuit wound up netting no confirmed enemy casualties. Perhaps there would be a blood trail, but little else. The Viet Cong and NVA were experts at evading pursuit and dragging away their wounded and dead.

The Viet Cong and NVA had also festooned the battlefields of South Vietnam with thousands of mines and booby traps. Some were quite rudimentary, including the punji trap – a hole dug in the ground filled with sharpened bamboo stakes, often tipped with urine or feces, designed to puncture the boots of the unwary and then cause infection. Others were quite lethal, including command-detonated claymore mines that fired a hugely destructive pattern of shrapnel, and "Bouncing Betties" – mines that bounded out of the ground and exploded at waist level for maximum effect. There were small mines, termed toe poppers, designed only to maim feet, and larger anti-personnel mines that blew off entire legs. The most common type of booby trap was simple, yet quite effective – a grenade, usually of Chinese manufacture, with its pin tied to a monofilament tripwire. The wire usually hung slack on the ground, or in the water, where it was virtually invisible. Mines were placed in high-traffic areas, often on trails or rice paddy dikes, and were sometimes arranged in patterns where men rushing to rescue a friend who had been hit by a mine would trip another.

Casualty rates in Vietnam due to mines and booby traps varied across the country and across time as the war changed. Estimates of the percentage of total US casualties from these sources vary widely, from a low of 17 percent to a high of over 50 percent. Regardless of their actual destructiveness, mines and booby traps were the bane of many Americans' existence in Vietnam. There were no enemy in sight, or even signs of enemy forces. Suddenly, and quite without warning, there would be a loud explosion and a man would go flying up into the air. Was it safe to move? Was this a single mine or an extensive minefield? Everything would have to come to a halt while the medics came up and the casualty was dusted off. Then it was time to move out again, until the next explosion. Perhaps the most maddening part was that soldiers took losses, often gruesome casualties involving traumatic amputations, without anyone at whom to shoot; there was nobody on whom to take vengeance. You can't shoot back at a booby trap. The fact that a mine went off sometimes just after US forces had walked past some Vietnamese villagers – who didn't warn them of its presence – was often the cause for suspicion. Had they known about the danger? Had they put the mine there? The maddening world of search and destroy forced many Americans to wonder who the real enemy was.

DARRYL NELSON
Member of 1st MP Company

I went through Long Binh before I went to the 1st Replacement Company. When I got to Long Binh I immediately got placed on the security force. That night, armed with an M14, two other guys and I were on patrol. We had somebody try to run the gate and I fired my first shots in anger in Vietnam.

I wasn't given a briefing [before going on guard duty]. I was just told, "Anybody tries to come through the gate or come through the fence are considered enemy, and they are to be stopped." They were cowboys and they had been coming in and stealing stuff, and they were chasing the gate guards clear out of there because a lot of the gate guards, they didn't want to be in Vietnam, and these guys come out there and throw a string of firecrackers at them and they were gone. Well they threw the string of firecrackers and this one [Viet Cong] was in the wire, and I can't remember if I shot three times and yelled, "Halt!" or yelled,

"Halt!" three times and shot. All I know is I fired three times, and I had two of them lying in the wire. KIAs.

All I know is that after I did it I was so sick for about three hours I couldn't believe myself. That's the first time I'd ever fired at anybody in anger, and it's amazing. It was amazing that I hit because I was probably 200 yards away. I just jumped out of the truck and came into a standing position and fired, and I took two of the three out and the other guys didn't even fire. The first thing I did was go out to check them both for signs of life. I checked to see if they had weapons first, and I found a grenade in one guy's pocket. I took the grenade out, ensured that it was safe, and handed it to one of the other people and told him, "Go back over by the truck with this and just stay there." I then checked the pulse, and I couldn't feel the pulse. I then put my hand close to their face to see if they were breathing, and one of them sort of, I guess a twitch would be a good way to say it. I backed off and then the next time I went there he had expired. The sergeant of the guard, the officer of the guard, and everyone else was out there immediately; took the M14 away from me.

I was taken back to the guard shack and they started to say something and I said, "People, you folks are going to have to excuse me because I am sick," and I went outside and I upchucked everything that I'd eaten in two days, I'm sure, and I came back in. I was afraid I'd be court-martialed. My biggest fear right then was I was going to be court-martialed for shooting these people. There was an old master sergeant around there. He gave me a canteen of water and he said, "Go wash your mouth out, son." I washed my mouth out, and I came back and he said, "Did you drink some of that?" and I said, "Yes, sarge," and he took me to one side and out of his pocket he pulled a little flask and he gave me a shot of whiskey and he said, "There you are." He said, "By God, you're a combat veteran now. Go talk to them." I went over and they asked me to give them a statement. I told them exactly what happened, what I had done, and the sergeant of the guard called the vehicle back in and put me back on it. The officer of the day or the officer of the guard said, "Definitely put him back on there!"

When the vehicle came back, there was a new driver and two new people in it and the only thing that was said was the driver said, "Oh, you're the new guy that just greased two of them?" and I said, "Yes, I was forced to shoot two people tonight," and he said, "I hear you're a damn good shot," and that was the end of the conversation and then the next day I went to the 1st Replacement Company.

LARRY LUKES
Member of 3rd Platoon of Charlie Company

At first when we got to Vietnam it was pretty calm, walking around in the jungle fighting mainly red ants and that kind of junk. I thought, "What the hell are we doing over here?" If we went into an area where an air strike or artillery had stirred them up, the red ants would just eat you alive. And the mosquitoes. At night you would just have to burrow down into the mud like an old pig to get away from them. The bug juice they gave us worked some, and it was good for getting the leeches off, and my wife Kay would send me some Off [insect repellant] and other really good stuff from home. And she would make this oatmeal/caramel type of cake. Everybody loved that stuff. Every time I would get a box they would all ask, "Man! Is there some more of that cake in there?" That cake never lasted very long. She was always sending me hot sauce and catsup and stuff that we didn't have over there; you know, to make our C rations taste a little better. Everybody's girlfriends and mothers were sending stuff that we could all share. Everybody kind of pooled everything together.

The Vietnamese sold about everything you could imagine. They would always sell us the Ba Muoi Ba beer. The military always told us not to drink it because they had bamboo shoots in it that would grow in your belly and kill you. As much as I drank I should have been dead a long time ago. And the girls. They had all kinds of hookers running around. Of course they had massage parlors in little shacks; basically what they were was whorehouses. This one lieutenant in another company put this one cathouse off limits because they had this one French-Vietnamese gal in there. I mean she was really good looking. That was his sweetheart, so he put it off limits to the rest of us. Of course you don't say that to a bunch of GIs – that was like telling us to go and open the door. He was always mad because every time he came in there were always ten or 15 guys from the company in there. Of course they gave us lectures on VD, but the guys figured, what the heck? We're in Vietnam anyway. May as well die happy.

Most of our first operations were in a swamp – just mud and water. We would go out on night ambush patrol, and the tide would come in. So you have to blow up your air mattresses and put all your web gear and your weapon and stuff on there and make sure that you tied rope to it and to a tree. A couple guys got on their air mattresses and went to sleep and didn't tie them to trees, and in the morning they were gone. I don't think that they ever did find them. Sometimes you would crawl up into trees to stay dry. It was just leeches, mud, and dirt. You would have leeches all over you and little cuts from where they had been. I'd seen leeches and used them for fish bait, but this was the first time I ever had them on me. You'd just spray the bug juice on them, and they would let go. We would often find enemy bunkers on our searches. One time we were taking a break, and I could hear some Vietnamese talking. I said, "Sergeant Marr. Do you hear those Viet Cong talking?" He said, "You have to be crazy!" But we ended up finding bamboo sticking up out of the ground. They called in the engineers and everyone, and it turned out that they had a whole hospital underground. They had lights down there and cook-fires going. They had been there, but they had hauled tail when they heard us digging, pounding, and jumping around. One night a tiger walked through our ambush – it scared Smitty [James Smith] so bad that he was damn near petrified. Next thing I know there are machine guns and rifles going off. I wondered what the hell was going on – seeing a tiger running through setting off trip flares and getting shot at. From where I was at it sounded like World War III going off. But I don't think that they ever did hit it. I laughed so hard.

Mines and booby traps were the big danger. We walked through the rice paddies, never on the dikes if we could help it. That is where they mainly had the mines. The VC would dig these pits where we would walk. They had these spears poking up out of the bottom of these pits covered in human urine so if you got poked the infection would kill you. One time McBride was right in front of me. I stepped in one of these holes and fell, and my rifle was cradled across the hole. Thank God that I was short, so I never hit any of them spears. McBride turned around, and he was laughing. About that time I went to move to get out of the hole, and I tripped a grenade. It was right there. And I'm looking, and I could see in slow motion the pin go flying through the air. All I could think was, "Aww, shit! This is it!" And it was a dud; it didn't go off. McBride reached down and grabbed me by the back of my shirt and pulled me up out of the hole. I said, "Damn! Did you see that?" And he could hardly talk; he only said, "Yeah. I seen it." That is the scaredest I have ever been in my life. That grenade was only about 8 inches from my face. If it wouldn't have been a dud, I would have been dead. But it never went off. I'll tell you something, I'm not sure what the good Lord had in mind for me, but I had a lot of deals where the guy standing next to me would get wounded real bad or step on a land mine and two or three guys would get wounded, but I would never get a scratch. It often made me wonder why. Here I am just an old country boy, no college education. We had all these guys that had had college; they had kids at home and money, and they had come from good families. And they would end up getting killed or wounded real bad, and I didn't get nothing. I thought, "What in the heck is the deal with this?" But I guess the good Lord had something else in mind for me.

When we began really to lose people some guys took it really, really hard. It was tough; it was hard on all of us. But I felt so sorry for our replacements who came in, because nobody would befriend them. You didn't want to get to like them because you didn't want to feel like that [the grief they felt at losing old timers in the unit] when they got shot or killed. It was tough on the new guys, because nobody wanted to be friends with them. You just didn't want that hurt when they got wounded or killed.

LIFE AND DEATH IN THE NAM

ANTHONY GOODRICH
Member of Mike Company, 3rd Battalion, 5th Marines

We were just doing patrols in the area. To be very honest, I never knew what we were really doing. We'd go on these patrols and go through villages. Sometimes we would check for ID cards, sometimes we wouldn't. I remember one time we were going up into the foothills of the Que Son mountains on a patrol one day. It was 95 degrees, humidity was about that much. I remember just blacking out. I woke up with the corpsman pouring water on me. For the most part, I didn't get teased too much. Everybody said this happened to everyone. I got pissed off at myself. Never happened again after that. They said make sure to drink plenty of water. When I first got there, I carried four canteens of water, and I ended up carrying six and eight the rest of my tour.

I was never asked what my MOS was when I got in country. I wasn't going to volunteer that I was a machine gunner. About three weeks into my tour, one of the machine gunners rotated home so they asked if anybody here was an O331 [machine gunner]; of course I learned very quickly, you never volunteer any information. They knew, Goodrich is an O331; we have his rosters right here. I remember my squad leader saying, "How come you didn't tell us you were an O331?" I said, "Because I knew better." He laughed. He took me over to this guy, who was the gunner. Probably the guy that taught me more than anything I needed to know to survive there. I went up to him and he said, "I'm so and so, you are now my assistant gunner, which means you feed belts of ammo into my gun and when I'm moving you're attached to my asshole. When I move, you move."

Anyway this guy basically sat me down one night and said this is what you need to do to survive here. This is what you carry. He took my backpack. Took everything else I didn't know I had. I carried extra utility uniforms, threw that away. He said, "You want to carry three or four dry socks; this is how you carry your C rations. This is where you put your frag [grenade]. This is how you carry your flak jackets." The guy actually sat me down and said, "This is what you need to carry. This is what you need to not carry." He said that we were a team. This whole thing about an FNG [Fucking New Guy], everybody doesn't want to get close, he said that doesn't work with me. He said, "You see the belt getting short you make sure you clip another damn belt on there." He said as an A-gunner, I'd have to carry I think 400 rounds. Which would be four belts. He said, "Just carry a pistol. You don't need a rifle because you won't be using it." So, I said okay.

Shortly, after that we got called back to An Hoa, where we were told we were going to go on a combat operation up in the mountains. The company had just come out of the mountains before I got there. They were not happy. They said the mountains were scary. There were lots of enemy there, they said. My gunner and I got together the night before we went up. He said, "This is a combat operation. This is going to be your first one; just follow me. Do what I do, pay attention to what I do. This is what you've got to look for. This is the way you've got to comport yourself. Ration your food and your water as much as you can. Carry as much ammo as you can. Carry as many frags as you can. We'll get up there and we'll do just fine." The choppers landed. I remember I had an upset stomach that morning. I was very scared. He said, "There's no doubt we're going to go up there and hit something. We're going to find some enemy. It's not going to be like we've been doing for the past two weeks down here." So, we got choppered up, Operation *Durham Peak*. Years later I found out that we were basically chasing a couple of divisions of NVA with a battalion-sized operation from our side of the Que Son mountains.

I should tell you the night before we went up there, they did an arc light [B52 strike] on top of these mountains that we were going to go to. My gunner said as these bombs are dropping, it was just an awesome sight, to see the whole sky lit up on the top of this mountain. A few seconds later the ground would start shaking; you could hear the rumble. It was just a truly amazing sight. He said, "That's where we're going tomorrow." I said, "Will there be anybody up there when we get up there?" He said, "Probably." Anyway, we chopper up into the mountain right where they dropped those big bombs from the 52s. Get out of the chopper; he trained me to be the last guy to get on the helicopter. He says, "We want to be the last two on the chopper, because we want to be the first two off. If this thing gets hit," he said, "if there's a hot LZ we want to get the hell off this thing. Besides they need automatic weapons to get off there quicker than the rest of the platoon so we can lay down a base of fire." So, that made perfect sense to me. We fly up there, wasn't a hot LZ. They were actually able to land these choppers up there on top of this mountain ridge. We got the whole company on this ridgeline. We started humping. We humped that day probably for six or eight hours to our position on another mountain. I remember the heat, even in the mountains; it was hot as hell up there. I remember just trying to gain footing. We were going straight up and straight down. It was double-canopy jungle. It was just tough. It was hard as hell. It was hot. It was humid. There were lots of bugs. There were a lot of little animals scurrying around. There was lots of noise. Lots of jungle noise, which my buddy said that's good, because if there's lots of noise, you knew that the enemy wasn't around. When it's quiet you've got to watch out for yourself.

I remember going up the side of these mountains, and there were vines grabbing onto your gear, onto the gun, everything. You would fall, slip and fall back, knock people down. It was just a miserable hump. Anyway, we got to the top of this other ridge. We got to our objective for the day. We set up guns. We set up good field of fire, actually by the LZ. We had a small LZ that probably wasn't wider than maybe 30 feet across. I remember the choppers came in for resupply. The front wheels would hover; the back wheels would touch down. They would drop the ramp and they would throw out C rations and ammo to us. The chopper skills were just amazing of these guys. A 300- or 400-foot cliff on both sides of this little LZ we had up there. I remember that. That was around the same time that man landed on the moon. Somebody had a radio up there. I remember he said, "We just landed on the moon. The United States just landed on the moon." There was no celebration. Everybody said, "Well fuck, so what? We wish they were here and we were there." That was July 20, I guess. July 20, 1969.

[On operations we would carry] not less than 60 pounds, probably closer to 80. We carried claymores [an anti-personnel mine]. Everybody carried a claymore. We carried pop-up hand illuminations. At least two of those. At least 2 pounds of C-4. I probably carried four to six frags. Four or five hundred rounds of machine gun ammo. Sometimes I carried an extra 60mm mortar round. Of course, my pistol. I had on my helmet and my flak jacket. Anything that they needed help carrying, I helped carry. Illumination, sometimes smoke grenades. Sometimes willy peter [white phosphorous] or thermal grenades. Six canteens of water. We were weighted down pretty much. The flak jacket weighed a ton. Those flak jackets we had; I thought they were worthless until I saw a guy get his life saved because it stopped shrapnel. They would get wet and they'd be so damn heavy. They were heavy dry, but they were really heavy when they got wet. I remember being in the jungle – out in the bush if you get a scratch on your hand or on your arm or face and how it would fester because there was no way you could clean it. We called those gook sores. Corpsmen would clean it quickly. They'd say pour water on it, but we hated to use water for something like that. Water was a precious commodity, one of the things you didn't give it away.

I remember one of the most surrealistic things I ever saw in Vietnam was at Christmastime, Christmas Day. It was raining like hell. We were in the Arizona [an area near An Hoa]; it was just muddy and rainy, just miserable, and we had a chopper come in that was bringing care packages from the States. I remember the chopper landed, the back ramp dropped down, and there was a guy dressed up like Santa Claus that started throwing packages out. He had this big bell, and he walked out and he was ringing the bell saying, "Ho, Ho, Ho," as he threw the bags out, and of course we laughed for about two seconds, and then we wanted to take him out. After it unloaded all the bags, all the mail, all the care packages, the chopper took off and circled our position, and this guy was leaning out the side window ringing this bell and saying, "Ho, Ho, Ho," and it was just one of the strangest things I'd ever seen. That, and the day we were on patrol during the Christmas season, and there was a bird dog, which is an observation plane, flying overhead that had a speaker and it was playing Christmas carols, and we were on patrol in the Arizona, in the middle of nowhere. He was playing "Hark the Herald Angels," and "Frosty the Snowman"; it was just another surrealistic thing.

Once we had to move people from a village to a safe area. I remember going into this village – this was something that really sticks out in my mind. We had to round up all the people in the village. We had to kill all their animals; we had to set all their hooches on fire, burn them down, and then we put them on choppers to send them to a relocation camp. I'll never forget the looks on these people's faces. We were shooting the water buffalo, shooting the chickens or pigs, and these kids were begging us not to do this, and that just always stuck in my mind. This is not the way to win these people's hearts and minds: destroy all their crops, burn down all their houses and put them on choppers and say we're going to keep you safe back in some other place. I just never understood that. I had to go around with my M14 and kill all the water buffalo, and that was tough; it was tough for me to do. I thought what if this was happening to me, and people came into my town and said okay, we're going to take all you guys, we're going to move you from Albuquerque to Santa Fe; we're going to destroy your neighborhood. And I'd been there for generations after generations; I just knew that was not right. We weren't doing the right thing there.

I have no idea why that order came down; even our platoon commander was baffled. We did not understand why we were doing this; it was just crazy. We even asked the lieutenant, "Lieutenant, why are we doing this?" He would say, "Don't ask me. These are orders from the battalion or from the regiment. We're here to save these people," and of course that was tongue in cheek. We were kind of giggling as we're saying we're going to save these people by sending them to someplace where they have no idea, taking them away from their ancestral land. We all questioned what we were doing, including the lieutenant. I remember we were killing animals and destroying crops and putting people on choppers, and they're in tears with rage and sadness in their faces, just incomprehensible.

RON VIDOVIC

*Ron Vidovic was from Tacoma, Washington. He dropped out of school
in the 10th grade and worked in a gas station. At the age of 19 Vidovic
married and later had two children. He worked in a cabinet-making
factory before getting divorced and subsequently drafted in the spring of
1966. Vidovic served in the 3rd Platoon of Charlie Company, 4th of the
47th Infantry with Fred Kenney, Larry Lukes, Elijah Taylor, Richard
Rubio, Terry McBride, Don Trcka, and Steve Hopper. Vidovic was
wounded in action in August 1967, losing a leg. After the war Vidovic
returned to Tacoma and worked for 20 years with a company that
manufactures school furniture and then worked for the Tacoma School
District in custodial services.*

We were searching each one of these bunkers, and we did not find
any VC in them or even in back of them. We waved to our platoon
leader that there were no VC. We were going to come in right
across the middle of the rice paddies. If there was anybody out
there they would open up on us, and the company would jump
them. We were going to be the decoys. So we come walking back
out. See, I did not want to wear my flak vest out there. It was
too hot, too heavy, and we were not seeing fire or anything.
Thank goodness I did put it on. When we were coming back, we
were just walking, and then all of a sudden – probably about
halfway back – there was a great big explosion. I thought someone
had dropped an artillery or mortar round on us. It hit me and
I could feel my hat take off, and my rifle flew out of my hand.
Felt like something hit me right across the chest.

I tried to get up and could not get up; I tried finding my gun
and could not find my gun. I was just more or less in a daze.
I looked down and saw my one leg was blown off and my other
was mushy black. I sat back down, and I think I yelled "medic!"
I had tripped a mine. Our old medic went on R&R, and I was this
new guy's first casualty. Finally they got out there to me and
[Terry] McBride was joking around with me. He said, "Dang, Ron!
Looks like you're going home." [I had been wounded in the groin
as well, so] he grabbed my pants and cut the front of them open
and said, "You're still good there, fella!" I said, "Boy, when they

make these movies about John Wayne, a guy gets wounded and the first thing that comes out of his mouth as he's lying there, 'God damn, I wish I had a cigarette.'" That was the last thing in the world I wanted.

The new medic guy didn't quite know what to do. I did not want to look at my legs; I knew they were hurt real bad and one was gone. The medic picked up the severed leg; it was still connected by a strip of skin. What hurt worse was my finger and the side of my mouth. Shrapnel went through the side of my face. I said, "For being one of your first patients this really turns your stomach a little bit, doesn't it?" He did not really say much. I do not remember his name.

Thank God I had a flak vest on. It was the only thing that saved my life out there. They finally threw smoke over there and got a helicopter in to get me dusted off. I cannot remember if the medic guy or the helicopter guy did it, but somebody asked how was I feeling and if I needed another shot. I said, "Boy, if you got one I could sure use one because there is going to be a little bit of aching here." He gave me another shot. I was in wonderland, and all I knew was that I was on a helicopter.

KIRBY SPAIN
Member of 1st Platoon of Charlie Company

In April 1967 we had been out on operation for a couple of days. So I got this squad out there, and everybody sets up at their designated spot. We were all up eating our C rations when the daylight comes up. We were over there by ourselves, had a radio with us. Anyway, this sampan comes floating down the river. This was odd; we could not see anything in it. We called Lieutenant Hunt and told him about it. He said, "Well stay alert and make a sweep." We would go out maybe 50 yards, spread out and make a sweep of the area to make sure nothing came up on us.

About a hundred yards from where we spent the night, we came up on this base camp. I let Lieutenant Hunt know, and he has us to hold still and brought the rest of the platoon in there.

We were going through the base camp, and the Viet Cong still had their rice cooking in the pot. The rice was still steaming. So I know they had spent the night there. It was more like 50 or 60 yards from where we had spent the night. We were making this sweep through the camp and Lieutenant Hunt is telling us to be careful of booby traps. All of a sudden we hear this explosion off to my left. Everyone is wondering what it is.

You can hear Lieutenant Black [the company executive officer] moaning in the middle of this thicket. I did not know at the time, but he had found this grenade strung up with tripwire. Instead of letting the engineers disarm it like we were taught to do, he tried to disarm it himself. It blew up on him; he was squatted down near the grenade and it went off. I was one of the near people to him, maybe 10 yards at most. The explosion got him in the legs, torso, and pieces of the grenade came up underneath his chin and were lodged in his brain.

Lieutenant Hunt told me, "Spain, take your squad in there and get him out." So we were very gingerly picking our way through, and Danny Bailey, bless his heart, tripped another booby trap. It got him real bad and got me in three places. There was a piece of shrapnel that hit the back of Lieutenant Hunt's knee, went in and lodged under his kneecap.

It stung, and, after you get thinking about, it kind of makes you sick to your stomach. Got me in the back, the right arm, and in the stomach. The area had 2-, 3-, sometimes 4-inch trees in it. It was the only thing we had for a landing zone to bring a chopper in. So everybody started hacking with machetes, and one of the guys from engineering squad that we had with us came up and started stringing detcord [an explosive cord] around as many trees as he could get. When he blew them, they fell in. That is what we used for a landing field for the dust off.

Danny was in real bad shape and I was real concerned about him. His wound started right at the top of his boot, went up his leg, and as it got up around his upper thigh, buttocks, and the small of his back. He took the brunt of it. He had one of them bush hats. We could not get through the brush real good with the helmets. So we would snap the chinstrap onto our canteen on our belts. The blast knocked holes in Danny Bailey's helmet that I could run my thumb through. Right there on his butt, his right cheek, looked like it has been run through a sausage grinder. In Bailey's own words, "It damn near blew my ass off!" If he hadn't been wearing that helmet hanging off of his canteen it would have blown his groin to bits.

I went and visited Bailey in the hospital when I got well enough to walk. On the second day I was in the hospital they told me that Lieutenant Black died. So he lived for a while. They brought him in there to get the shrapnel out, but he did not survive the surgery. I saw his wounds. The wound that killed him went in underneath his chin and upper throat, right there behind his jawbone, and went all the way through into his brain.

GARY FRANKLIN
Member of the 198th Light Infantry Brigade

I did a lot of talking [with our supporting artillery units] when I was RTO. I knew our artillery was normally very good, real accurate. They could really put a round where you wanted it. I think part of that was pressure on them, because about my fourth month there we figured out that the standard procedure was to call first aerial bursts of smoke, white phosphorous, and we'd have a 100-meter aerial burst, and by that we could tell where the HE [high explosive] was going to hit. The whole idea was safety. You called a first round 100-meter aerial burst, and then you made sure that you were on target. Well, the NVA, they knew as much about where the artillery was going to hit as we did. They would see the first round of white phosphorous at 100-meter aerial bursts and they knew when the first HE round was going to hit and they'd be gone before it hit. So we gave up on that; I guess it was about October '68. We started calling first round HE on the ground and we'd just call HE on the ground, first round, and make sure that we knew where we were, where we were calling artillery, and made sure that artillery understood that they'd better hit where we called it.

[After about four months in country] Tim [my squad leader] was going home and got together with Ordway, one of the fire-team leaders. They got a little pow-wow, and I knew from what they'd been talking about for the last three weeks they were going to decide who was going to be the squad leader. I naturally figured it was going to be Ordway because he only had about four months left in country, and they got through their little pow-wow and I said, 'Okay, who's it going to be?' and they said, "It's going to be you," and I said, "I don't think I'm ready for that," and Ordway said, "I'll train you. Don't worry about it." What they decided was since he just had four months left that he was going to be a short timer pretty quick, too, and I still had nearly eight months left, and Ordway's going to train me since he was an experienced guy, and he did. He'd answer and advise me on anything I needed to know. He made sure I didn't screw up. So, I became a squad leader pretty early in my career in Vietnam. I was a squad leader for about the last seven months, and it worked out, and it didn't help Ordway that much anyway because about the second month we got a new lieutenant. We got a couple of guys hurt and all of a sudden we had to have a squad leader in I think the second squad and he was it. You did whatever worked at the time for everybody. Whatever was important for the platoon, that's what you had to do. He was a real good, experienced guy and taught me a lot of things, and somehow Tim came home. Tim was wounded I think four times, and I was wounded three times; everybody I knew was wounded three or four times nearly. But Ordway came home and he was there the whole year, from January '68 to December '68 and was never wounded, which is miraculous how he did that. He was lucky. It was pure blind luck.

We normally were able to keep 18 to 25 guys in 3rd Platoon [at full strength a platoon numbers roughly 40 men]. I can remember getting down to 12 or 13 once or twice and I can remember having 28 or so a couple of times, but normally we ran around 22 to 25 men if we were able to keep that many in the field. We thought we really had a lot of people if we could get 25 people in the platoon. We didn't even get close to what the Army considered a standard fighting unit. We just couldn't keep that many people out in the field all the time. We were constantly getting new people, somebody would be on R&R, somebody wounded; just never could keep that many people out in the field.

We were always glad to see new people come in because we were always needing people. I really had a squad with quite a few experienced people, thank goodness, and everyone tried to help the new guys learn what was going on and train them as fast as they could, hoping that they'd become experienced. Unfortunately, most of the new guys didn't last anywhere from a day to two months. It was hard to get new guys trained enough to get them experienced enough to last. One thing I know was true, even in my case as a squad leader, you didn't get to be close buddies with a new guy until he was there two or three months, because he just didn't last. That kind of made it tough on the new guys, too. I was one at the time, and your first thought is, '"Do I have the plague? Nobody wants to chum around or be buddies much with me." Well, they're all scared you're fixing to get blown away. So, you had to kind of get over about a three-month hump. We were always glad to see new guys because we were always needing personnel. Even if all they knew was to follow around and shoot a rifle, that was a help. It seemed like we had a lot of turnover of new guys, and you always had a core of old guys that seemed to last.

My [friend Jerry and I] were squad leaders and I guess we'd been to a briefing or something. We were a close enough platoon where if the mail arrived and somebody wasn't there, we'd read their mail for them. We'd let them know what it said when they got there. But, if you didn't get your mail first and open it, there was liable to be somebody else reading it. Well, Jerry and I got back over there, and the whole squad was eating cake. We were lucky; a cake that got there was usually a week old but still tasted good. Sometime it is kind of half squashed and a lot of times they never got there. A fresh powder cake, if the guys in the rear could smell it, they knew what it was, they'd open it and eat it and it would never make it to the field. Anyway, the guys were sitting around eating cake and we walk up and somebody says, "Hey Jerry, we saved you a piece of cake. Grab a piece of cake!" We thought, "Oh, this is great." One of them said, "Happy birthday,

Jerry!" It was Jerry's birthday and the guy said, "Your aunt sent you a cake, wrote a nice note, too." They'd already opened the care package. Luckily for us they at least saved us a piece of cake for Jerry's birthday.

We didn't have a real good relationship I guess you could say with the rear-echelon base camp commandos because we thought they lived the luxury life, and they seemed to always have things we didn't. They took advantage of the situation, I guess you'd say. We went once during monsoon season and were trying to get poncho liners, and those things were fantastic because they'd keep you warm even when they were wet. That was the best thing the military had was those poncho liners. We couldn't get any. Finally found out they had got a big supply the last month before. Our supply sergeant back there had given them to his girlfriend, so they all went on the black market, and a lot of that stuff that should have been out there, like ordnance and weapons, a lot of it ended up being sold or given to the villagers by one of the rear echelons.

One time we found a big weapons cache. We found way over 100, mostly bolt-action and little carbine and SKS rifles, and we tagged them all, tagged one for the colonel, and then the captain got first choice and we just worked our way down by rank and privilege and everybody tagged one and the captain called the armorer back in Bayonet [a base camp] and told him they were on the way in and the colonel knew about them. We had a nice bolt-action rifle souvenir. Well, about half of them got retagged on LZ Professional when the chopper stopped on Professional. When they finally got back to Bayonet I think Captain Hall was the only one that got a rifle. All the rest of them went out to base camp commandos. They registered them for themselves and sent them home.

Every once in a while everybody chipped in to buy beer for stand down or something and an officer would call in and say, "We've got 70 people on the firebase, I want 70 beers." We'd go back there to Bayonet to the supply room; they had stacks of Budweiser and Coors. But they would drink all the Bud and Coors and send us the Ballantine, the junk. So, we just didn't have real warm feelings toward the base camp command. Of course they kept their distance from us. We usually came in from the field – we'd been out there for two weeks and we were grungy and smelled – and they all kept their distance from us and that was fine with us.

STEVE HOPPER

Steve Hopper was from the rural area near Greenfield, Illinois. After high school he went to work for Caterpillar in Peoria, Illinois. Hopper was drafted in the spring of 1966 and served in the 3rd Platoon of Charlie Company, 4th of the 47th Infantry with Fred Kenney, Larry Lukes, Terry McBride, Elijah Taylor, Richard Rubio, Don Trcka, and Ron Vidovic. Hopper was wounded in action on July 1, 1967, and again when his squad was pinned down in battle on October 6, 1967. After the war Hopper returned to Greenfield, married his sweetheart, Jennifer, and went to work again for Caterpillar.

I was scheduled to go on R&R in the first week of June. But what happened was we had a one-day patrol out on an island not too far from our base camp that we called Booby Trap Island. We knew that the area was full of booby traps and punji pits, you know? The day we went out on that patrol I walked up to my platoon sergeant, Joe Marr, and said, "Joe, I've got a really, really bad feeling about today. I don't know how to explain it, but I just have a feeling that something is going to happen to me. This is gonna sound odd, but can you permit me not to go on today's patrol?" He looked at me kind of funny, and I looked at him. He said, "Steve, I know what you want to do, but we've got to have you. You are the squad leader and we've got to have you." I said, "I understand. I'll go." I just had a really strange feeling, and I had to express that to the platoon sergeant.

Even before we landed on the island there was sniper fire. We got out onto the island and scattered, looking for cover. Just trying to stay scattered to make a smaller target. We kind of cleaned a few areas out and moved right down the island. We entered kind of a wooded area, and we had a guy step into a punji trap. We moved on through the woods, and there wasn't a lot of activity, just a sniper here and there. It was actually kind of a pretty calm day. Then we stepped out into an open area with tall grass in it. The grass was maybe a foot and a half high, and there were a few paths out in it. As we moved out, we kind of stuck to the paths. I was moving off to the left flank and was on a path. Then I moved a couple of steps further and tripped a booby trap or a land mine. It literally blew my trousers almost completely off of me. It went off a foot or two behind me. I can still smell it, the explosion. I can still smell the blood. I can still feel the hot metal hitting me. The fragments hit my legs and ankles all the way up to my buttocks area and my lower arms from the elbows down. Fortunately I had a flak jacket on, so I didn't get any in my back. Doc Taylor came over and started cutting my clothes off of me. There wasn't much left of my trousers. They were Taylor's trousers I was wearing that day. I had borrowed a pair from him. To this day when I see him he asks me when I am going to give his trousers back.

I started to sit down, and Taylor told me not to, that there was some shrapnel that he had to pull out of me. He pulled several pieces out of me in the field, and they got me over with the rest of the group. Joe Marr had also caught a piece of shrapnel from this thing. And Alan Richards got a piece of shrapnel from it in the jaw. Marr got a piece in the groin area. They started bandaging me up, but it was like where do you start? I was peppered all the way up and down my body. The chopper came in, and I got on. They dropped me off at the hospital, and when I got off of the chopper there was a couple of guys running out with a stretcher. I said, "I'm okay. I can walk." And they told me, "No, get on the stretcher." Here I was kind of naked from the waist down, you know? So I got on, and they carried me into the hospital. The nurses were raising my legs, examining me, and looking me over. I remember being embarrassed; I mean here are all these nurses checking you out, and you are naked from the waist down.

They asked me if I wanted my parents notified, and I said, "Yeah. You had better let them know." They examined me and told me that it looked like I would be going home, and I said, "Well, that would be nice." But it didn't turn out that way.

They took me into surgery and numbed me with Novocain. Then they had to go in and dig the shrapnel out. I just watched them. They would take a knife or scalpel and slice me open to the point where they could get the shrapnel out. Then they would dig it out with their tongs or just get their fingers in there. They didn't stitch anything up; they left everything open to heal from the inside out. I got into my room later that night and was counting the wounds. Some were pretty small. I counted 30 or 40 marks just in my arm alone. Most of that shrapnel is still in me today. The next thing I sent a letter to mom and dad telling them that I had gotten wounded but that everything was okay. I told them a little bit about it. Alan Richards and I were supposed to go on R&R together in three days, but that got delayed because I got wounded and he got wounded. Richards wasn't too bad. What was terrible about it – it was a very minor wound, but they opened him up. And here he was with a long scar right along his face. Because of me. That bothered me greatly. I blame myself. It was one thing for me to be wounded by my tripping off a land mine or booby trap. But when you get others involved in it, it takes a little bit of a different appearance. I've thought about if for 40 years.

TERRY MCBRIDE
Member of 3rd Platoon of Charlie Company

[In June 1967] I remember when we landed that day there were trees everywhere, and just after we landed somebody got hit by a sniper. I don't know who. He wasn't in our platoon. We were on patrol, and Bob Sachs tripped a booby trap, and got hit by fragments. There was a big tree between me and him, or I'd of got hit right in the face. I [as a machine gunner] was with the point squad most of the time, and he was one of the point guys. Sachs got screwed up pretty bad, and that was the last I seen of him. He got dusted off and that was that. As machine gunner they usually made me wait while they crossed these little canals on little poles [monkey bridges]. Well your average Vietnamese weigh about 98 pounds. And they crossed the canals on these suspended sticks.

The platoon would always wait and make me cross last; then they would all stand there and watch me cross, hoping that the thing would break. Everybody else would be dry, and I would be wet and nasty, you know? Just because I weighed a little bit more than everybody else.

After Sachs had gotten hit we were going on a file down this path. You really felt at home, because on each tree there was like this piece of tin that was flattened out with North Vietnamese flags painted on them. People were wanting to tear them off, and I told them not to. You never know, there might be a grenade dug in right behind it. Then the point squad got hit with automatic fire. I happened to be right by this little hooch, so I jumped inside of it because they usually have mud bunkers in them. So I got low in the bunker and make a hole into the side wall [of the hooch] so I can see out. I had just gotten a new ammo bearer named Halsey. He was peeking out the side of that hooch, doing a World War II thing, like he had something in front of him strong enough to stop a bullet. But it was only a thatch hooch, and he got struck through the gut.

I'm looking to see where this fire is coming from. I can hear it; it is off to the right front of the trail we were going down. But I couldn't see any flashes or anything. And they were firing pretty good at that point in time. About that time this big old pig comes walking down the trail. Like a 500-pound pig. The hooch we were in had like three placemats with bowls of rice steaming on them, so I knew that whoever had been there had just left. So I was in their home, of whoever was shooting at us. And this pig has come down the same trail we had been walking on, and I told everybody to pay attention. I was going to shoot the hog, and if it's theirs they are probably going to be pissed off and are going to fire back as soon as I shoot it, and then we will look for their flashes. And as soon as I knocked that hog over, I looked to my right front, and I saw the flashes from where they were coming from. I hollered at the squad leader and told him where the flashes were at and that I was going to put a burst on them and was going to keep it on so he can have some people come up to the right of where I was shooting to throw a grenade in that bunker.

So I'm shooting at this bunker and they came up on the right flank and fired a 79 round [from a grenade launcher] and then threw a grenade in there. It killed them all and caved the bunker in on top of them. It was kind of like a big spider hole. Then they told us to get in there and get the weapons and stuff. But it was caved in, and nobody had a shovel. So we start digging it out with our hands, and lo and behold I see this hair. So I thought I would just grab this sucker by the hair and pull him out. When I pulled on the hair, I just got this whole chunk of skull with skin and hair on it. I thought, "Jesus Christ, this hair is really long." Must be a hippie dude. Then we got it dug out and I realized it was a chick. I got the scissors from the medic and cut off, I don't know, about 18 inches of it, and got some tape and stuck it to a slit in the back of my helmet. It kind of looked like Attila the Hun. I wore it for maybe a month and a half, until it got kind of funky looking. At the same time it reminded me that it wasn't just dudes that were fighting in the war. It was a little deeper than that. I mean she had web gear on and a weapon and the whole thing. So the war just got a little deeper at that point.

I know what that day meant to me; it meant I really had to watch my ass, you know? And everybody else too.

On July 4, me and Larry Lukes were going along with the platoon and were right next to the headquarters section, the lieutenant and all that. And Lukes says, "Hey, I see something moving over here to my right." And I look where he is pointing, and I don't see nothing. He said, "Well, I just seen two people." And I said, "Larry, I don't see nothin'." And he said, "Let's go over and look, okay?" So we got the rest of the platoon stopped and then we kind of cruised over to our right there and I said, "I still don't see nothin'." And then I look and see this little hooch, kind of like a storage shed. Just an angled roof on one side. It had three sides and the front was open. I thought, "That's a weird-looking hooch. They built half of it and that was it." Right by this thing I look down and there are these two pairs of sandals sitting there, and there is like water where they had just come out of the paddies. And it is fresh, there are drippings right behind the sandals. I looked up in the air and said, "Well, they aren't up there." And Lukes puts his finger to his mouth like quiet and I whisper, "What?" And he points down at the ground. Then I look and think, "Well, that makes sense."

So we start looking, and there is a perfect circle like someone had taken a pencil and drawn a circle on the ground, but it is like 36 inches in diameter. It was like the size of the covering of a sewer. They had jumped in this hole and taken the top and set it down and it had blown the dust up around the edges of it. Lukes says, "They're in here." So I took the safety off of my machine gun and I said, "Open it up." So he opened it, and as soon as he did there's these two guys in there. One has got a grenade in his hand and the other has an AK [47]. So I just blasted both of them right there, and now a couple of guys from the platoon come over. The lieutenant and somebody else say, "What's up?" So I say, "Well, look." Lukes had dropped the top back on it as soon as I fired. He was thinking that the grenade was going to go off too. But it didn't, and the lieutenant opened it, and we took the guns that were in there. One of these guys had an information packet or something, turned out he was an officer or something like that. He was headed to some battalion meeting.

Right after that we went further down the trail, and Porky Johnson was on point and comes up on a couple of guys sleeping on the trail, and he cuts loose on them. I was with the point squad and we were in a tree line, and they took off. I figured that they had to come out of that tree line, so I moved to the right of the trail. All of a sudden, about 50 feet in front of me, this guy comes hauling ass out of the tree line. He's running like O. J. Simpson going through the airport. My machine gun is almost pointed straight down, and the first thing I do when I see him is pull the trigger, and the first rounds were landing like 3 feet in front of me. Then I just took the gun and leaned back and pulled up on it, and I hit him one time in the hand and knocked him right off the dike. We went over there and looked for him, and this is like 30 seconds after it happened. But it was just like he disappeared. I don't know where he went. We didn't find any blood or nothing. I knew that I hit him in the arm or the hand just by the way he spun when I hit him. But he was gone. We looked for him and couldn't find him anywhere.

FRANK LINSTER
Member of the 188th Assault Helicopter Battalion

The 188th was involved with a big operation at that time with the special forces out of Tay Ninh in the Parrot's Beak, which was right on the Cambodian border. The battalion commander that was running that operation up there believed that the Viet Cong had a headquarters in the Parrot's Beak. I remember one of the missions; the hole [to land the helicopter in] was only big enough for three helicopters at a time. So we would fly in with nine helicopters, three would drop off, circle around, the three would come out and another three would drop in the hole and we basically put the entire special forces battalion and their Montagnards in that hole in one day, three ships at a time.

One of the LZs that we used during this period of time was an enemy camp. We actually sat them on top of Charlie. So it got pretty intense. One of the SF [special forces] guys was calling that "I got the Viet Cong exactly where I want them," and the guy says, "What do you mean?" and he says, "They got me surrounded, and I'm popping red smoke." That was totally contrary to what you'd do. Normally what you'd say is, "I'm going to pop smoke," a pilot would identify the color, and the guy on the ground would verify it. Well, he says, "I'm popping red smoke," and I mean red smoke came up everywhere. I said, "I got smoke everywhere!" and he said, "I didn't pop any smoke at all. Shoot it all!" So, we just rolled in and just annihilated that place. I mean, we had all eight gunships up that day, and we were shooting all around this guy, in a jungle, and when we got done he didn't have a scratch. That was the mentality that we picked up as a company because we worked a lot with SF. We had the same kind of mentality that, "Yeah, we're surrounded, big deal; no big thing. We're going to take them on anyway," and I think that's probably why we got away with as few a casualties as we had because we were more obnoxious, if you want to call it that. We just figured, "Hey, we're going to win this thing. We've always got more bullets, and we can shoot faster and we can shoot straighter than the enemy can, so we're going to win any confrontation that we get into," win-win attitude, and I think that had a lot to do with the make up of our company. It wasn't something that we started; it was something that the first guy that went to country started and it just never stopped.

When we weren't in action we did the things that the kids did, you know, the young pilots; we had a lot of fun. I mean, we partied hard. We would buy a quart 100-proof Smirnoff for 95 cents, put it in the club, and sell it for 25 cents a shot. Well, by the time you got the neck empty you'd made back your cost so the rest of the bottle's all profit. We would sell beer for ten cents a can when we bought it by the pallet load, 100 cases to a pallet; we would pay eight cents a can. Well, when you got 500 guys drinking beer you can drink a lot of beer in an evening. So, we had a lot of money at Chase-Manhattan bank as a company from the officer's club, the NCO club, and the EM [enlisted men's] club. Well, when we [in a command reshuffle] were going to become part of the 101st, the rules were that anything we had in the club fund over $10,000 became part of the 101st club fund, not the Black Widow [the nickname for Linster's unit] fund. The guys weren't having any of that. We weren't giving them our money.

Colonel Dreer told me as a supply guy to figure out a way that we can legally spend this money. Well, I had some contacts down in Da Nang, and one of the things they had down there were these 35- and 40-foot freezer trailers full of filet mignon for the Navy. I found out I could buy that stuff, 55 pounds of filet mignon to a box. So, once a week I'd fly down there with the helicopter and I'd pick up enough filet mignon to feed our entire company out of the officer's club. I would take money from the NCO club and they'd buy the French fries, and I'd go to the enlisted club and take money out, and they would buy them wine. So, once a week we would have a cookout. We'd go down to the local village and buy charcoal, and we would have steak and French fries and wine for supper.

Well, the first time I did this we hadn't had any class-A rations or fresh meat for maybe a month or so. We'd been eating Cs and Bs. I remember Willie and Jackson coming through the line, each of them had a plate. Willie had seven filets on his plate, had this plate full of French fries, and he had a bottle of wine in each pocket. They was going to get all the fresh meat that they can get their hands on because they may not get it for another 30 days or so.

We had a kid that the Army had sent to the Hilton Baking School, and had graduated number one in his class. He came to us in Vietnam, and he was a first cook as an E5, the meat and potatoes guy, first cook. So, he went and talked to the colonel and let him know that he was qualified to do this and he says, "You let me cook at night and I'll cook pastries for breakfast, and I'll take care of all the air crews that come in after regular mess hall guys get off," because these guys are up at two o'clock in the morning to feed these guys that are getting up at four, so their days would be pretty long. I find out about this when the colonel calls me into his office and hands me this legal pad and says, "Here, Linster. Go get this." I look at it, "flour, yeast, syrup," you know, on and on, "nuts, walnuts, jam." I looked at Colonel Dreer: "Sir, where in the hell am I supposed to get this stuff?" and he looks at me straight-faced and says, "How in the hell do I know? You're the supply officer, go get it!" "Yes sir. I need to pick up some liquor out of the officer's club and NCO club so I can trade for this stuff."

It didn't take long before everybody in the company knew I was going out on a scrounging run. I mean, everybody that had any information about anything was passing it on. Well, the Marine Corps had just opened up a bakery at Wonder Beach, right up on the DMZ on the ocean, so I thought, "Oh, we'll go there first." So I take the helicopter, we take off at first light in the morning and we land in the yard where the bakery is at and this gunny [gunnery sergeant] shows up all covered with flour and he says, "What can I do for you, Lieutenant?" and I says, "Are you a drinking man, gunny?" "Yeah." "What do you drink?" "I drink scotch." "You like Chivas Regal?" and he says, "Yeah, why?" and I says, "What can I get for a fifth?" and he says, "What do you want?" so I tell him what I'm doing and he says, "Okay, I can handle that. I'll give you 1,500 pounds of flour and two cases of yeast for that bottle of scotch."

He says, "How many guys you feeding?" and I told him and he says, "You need to be back here in three weeks, and bring another bottle." So, he picks up 1,500 pounds of flour in a forklift, puts it in the helicopter, crams it in there and gives me two great big cases of yeast, and that's all I can carry. I pick up my helicopter and I go home and I land at the pad and I call on the radio and I say, "Hey, bring the forklift down to such-and-such a hole." He says, "What for?" and I say, "I need you to unload a pallet of stuff I have for the mess hall." I mean, when I showed up with that flour and yeast the guys in the mess hall's eyes went wide. The baker drooled at the mouth because he knew tonight he was going to be doing some baking, so he made rolls, hot rolls for the morning breakfast. We had guys coming in at ten o'clock at night and all they wanted was hot rolls and butter: "Don't feed me nothing else, just give me hot rolls and butter." So, we went down a couple of other places and we spent about a case of liquor, 12 bottles, and we ended up picking up enough stuff for the guy to bake for a month, basically, and we did that until I went home. Once a week we'd take the helicopter, once every ten days, and go out and do this run, pick up all this stuff for the mess hall.

One of the things that we had in our hooches was praying mantises, and they got really big. We was in playing either poker or something in the hooch, and we had sodas and beer cans sitting around while we was playing, and a praying mantis drops off the ceiling and is sucking on a beer can. We said, "Oh, we've got to get this guy some water." We've got maybe half a dozen inside the hooch, and so we start sitting out a little tin of water for them every day. We had a little box with a light in it to put the salt and the sugar and the pepper in so they wouldn't get hard, and the praying mantises would sit by the light waiting for the mosquitoes and stuff to come around. By accident one of the praying mantises got stuck in the door and got killed. I mean, the guys were devastated. We got Father Red to do a memorial service for our praying mantis when we buried him. Father Red, he was dead serious about this because this guy was one of the members of the family; he was an integral part of not getting bit by mosquitoes.

LIFE AND DEATH IN THE NAM

JOHN YOUNG

John Young was from St Paul, Minnesota. After high school Young attended the University of Minnesota but dropped out to enlist in the military. Young served in the 1st Platoon of Charlie Company, 4th of the 47th with James Nall, Carl Cortright, Steve Huntsman, Kirby Spain, and Ernie Hartman. Young was wounded in action in the fighting on June 19, 1967. After the war Young held down many jobs before reenlisting in the military and serving until 1982. Young now resides in Picayune, Mississippi.

Our company was running a regular operation, by that time they were called reconnaissance in force, and the company was paralleling the bank of a rather large canal. If you walked along the edge of any good-sized canal, those are generally highly booby-trapped areas, because the enemy kind of figures that you are going to be in that area. So you have to be extra careful when you are going along one of those canals. And my squad happened to be on point this day; I think it was in the morning. When you are on point, there are a lot of things you are looking for. The main thing, of course, is the enemy presence: snipers or any real enemy contact. But not quite secondary to that are mines and booby traps. You will almost never find a land mine as such, a buried explosive device; you are just not going to see that. Most of what we had to worry about was booby traps. A booby trap is anything set off by a tripwire. You have a tendency to think of a tripwire as being a taut wire, and usually they were not. They were usually nylon, monofilament fish line, which is very hard to see anyway, and they were usually laid slack across the path of wherever you were likely to walk. And very often in water. Occasionally you'd get lucky and see the tripwire.

You're in enemy country, and you don't want to make any more noise than you must. And this is November. We had been in country for 11 months, and we had gotten pretty good about knowing how to operate and do things right. Well, we'd been on point and moving along for an hour or so and hadn't found any signs of danger, when suddenly in one of the platoons behind us there was an explosion, and we all stopped automatically.

It turned out that one of the guys in the platoon immediately behind mine had tripped a booby trap. Well, my automatic suspicion is that is one that I've missed somehow. I'm supposed to be looking for those things on point. But the guy had wandered off the main path that most of us had been following. Nevertheless it makes you worry all the more when you are up there on point, because now we know that there are booby traps around.

So there was a delay when the file came to a halt as they called in a medevac to get the casualty out. So we had to wait 15 or 20 minutes to get a medevac in and out. While we were standing there waiting, I had a point man out in front of me and another new man in my squad named Brookins, and me and the rest of my squad behind. Brookins was a replacement who had come in only in the last month or so, a guy from Houston I had not gotten to know very well, so I thought, "Well, we have this little break here, I'll just step up here and talk to Brookins." He and I stood there together, and we each had a cigarette and talked. Brookins told me a little bit about himself. He was separated from his wife and had one child, and while he was separated he got drafted. Between the time he got drafted and he went to Vietnam, he and his wife had gotten back together. But it was too late, he was already on his way to Vietnam. We just stood there very casually talking and waiting. You are not totally relaxed during this time; your point man is still watching the area out in front and you are still listening for sounds and so on.

Then word was passed back up the line to move out. So I waved at my point man to move out, and threw down my cigarette butt and put my hand on Brookins' shoulder and I said, "Okay, let's move out." And BOOM! Something slapped both my lower legs, and I went up in the air. I remember thinking, "Crap, I can go home next month, and I've just blown my leg off." I came down against a palm tree, kind of stupefied, kind of stunned. My head cleared, and the dust and smoke in front of me cleared. And I looked down; I had been knocked into a sitting position. I looked down, and both of my legs were still there. About the time I realized that, Brookins came down out of the air and landed in the canal. I jumped up, and my point man came running back, and we grabbed Brookins, each by an arm, and dragged him out of the canal. When he came clear of the water, one of his legs, from about halfway beneath his knee, was just gone. Just gone. Nothing there but some splintered bone and some pieces of meat. A traumatic amputation is a shocking sight. To suddenly see just a stump, where seconds ago there was a limb: it is a very ugly, shocking thing to see. Brookins was kind of moaning, and right away the medic was up there on hand. I remember looking at the stump of his leg. Never before or since have I seen bleeding like that. Blood ran from the stump of his leg just like water from a faucet. He was losing a lot of blood really fast. The medic wrapped a tourniquet around that leg and was wrapping bandages all around the stump to stop the bleeding. And within a minute or two he gave Brookins some morphine. All this while, which hadn't taken more than a couple of minutes, Brookins was afraid to look down at his legs. He was just lying there flat. He was obviously extremely scared and very frightened. Who wouldn't be? Remember, he'd only been in Vietnam less than a month. I lit a cigarette for him. By this time I'm talking to him, trying to buck him up a little because it helps to keep a casualty alert and talking because they can just kind of slide off into shock. That's a dangerous thing, if you let a guy slip away. Just going into shock can kill him, rather than the wound itself. Pretty soon after the medic gave him morphine, he was calmed down a good deal, and the platoon leader was on the radio calling another medevac. About that point Brookins looked up at me, and he said, "My leg's gone, isn't it?" And I said, "Well, part of it is." He looked kind of resigned and said, "Well, get me the hell out of here." I told him that that was what we were doing; we're getting a medevac now.

Within a few minutes some guys got together and put him on a stretcher and hauled him off to where they were going to bring the medevac in. Once they walked off with Brookins, it all just sort of hit me – how close I had been. That had almost been me. In fact I had heard the fuse go off on that mine. Here I was 11 months into a 12-month tour, and I was only inches away from that being me instead of being him. And I got down on my hands and knees, and I vomited. I was just sick from the fear. I remember being really embarrassed with my men scattered around able to see that. I was really ashamed.

So we waited another few minutes for this medevac to come and go, and they passed word up the file again to move out. And so I called to my point man to move out. And a guy had come up to replace where Brookins had been, a guy named Bob Eisenbaugh. And Eisenbaugh took about one or two steps and there was an explosion, and he went up in the air and came down in the canal. Eisenbaugh got his head above the water really quick. Me and Benjamin Acevedo went over there and got half in the water and half out and pulled him out. This time when we pulled him clear of the water, he was intact. Both his legs were there; even his boots were still there. Eisenbaugh looked down at himself and broke out into hysterical laughter – just laughing uncontrollably, because he had been afraid that something was going to be gone. And he looked down and realized that everything was still in place. He had stepped on what we called a toe popper, which was sometimes nothing more than a .50-caliber cartridge set in the ground so that when you step on it, it will fire up through your foot. Sometimes toe poppers were only small explosive charges that weren't designed to do anything more than shatter some bones in your foot. And that's what he'd stepped on. He wasn't gravely wounded, but he had several broken bones, so we had to call yet another medevac.

At this point, in a total of 20 or 30 minutes we've lost three men here. And one had lost part of a leg. A series of incidents like that in a very short period of time just beats your morale to pieces. At that point everybody was just looking around them, wondering where the next booby trap or mine was going to be, and everybody was just kind of scared to do anything, afraid to take a step in any direction. And the company commander, Captain Lind, sort of had the same idea. This area just wasn't worth working. And he wanted to get us out of there. He was on the radio by this time and had to do a little arguing with the battalion commander, but he finally got permission just to get out of there – to pull us out of the area entirely. Because this was just not going to be a worthwhile area to work. All we were doing was losing people to no effect. So we were all greatly relieved to be leaving that little piece of terrain.

Everybody was very careful making their way to the canal to get on our boats. We hadn't accomplished a thing in there except to lose people.

ELIJAH TAYLOR

Elijah Taylor was originally from Highbank, Texas, where he worked on cotton fields until his family moved to Dallas. After graduating from high school, where he enjoyed playing baseball, Taylor got a job working at the US Post Office until he was drafted in the spring of 1966. Taylor served as a medic in the 3rd Platoon of Charlie Company, 4th of the 47th with Fred Kenney, Larry Lukes, Steve Hopper, Terry McBride, Don Trcka, Richard Rubio, and Ron Vidovic. Taylor also went through medical training with Bill Geier, the medic for the 2nd Platoon of Charlie Company, who died in Taylor's arms in the battle of June 19, 1967. After the war Taylor returned to his job in the Dallas Post Office from which he retired in 2004. Taylor married and helped raise three daughters, one of whom served in the Persian Gulf War.

I was a medic, which meant that I didn't have to do KP in training. But when we got to Vietnam, I pitched in just like the regular infantrymen – digging and filling sandbags. Being a medic didn't make me exempt from Viet Cong mortar fire. I needed a place to hide too. And they all said, "Doc, you don't have to do that." And I said, "Yes I do, man. We all have to get out of this thing together." I was proud of being a medic; it was a good thing. I actually took a whole lot of chances, because I felt that way when my guys would get hit. There is nothing like going through a jungle real quiet like and all of a sudden you hear an explosion go off. And all of a sudden you hear, "Doc! Doc! Medic! Medic!" And in thick jungle you went single-file. Man, when I heard that cry, I wouldn't think about my own safety. I would just take out running to where that voice was coming from. I could have stepped on a mine or a booby trap or anything. But it was just reaction; I never thought about it much. The infantrymen knew that I would come and get them. I never thought once about not going to get them. In fact I took so many chances that somebody told me once, "Doc, you really scare me when you go out there like that." And I said that I couldn't lie back, that I would want someone to do the same for me. I never could live with myself if I ever refused to go out and get a man. I just couldn't do it.

Lieutenant Hoskins saved my life one day. I couldn't swim – you know the white folks wouldn't let us use their pools [so we never had a chance to learn]. In Vietnam we were working an area called the Rung Sat Special Zone. It is full of nothing but streams running off of the main river. Every 30 meters or so the point man would send the word back that we had a stream to pass. My question always was "How wide is it?" I carried an air mattress. The good swimmers would go across and secure the far bank. Then I would come along and blow up the air mattress. Man, I got so sick of blowing up that air mattress. Then I would just paddle on across the river. This one day they passed the word back that it was a stream, and it was wide enough for me and the other non-swimmers to start blowing up our air mattresses. But one of the guys said, "Naw. I think we can get across faster if one of the guys ties a rope to a tree on the other side." And I said, "Yeah. Let's go across like that." It was working. Then I get in and start going across. It was okay when I could feel the bottom of the stream, but I got a little leery when I couldn't feel the bottom of the stream anymore. Man, that doggone rope came aloose, and I went down. I guess I saw heaven down there. Man, I had on all that equipment, and I panicked. I was trying to get back up, and the more I was trying to get back up to the top of the water, I was sinking. Man, a hand came down and grabbed me by the collar and pulled me up. It was Lieutenant Hoskins. He said, "Float with me, Doc! Float with me!" I couldn't even float, and we went under. Man, he came up in there and saved my life. We got to the shore there, and, man, I was so relieved.

A month after that we were in a firefight, and somebody yelled out that Lieutenant Hoskins had been hit. Bullets were flying everywhere, and I said, "Where is he?" And somebody hollered out that he was over there in the rice. And, man, nothing could stop me from going to Lieutenant Hoskins. Man, there was all kind of rounds coming after me. I got to him and he said, "Doc,

I've been hit." And I said, "Where, lieutenant?" He said, "Someone shot me in the damn butt!" There was still bullets flying around everywhere, but I couldn't help but laugh. There wasn't all that much bleeding because it is all muscle back there. I patched him up and said, "Now we're even, lieutenant." And he said, "What do you mean by that?" And I said, "Because you saved my life."

One day Varney [a buddy] told me, "You know, Doc? We are the only American soldiers down in the Mekong Delta." And I said back, "We must be some lucky buggers, don't we?" One day we were walking through the rice paddies near a clump of vegetation with a stream running through it. The point man passed the word back that when he had gotten around the corner he had seen three VC, and last he saw they had crawled into the water but had never reappeared. One of the sergeants said, "They are still down there breathing through reeds." So Lieutenant Hoskins told a couple of guys to throw grenades in there. 3rd Platoon was a platoon that was going to overdo stuff. If you told half the platoon to do something, the whole platoon would. So about half the platoon threw grenades off in there. Man, those guys popped up out of that water. Because of all of that concussion they were just dazed. The blast was so tremendous that blood was coming out of their ears. We had to stop and have them air-lifted back to where they kept POWs.

The M16 jammed so bad back then. Sometimes I wonder how many American soldiers got killed by trying to reload and unjam that doggone M16 while at the same time the VC came up on them and killed them. Man, that thing would jam. I don't care how much you cleaned it. But I had me a back-up plan. On operations I carried six grenades. My plan was if I got in a situation in which that doggone thing jammed on me I would just reach for a grenade and pull them off until I could get that thing unjammed. That thing was unreliable.

MEDCAP [Medical Civic Assistance Program] missions were part of a medic's job. It was a goodwill thing toward the villagers. We would go in and help fix up the children. They always had sores, because they were always barefooted. We would come in, and the little kids would come running up to show you where they had been hurt. We would put some salve on it, and if it required a dressing we would do that. We would give out some medicine, but there was a language barrier. They would try to talk to you, and some of the medics would find out what they meant. Sometimes they just wanted an aspirin to feel better. I went on a few of those, and it was a lot of goodwill. You had to secure the village before we went in. That was part of a medic's duty. I believe that we did a good thing for those villagers, but we would be there in the day. And if the VC came in at night they then have to go along with the VC. It was a 50-50 thing. The VC would come in and take all the supplies from the farm for their men. The older men were too old to be VC anyway, so they would leave them and the mamasans. So it was a goodwill thing that we did, but the VC would come in in the night. In order for the villagers to live they probably had to tell when we had been there and how many people we had. But we were trying; let's put it that way. We were trying. [During the MEDCAPs] the children would always want candy, or offer their sister to us. "She is number one, GI!" One day we were in a village and I saw these kids. They were running around a hut. And I'm looking close, because if you see anybody running in Vietnam you want to know what's going on. I look up and there is this rat as big as I don't know what with a long tail. And these kids were running after that doggone rat. They had a long bamboo pole with kind of a spike on the end of it. That rat ran up in a hole, and they were so happy. They got that bamboo pole with the spike and stuck it up in the hole and twisted on it. And, man, they got that rat out of there. I'm looking at it amazed, thinking that they are going to throw it away. Just for fun, for sport. And these kids looked at me and said, "Chop chop number one!" And I said, "Aw, man!" They were going to eat him, but I didn't want to stay around to see what happened next. They probably had him with rice and had a good meal.

5 COMBAT

Although the Viet Cong and NVA were often best characterized as elusive, in Vietnam, as in any other war, there were large, sometimes set-piece, battles – great moments of destruction when opposing forces met and refused to give way. Such battles in the Vietnam War were many – the Ia Drang Valley, Hill 875, the siege of Con Thien, the Tet Offensive, the struggle for Khe Sanh, and Hamburger Hill. Regardless of the attention that these battles received, from media at the time to historians and filmmakers today, in general they stand as important exceptions to the Vietnam War rule. While important moments in history, and sometimes pivotal events in the war, these battles are not truly representative of the overall Vietnam combat experience. At its heart Vietnam was most often a small-unit war where even major military operations, such as Operation *Junction City*, or Operation *Coronado II*, or Operation *Buffalo*, resulted in bitter combat contested in the main on the small-unit level – sometimes between battalions but more often than not between companies and even platoons – battles in which hundreds of men died, not the tens of thousands of earlier wars. Most of these vicious small-unit battles in Vietnam are not even graced with a proper name. They were battles for forlorn pieces of ground that only had value because the enemy was there; ground that was abandoned as soon as the battle was over, while the larger operation went on.

The small-unit battles that best typify the Vietnam War took place in a variety of geographic settings. The fighting in the Mekong Delta and in the coastal littoral of the country often took place in the flat expanses of rice paddies, with open fields of fire and in close proximity to population centers, and often involved clashes with the Viet Cong. Combat in the highlands and along the Demilitarized Zone was quite different, involving struggles for hilltops and valleys, often in densely vegetated and unpopulated terrain, and often involved fighting against North Vietnamese regulars. The chronology of the Vietnam War also played a major role in determining the types of battle faced by US forces. The years of the build-up, 1965–67, were the years of the "big-unit war," often involving major US troop concentrations sweeping through the countryside trying to lock the communists into pitched battle. The massive series of communist assaults during the Tet Offensive in 1968 stands alone as a distinct period, followed for the remainder of 1968 and much of 1969 by a renewed series of US big-unit ground offensives. During the years of American withdrawal, 1970–73, the tempo of US operations slowed considerably, with American troops operating in ever-smaller concentrations.

While the varied elements of geography, time of service, and nature of opposing forces mean that there was no dominant single combat experience for American soldiers in the Vietnam War, at least one theme holds true for very nearly every occasion on which Viet Cong or NVA forces offered pitched battle. In an attempt to offset the lethal US edge in firepower, enemy fighters in Vietnam engaged in battle in as close proximity as possible to their American foes. Fighting in and among the Americans made the battles man-to-man affairs of small-arms fire – the Americans could not call in their mighty artillery and air support on their own positions. Battles in Vietnam, then, were often fought between small, and often isolated, units at very close range – certainly within sight of the enemy and often in among their defensive positions. Battles at such close range tended to be brutal, and, when death hovered so close by, quarter was rarely asked and rarely given.

In the battles of the Vietnam War, the initiative all too often rested with the Viet Cong and NVA. Sometimes US and South Vietnamese searches caught them unawares, but it was much more typical that communist forces were aware of impending US and South Vietnamese military actions. The Viet Cong and NVA tended to offer battle only when they felt that they held a tactical advantage – if they didn't they usually hunkered down in their nearly invisible bunkers and let the Americans pass. Communist forces also often offered battle as a delaying action for retreats or as a diversion for their own attacks. The diversions often heralded a staple of the communist military strategy in Vietnam, attacks on inviting, stationary targets, especially remote US firebases, landing zones, and special forces camps. Such attacks usually took place at night and were undertaken by specialist sapper units, which, often under the cover of a mortar barrage, first broke through defensive barbed-wire entanglements and then assaulted bunkers and command posts with grenades and explosive satchel charges. Both battles in the field, whether instigated by American or communist forces, and attacks on US and South Vietnamese emplacements were usually quite transitory affairs. Once their perceived tactical advantage was lost, communist forces usually attempted to break contact and flee – again often under the cover of darkness. Disengaging from battle was dangerous and was often the most costly moment in any battle for the Viet Cong and NVA, because it was the moment when the American edge in firepower could most easily be brought to bear.

The overwhelming and lethal firepower support upon which American forces relied took several forms. Most battles took place within the effective range of the artillery from at least one fire support base. American forces locked in battle could also call on the might of massive air support, from carriers off shore or from the many air bases dotted around the region. Fixed-wing aircraft could deliver everything from pods of 2.75-inch rockets, to 500-pound high drag bombs, to canisters of napalm in support of troops on the ground. In the biggest battles US forces could even call on the might of B52 bombers, capable of vaporizing entire enemy units in an instant. Nimble helicopter gunships could also provide machine-gun and rocket fire to support troops on the ground, augmented by fire from the door gunners of troop-transport helicopters. Even more importantly, though, the choppers were capable of bringing in reinforcements and supplies to troops cut off from ground sources of supply. The choppers were also the last hope for many of the wounded and dying.

American battles in Vietnam were often a chaotic symphony – a clatter of small-arms fire followed by bellowed orders and attempted maneuver. Then the brutal music quickened its pace as the first artillery shells began to fall and officers on the scene worked to "walk" the artillery fire closer to their own front lines. The artillery had to pause to allow helicopters to thunder in with needed supplies or to allow medevac choppers the desperate chance to get the wounded to safety. Everything had to stop, and the men had to hug the ground, when the jets began to arrive to unleash their payloads. For the American soldiers on the ground the battlefield in Vietnam was an amazing, adrenalized place. Death cracked past in the air, men were screaming – some shouting orders, others yelling in pain, others just screaming – bodies of friends jerked and fell, bombs shrieked in, tossing trees around like matchsticks. The enemy, usually so elusive, was right there where you could see him – sometimes just a rifle muzzle in a firing position, other times running at you with a grenade.

The battlefield was a place of primal thoughts and visceral emotions – an intensely personal place. Personal reactions to combat varied and, try as the military might, could not be replicated in training. A few soldiers couldn't take it and broke down mentally under the strain, others fought like madmen, some lost control of their bowels, but most fought – and fought hard. Battle – the dire risk of a violent death – focuses the attention of most soldiers to a laser point. To survive, soldiers tend to fixate on their immediate surroundings – the firing position to their front, their ammo bearer, their RTO. Quite commonly the moments in battle are those that are most indelibly imprinted on a veteran's memory. Even if that veteran cannot recall much else about his tour in Vietnam, those fleeting moments of battle are often recalled with crystal clarity. But those moments are usually severely limited in scope; for many veterans what was happening only a few yards away on the battlefield might as well have been happening on the moon. Their recollections of battle are of their rice paddy dike, their bunker, their threat of death. What was the rest of the platoon doing? Who knows? They were busy surviving.

By their very nature, then, oral histories of battles in Vietnam are like individual pieces of a vast and violent puzzle. On their own the pieces have immense value and are indispensable in understanding the reality of combat. But those pieces only hint at the overall story. The pieces, the individual life-and-death struggles, are inextricably interwoven and must be reconnected to achieve a fuller understanding of the face of battle in Vietnam and the effect of cumulative battlefield experiences on the soldiers themselves. This chapter will focus on battle in Vietnam in a number of ways. In part it will examine the cumulative battlefield experience of a single unit, Charlie Company, in an attempt to interlink the puzzle pieces of combat and to provide depth. The second group of oral histories in the chapter will examine some of the vast breadth of combat experiences in the war with more individual accounts of other battles that typify the small-unit combat seen in Vietnam, both from the ground and from the air.

On May 15, 1967, Charlie Company fought its first major battle of the Vietnam War, one that resulted in one fatality, 14 seriously wounded, and over 100 enemy killed in action.

STEVE HUNTSMAN
Member of 1st Platoon of Charlie Company

We went up this river; I don't know which one it was. This particular day they had jets out there just bombing the crap out of this area. Then, when they got done with that, they let us off on the shore there. There was a little hooch there that was just blown to smithereens. Nothing was left but scattered debris, and the ants were so hyped up. They were all over the ground and we were hot-stepping it. You had to keep those ants from getting on you, because they were ready to bite anything. We stood there on the shore of the river until they got everybody off, and then we started moving inland and started taking on light fire. I remember we got down; I was sitting there in the grass and you could feel those bullets going by, the concussion; the crack and then the pop. I remember thinking, "Man, this is the real shit. Why are these people trying to kill me? This is the real deal." I'll never forget thinking that: "Why are they trying to kill me?"

We were down there for a little while, and then we got up when the firing slacked and moved across this dry rice paddy. There were a bunch of trees out there on the other side of it. We got right out in the middle of that rice paddy, and they opened up. And that's when they got Don Peterson. They shot Charlie Nelson. We were probably 50 yards out into that rice paddy, out in the open. I was close enough to Don Peterson to hear what he said. He said, "Oh, my chest." That's all he said and hit the ground. He was over to my right a little bit. We all hit the ground. Charlie Nelson was up ahead of me. Jarczewski was up there. We all hit the ground. There was a little dike to the rice paddy back about 50 yards. We all tried to make it back to that dike. I remember jumping over the dike. I remember that it was hot and miserable, and I had lost all my strength. And I remember thinking, "Boy, if they come at us now they are just gonna have to kill me," because I couldn't move. I remember being so exhausted. Maybe it was being in the firefight too. I don't know how much it was. But I remember taking out some of those salt tablets and gulping down a little bit of water to try and get my strength back.

COMBAT

I remember looking over the dike and the rest of my squad; James Nall was out in front of me a little ways. I rolled over and looked over the dike and I remember him running, and he was kind of zig-zagging so they couldn't get a bead on him. The bullets were kicking up the dirt by his feet. I remember his eyes were about as big as saucers. He made it over the dike, jumped over, and the ones that didn't make it back were Jarczewski, Charlie Nelson, Peterson, and Cortright. After that we were just taking small-arms fire, and we were firing back. I remember that they called in a helicopter gunship, and it was strafing over to my right because there was a machine gun nest set up over there.

I had my head resting on my arm, and all of a sudden I felt this thing hit me. I felt the burn and the pain. I looked down at my arm, and it was really kind of surreal. I saw the blood; they must have hit an artery. Every time my heart beat, blood would spurt. All I remember thinking was "Oh, my hell; I got hit." That was my only thought. So I took out my bandage and wrapped up my own arm. They pulled the guys who were wounded back to this tree line. I remember getting back there safely. Jarczewski was already there. I remember him not having any shirt on. He was covered with blood from his head to his waist. And he was sucking air; one of the bullets had punctured his lung. I remember him lying there on the ground about 3 or 4 feet from me and every time he would take a breath hearing "gurgle, gurgle, gurgle." Jarczewski and I were pretty good friends. I remember saying to him, "Hang in there, Jarczewski." I never thought I would see him alive again. I just said, "Hang in there, Jar."

DON TRCKA

Don Trcka originally was from League City, Texas, where he was the only student in high school to letter in all four major sports for all four years. Trcka was drafted in the spring of 1966 and served in the 3rd Platoon of Charlie Company, 4th of the 47th with Fred Kenney, Larry Lukes, Steve Hopper, Terry McBride, Ron Vidovic, and Elijah Taylor. Trcka was wounded in action in the battle of May 15, 1967.

After recuperating, Trcka married his sweetheart, Beverly. Trcka eventually moved to Houston where he worked as a director with a major auto sales firm until his retirement in 2006. He and Beverly now boast six children and 11 grandchildren.

May 15 is when we first got contact. They put us out on boats, and the whole battalion was going to do a search and clear mission because they had information that they had Viet Cong held up there. We could even see them dropping napalm in the distance. When we got nearer we were fired upon and returned the fire. My squad, following Lieutenant Hoskins who was in front of me – a real gung-ho West Point officer – went through a small canal. We were trying to get around where the Viet Cong were. My squad was following me, and the doc was with me. But the Cong were hunkered down in like cement bunkers. The jets came over with napalm and you could see it. Then I did a thing that you were not supposed to ever do. Because we were low crawling and I had lost sight of my squad – I knew that they were behind me – and I was trying to keep up with Lieutenant Hoskins. I was already out of the canal and into some rice, and I stood up to see where in the hell everyone was. When I stood up – BOOM!

I landed on the other side of the canal. I was in a haze when I was first hit, but I thought to myself, "You can't die." I had taped a picture of my girlfriend [and later wife] to the butt of my weapon, and I came to staring her in the face. Then I knew that I wasn't going to die. Doc Elijah Taylor came to me; he knew that I was hit, and he knew that I was bleeding. So he gave me morphine. Then my squad caught up to me, and I crawled back to the company command post. There was still firing going on all around us. When I got there they knew that I was hit, and they had a chopper coming down. I had been hit 11 times. Most of it was shrapnel from a rifle grenade, and I had a bullet through the arm. The rifle grenade had gotten me all in my stomach and jaw. All that just by standing up one time. Stupid.

There were two other wounded men on the chopper with me, and there was a guy who was just so scared that he couldn't lead his squad or anything. He had flipped out. They had me on a stretcher and were putting packs on me. They flew me to Bear Cat, but I was completely out.

CARL CORTRIGHT
Member of 1st Platoon of Charlie Company

We walked for maybe a couple of hours or so; it is hard to say exactly. Then this replacement lieutenant starts going out in the open more, kind of like a dry rice paddy. It was open where we were at, and I think that we shot a few rounds into the nearby trees and brush. I thought, "What is this damn idiot doing out here in the middle of the open?" The guy had no conception, and I'm not an expert. Then we start pulling back. We got back about 60 or 80 feet, and that is when all the fire started happening. Charlie Nelson was almost immediately hit in the neck; it looked worse than it was. He was like, "Aw, it's nothing." And we were still all on our feet yet. Some guys are running, and others start to get hit already. Then someone yelled, "Pete's [Don Peterson] dead!" Just that quick. When two seconds later I thought, "What the hell am I doing standing here?" I was still standing up like an idiot. That's a replacement for you. First thing that came to my mind was cover. At least I learned something in training. I should have dropped right where I was instead of trying to run someplace. I ran maybe 3 or 4 feet and was just ready to crouch down and I got hit. It felt like somebody had hit me in the back with a sledgehammer. My gear went flying somewhere. I landed on my back, and lay on my back. I had no feeling at all; I couldn't move. Thought I was dying really. I thought that might be the start of the dying process, not being able to move. I asked one guy to shoot me, because I was gonna die anyway. I said, "Just shoot me." Maybe I said it twice. He just kind of paused and said, "Aww hell, you got a million-dollar wound. You'll be home soon."

So I basically just lay there. We were under such heavy fire that the platoon left. Somebody did put a patch on me somewhere. It wasn't the doc; it was someone else. I laid out there alone for hours.

Time is hard to decipher when you are in a situation like that. Somebody told me that they were going to be firing artillery, and I told him that I couldn't move and to go back and save yourself. I remember smoke, and gunships coming in, helicopters with missiles, but I don't remember artillery hitting around me. My brain might have been on overload, though. I don't think that the Viet Cong were shooting at me anymore, because I was lying on my back. Finally, I swear it was almost three hours, I heard this noise, and I look and it was John Young on his stomach looking at me. He tells me he is going to get me back to the rest of the guys. He said, "Can you walk?" And I said, "No." And he took my left arm around his neck and shoulder and tried to drag me, but he couldn't drag me very far. I'm a lot bigger than he is. So John said, "I need your help. Use your right arm too, kind of like an alligator." And I did. [Young crawled through the paddy with Cortright on his back.] I don't know how far we went. Seemed like the damndest, longest ways. We would move 4 or 5 feet and the bullets started flying over our heads. We would drop and wait for three or four seconds and the bullets would hiss by us. It would be like "hiss, hiss, hiss" and we would drop. We got about halfway and John gave me his helmet. We must have been a hell of a sight. They were all watching us out there [on both sides] going up and down and up and down. We finally made it. I was just dragging along there, my feet useless, but we made it. About the last 20 feet we got covered; a couple guys jumped out [from behind a rice paddy dike] and dragged me back. They threw me back on my back again. I figured that the spinal cord, this wouldn't do it too good. But what can you do?

I was there about another two hours before a helicopter comes, because I had missed the first one. Doc was giving me some attention, and I wanted some morphine. The pain in my leg was really pretty bad. The bullet wound itself wasn't very painful – that was the kind of reaction I was getting from it, because it [his spine] was crushed. But it was like a steamroller was going up and down my legs the whole time I was out there. I don't know why it was doing that. I asked for pain medication, and he said, "No. With a stomach wound we can't give you morphine." And I said, "The pain is almost already killing me the way it is."

The bullet went through at a 45-degree angle from my front to my left side and right straight out. It went in the front and came out the back. Only thing I can figure out is that a small portion hit part of my belt and that the small portion went through my spine. Today when I take an x-ray you can still see it. It is smaller than half a dime. They never took it out.

All the doc in the field could do was bandage me a little bit more, and then they moved me to the area where the helicopter was coming down. It was good to be back with the guys. At least there were some familiar faces again. But there was very little talking going on. The guys that were wounded weren't in too good a condition, any of us. I knew it was going to be a quiet ride. One of the guys sitting in front of me had two or three bullets in him. We just looked at each other. None of us felt much like talking. When we got about 1,000 feet up in the helicopter I breathed a sigh of relief, because near the ground they can still shoot it down. When we got up to 1,000 feet I thought, "Well, my chances are looking better."

On June 19, 1967, the companies of the 4th of the 47th became involved in their biggest battle of their one-year tour in Vietnam. Alpha Company became enmeshed in a U-shaped ambush, while Charlie Company was locked in battle by a Viet Cong force protected by both strong bunkers and a canal. The battle raged for an entire day, and resulted in Alpha Company losing 28 dead and 76 wounded, while Charlie Company suffered ten killed and more than 40 wounded. US forces inflicted 256 fatal casualties on the Viet Cong.

MIKE LETHCOE
Member of 2nd Platoon of Alpha Company

We crossed 2 or 3,000 meters or so it seems like, and we came up to a canal that went from west to east with a bend on the east end of it. We were a company-sized unit and stopped there. We had swimmers cross with ropes, and they secured ropes on the other side, and we started crossing the canal. We had about two platoons across; we were crossing in two different places, and most of my platoon was across. The weapons squad and our company commander were still on the other bank. And as we moved away we were slowly spreading out in this open field. To the south of us there was a tree line about 5 or 600 yards away from the canal. To the east of us there was a bit of a tree line and a haystack on the corner of a bend. As we moved out across this open field, my squad, 2nd Squad, was in the forward element. As we moved toward the tree line, there were three or four burial mounds off to the east of us as we were moving across. As we moved forward I noticed that one of the mounds on the southeast corner of this open field had some bushes on it. And as we crossed close to it, I saw one of these Chicom claymores sitting in a bush. It was on a tripod. They would take the bottom of a 55-gallon drum and fill it about 6 or 8 inches high with explosives, then put in nails, bits of metal, rocks, and everything they can in the face of it. Then they would put a C-ration can right in the middle to use to detonate the explosives. They would set them up on a tripod and aim them. One of these things was sitting in the bushes on top of one of the grave mounds. I saw the thing and was trying to be nonchalant and casual about it. And I was scanning the dike line that that thing was in front of. And I saw a Vietnamese – just the top of his head and his eyes – looking at me.

I started running out to the right front of this claymore. I didn't want to run right at it, and we were in an open field, so I started running out to the side and toward it. I was trying to get out if its kill range. As I was running I saw this Vietnamese raise up, and I started firing from my hip at him while I was running. Well, he ducked down back behind the dike while I was running and set this monster off. I had gotten around the side of it, but the blast knocked me down, separating me from my weapon and my helmet. It cut the company in two; we even took casualties 4 or 500 yards away from that thing. That initiated the ambush.

I was sort of addled. I was lying on my back looking around, and I rolled over and looked, and all I could see was RPGs [Rocket

Propelled Grenades] and tracers and everything crossing this battlefield. I thought people had panicked and were shooting themselves. There were tracers flying everywhere and people out in the field getting hit, and I started waving my arms and yelling, "cease fire, cease fire!" Then I turned around and I saw that the fire was coming from the tree line. There was a bunker in front of us, one down the left side, and off to the right about 500 yards away was another line of bunkers. We'd walked into a U-shaped ambush.

I was about 60 feet away from the burial mound off at my ten o'clock. I didn't have any cover, was just lying in the mud in that open field. The tide was out, but the mud was ankle-deep. We were out there in the open, and they were having a turkey-shoot; they were picking people off. Even that haystack was a VC bunker. You would see AK47 rounds stitching through the ground; they would start in front of people and raise the weapon as they fired and just stitch rounds across them. We were caught out. I looked over at one of my team leaders; he was about 20 yards out to my right. He looked at me, and I looked up and looked around and crawled over and got my weapon and got my helmet. I looked back at my team leader and motioned for him to move forward because when you are in an ambush like that in the open the only thing you can do is overrun the bunker or you are gonna die where you are at. I motioned for him to go forward, and just as I did that those AK rounds stitched across him. Shot him right across the lower abdomen. He turned over, and he screamed and he screamed. Shit. I could see people all over getting hit, and my hearing was a bit off [because of the mine blast], but I was seeing all this happen.

I started looking around for cover, because I was out in the open and they were shooting us everywhere. Evidently the VC thought that the claymore had hit me when it knocked me down, and they didn't want to waste bullets on me or something. The only cover I saw was that mound that the claymore had been sitting on top of. I could tell that there were bunker lines all in the dikes that were about 20 feet in front of this mound. So I got up and ran over to that mound of mud. That claymore had cleared the top of the thing; there wasn't any foliage on the top anymore.

But there was a mound of dirt about 2 feet high with a crater in the middle of it. I got up and ran over to that. There was rounds hitting around me as I was running, I could also hear them going by in the air – automatic fire. They were shooting at me really hard, and I went over and hid behind the mound. I could feel the rounds hitting the mound and started digging in. I was there most of the afternoon. It was about ten o'clock in the morning when the ambush initiated.

It didn't take long, and I had a decent fighting position dug. But I was face on to this bunker line. The mound was 35–40 feet wide and about 2 feet tall. I would ease around one side of the mound and look up and they would shoot at me, and I would ease around the other side and look up and they would shoot at me. There was a .51-caliber [machine gun] right in front of me, about 50 or 60 feet away. They would shoot out in the field and then turn around and shoot into my mound. Then they would shoot off into the distance and then turn around and shoot my mound. Well, that got old, so I started shooting the people off the .50 [machine gun]. Every time they would swing that gun somewhere else I would raise up and put fire on them. I knocked one gunner off and the assistant gunner took his place, and I shot him off and somebody else took his place. I shot him, and he stood up when I shot him and then fell back down across the gun. Then two others came up; they had paths in there behind and would run up and replace the people. Then I threw a grenade in there and knocked that gun out. There was a reed stand, bamboo reeds, just to the left of me, and there was people firing from there, and when the machine gun was knocked out I directed fire on them. That is what I did pretty much all afternoon – try to keep those positions empty.

Later in the afternoon the landing craft came in and beached itself on the canal behind us and started supporting us with its .50s and its 20mm gun. The Navy was great during the whole thing. But they were 500 yards behind me. One of these monitors [a brown water Navy gunboat]. That was fun. It came up on the canal and started firing on this field. They were firing on this front bunker line that I was face up into. Evidently they didn't know that I was out there, so I was taking fire from both sides. That's when I had to hunker down. A monitor has a 40mm gun on the front and a mortar amidships. They were using the gun and the mortar, pounding on this haystack on the bend in the canal. They pounded on it all afternoon, but they didn't have any armor-piercing rounds. Everything they had was HE and point detonating. So they were just blowing dust off the top [of the haystack bunker]. The thing was a pile of mud 10 or 15 feet tall with hay all over it. They blew all the hay off of it, and they kept pounding on the big pile of mud. They finally blew it down until it was a pile only 6 feet tall that was actually the bunker. These were prepared battlefields. They had spare barrels [for their machine guns]; they had cases of ammo. There was a log bunker under the haystack with another .50-caliber. But they couldn't depress their barrel far enough to get me, evidently.

There were group firefights going on all around me. In the afternoon we had F-4s [fighter bombers] come in. That was fun. They would direct the F-4s onto this bunker line. Down from me a little way was a recoilless rifle. Somebody from back behind me was directing these aircraft to try and hit the recoilless rifle position. They came in first strafing, and when they peeled off the enemy would get up and run from the bunker line because there was another F-4 out there lining up to come in. When they got up, I would shoot them. I was out there having a turkey shoot. Every time an F-4 would come in I would raise up immediately and shoot these people who was trying to run away from the bunker line. They were taking a lot of hits, because after the air strikes there was much less fire coming from that bunker line. It was exciting. One of the planes came in; he was a little bit wider and higher than the others. I was watching him out of the corner of my eye. He came winding down through there, and this big egg dropped out of this thing. The fins popped straight out on it and I said, "Oh hell." Looked like it was falling right on me. It was a 500-pound bomb. This thing hits 30 yards in front of me. I saw it come in and knew what it was, so I just collapsed myself down in my hole that I had dug. I went down inside the hole, looking up at the sky and put my hands over my ears and opened my mouth. That thing went off, and the next thing I saw was this wave of mud come over me. The hole compressed around me and this wave of mud went kasploosh! over me. Undoubtedly it saved my life, but I almost suffocated trying to dig my way out of it. The edge of the bomb crater wasn't 10 feet from my mound of mud. I dug my way out, and as soon as I broke the surface somebody started shooting at me from over yonder somewhere. It was a bad day.

I had to go to the bathroom really bad, but I held it because I had nowhere to go. But eventually I just shit in my hand and threw it out of my hole. The tide came in in the afternoon and flooded the area about 2 feet deep. Every time I moved it left ripples in the water and somebody off to my right front about 200 yards would shoot at me. I just laid there with my head raised on the mud so my mouth and nose were exposed from the water and I could breathe. I just laid there still because every time I moved somebody shot at me. These were trained troops we were fighting against. We had had a lot of contact with Viet Cong who would fire half a dozen rounds and run. These guys hunkered down and fought. They were ready for a sustained battle. They fought hard. They were good shots and hardened troops. When we went out I had 28 loaded magazines, 1,000 rounds of ammo. I used most of it. When we got back to the boats later in the evening I had maybe two magazines left. I don't know how many I hit that day – a couple of dozen, I don't know.

Later in the evening, just before dark, a chopper showed up with a FAC [forward air controller] in it. It came in to direct artillery fire. That is when things started clearing up. When that thing showed up, it would stand off and direct artillery fire, walking it down the bunker line. Just wiping them out. They saw me up there. Saw me in a fighting position. They came in. They fired smoke, and just surrounded the area with smoke. Then this helicopter came down in the smoke, and the pilot leaned out and waved for me to go on back while all this smoke was around me. So I got up and ran over to a dike line to my left about 30 or 40 yards – you can't run far in this mud. But I ran as far as I could and fell down by this dike. Well the .50 over on the corner opened up on me a few times while I was running. And the chopper backed off and laid a barrage on it. I crawled along this dike line. Behind me about 50 yards back were some other grave mounds that some of my people had taken cover around. They had all dug in positions over there, and I crawled back to those positions. I got in a position with a guy called Matthison. He had a pretty good-sized hole dug. Off to my right side was an M60 [US machine gun] sitting out there in the open. The machine gunner had opened up right after the claymore had gone off. They had fired an RPG at him. The blast had torn off his cheek, and both of his eyes were swollen shut. He was in a position by Matthison, and his gun was out there in the open.

During an artillery barrage, I ran out and got the gun, because I figured we needed it. We used that for a while, but then everything was calming down, because we were still getting air strikes and artillery fire. They were dead on. That probably saved us. We stayed there until around dark. People were just out there. There wasn't any leaders. They were shot, or dead, or were across the canal. I decided that we needed to go back. I started organizing the guys who had taken cover in the grave mounds to get them ready to go back to the boats. We started crawling back. I took Strickland, the machine gunner. Both of his eyes were swollen shut. The blood had caked on the side of his face, and somebody had put a dressing on him. But he couldn't see. We were crawling back across this open field, and I had his hand on mine. We had a couple of hundred yards to go. We crawled back about halfway and Puff the Magic Dragon [an AC-47 gunship] shows up and kicks out a million candle-power flare and lit up the world. And the .50 on the corner out there saw us and opened up on us. It was shooting through the dike. A couple of guys laid down there and it shot them out, shot through the dike. We were crawling across there and I told Strickland, "They seen us. Can you run?" The guy behind me got hit just as we got up to run, because I heard him go "Uhhhhh!" I looked over my shoulder and he was flailing away. And we ran up to the dike line in front of the landing craft and tumbled across that.

The Navy immediately came up and gave me hot coffee, gave me some hot soup, and took my M16 back and cleaned it and my magazines and reloaded my magazines and brought my weapon back to me. We set up a position around the landing craft, and that's where we spent the night. Puff was there all night long firing a lot. Evidently after dark the Viet Cong started collecting their bodies and taking them out by sampan on these canals. Puff was just having a field day. Ten or 12 guys had made it back to the boat. The enemy was out in the field in front of us policing up equipment off of our men's bodies. When Puff would throw out a big flare you could see them out there. Guys back where I was at would fire on them. So they stopped that and went away; the enemy withdrew during the night.

The next day, just after daylight, another unit came in to relieve us. They came sweeping across the field from the south. Then we had to go out and police up the battlefield. It was a terrible thing. It was terrible. Because I knew all these guys; had been associated with them for over a year in close proximity. Out of my ten-man squad we lost six. They were caught in the open. Everybody was wounded. I had a few shrapnel things in my arms and stuff from the firing that had come from the rear. I didn't even report it. It was minor. There were dead people all around me, shot all to shit. Mine didn't matter. We took 80 or 90 percent casualties in the first two minutes, in the initial ambush. When the ambush was initiated by the claymore there was sustained fire that went on for ten or 15 minutes. They were shooting everything they could see, and they were good at it. There were 28 or 30 bodies on the field. We lined them up on an area off to the northwest that was a little bit drier. The bodies were assembled there and lined up and covered with ponchos until choppers came in and took them out. Charlie Company who came in did a lot of it, because our people were exhausted. Morally depleted. Everybody we picked up was somebody I knew by name. I knew everybody. It was a tough thing to do. My team leader, who had got shot across the gut, I knew he was dead. But when we went out the next morning he was alive. He had fought off a Viet Cong and killed him who was coming out to take his weapon during the night. The man behind me who got hit by the .50 was still alive and was crawling across the field. He'd been hit by a .50 in one side and it came out the other and he was still alive.

TERRY MCBRIDE
Member of 3rd Platoon of Charlie Company

We were going down the river there, cruising along, and I was standing along the side rail, and I remember seeing a couple of mamasans grabbing their kids and hauling ass into their hooches. I thought to myself, "Something is gonna happen soon." The local civilians were usually just real nonchalant, acting like nothing was going on. They usually couldn't care less if we were there, but today, these guys were definitely on the move. Grabbing their kids and everything was kind of a sign that something bad was about to happen. I knew something was up.

Well, we got off of the ATCs [Armored Troop Carriers] and started taking fire, so we started heading toward the fire – toward a canal on our right flank. My gun team [M60 machine gun] was on the far left flank of Charlie Company. 1st and 2nd platoons were to our right, and I was watching their M60 gunners firing – doing fire and maneuver. They would fire, and some of the squads would move forward; then they would leapfrog and get beside them or in front of them to cover their forward movement. I saw the beaten zone [where the enemy fire was coming at Charlie Company with the most intensity]; me and my team low-crawled through the beaten zone up to this hooch on the far left flank and tore a hole in the back wall of it. We slid inside that hooch, and they [the Viet Cong] never saw us get in there. This hooch was full of hundred-pound rice sacks. We took those sacks, and part of the wood off of the bed and the bunker that was in the hooch, and stacked them up so that they were chest high. Then I tore a hole in the side wall of the hooch and looked out and got a good visual. [From this elevated position] I could see right down the line they [the Viet Cong] were on. I couldn't see people, because they were in bunkers, but every now and then I could see smoke coming up from the bunkered rice paddy dike. Then I saw a hole that they would come out of on this paddy dike, and they would then jump over into this tree line along the ambush line. So I started watching that hole, and when someone would come out I would fire a three- or four-round burst. I probably hit four or five of them coming out of that hole, and then they stopped coming out for a while.

The rest of Charlie Company was down behind the rice paddy dikes. As best I knew I was the only guy up high. I could see enemy heads coming by as they low-crawled down the dikes they were behind. I must have been there for four hours before the Viet Cong figured out where I was at, partly because I never stuck the whole muzzle of the M60 outside the hooch. I dinged quite a few of those heads crawling past before they figured out where I was at. I was reloading the gun at one point, and all of a sudden the gun jumps in my hands – BAM! It was just one round, and it knocked the leg off of my 60. And I said, "Oh shit! They know where I am now!" So I got a fresh barrel and started firing again and, WHAM, another round comes through. They really know where I'm at now. So I tried to move our rice-sack bunker a little to the left of where I had been. But they must have fired an RPG at us or something that hit outside of our bunker. I definitely knew that I had been bracketed at that point. In the meantime my assistant gunner, Bill Riley, got hit right in the thigh with a .50 [.50-caliber round]. It flipped him about 15 feet in the air. Then he landed back down, and he was in shock. He had his leg almost totally blown off, except for a strip of meat. A 3-inch wide strip of meat was the only thing holding his leg on. When he landed, he landed on his back, and his leg was lying up over his arm. He was unconscious for a minute, and when he came to he yelled, "Hey! Get off me!" He flipped his leg off of him, and realized it was his and not somebody lying on him and went right into shock. As traumatic as that wound was, it didn't hardly bleed at all. That was really amazing. I guess it didn't get the main artery or something. The only reason that I think that Riley didn't die of shock was that Mario Lopez and a kid named Johnny had him, and they kept slapping the shit out of him to keep him from going too deeply into shock. The docs got some morphine into him, and that mellowed him out. Somebody blew up some air mattresses and slid him back and out of there.

Then helicopters started coming in to dust people off. When they loaded everybody into the helicopter, and it started to lift off, it got maybe 10 feet in the air. This was happening just to the right of the hooch I was in. A round went right through the top of the helicopter's windshield. I guess it hit the transmission or something, because the rear rotor blade just stopped and the helicopter started to spin around. Everybody who was inside who wasn't strapped down got slung out of the helicopter. It landed right back down from where it had taken off, and all those people who had been slung out and the crew of that helicopter were stuck with us. I was going, "Shit. Great, man!" There were two 60 gunners on that chopper who had great big cans of ammo. I was low on ammo at that point, and I knew now that I wasn't going to run out of ammo. The crew jumped out of that helicopter in a real hurry, except the pilot. I remember watching him. First he took his flight helmet off and put on his steel pot [helmet] that was behind his seat. Then he took his flight helmet and slammed it on the dash of the Huey, and then he jumped out. Here he is in his flight uniform; it don't have any mud on it or nothing. He grabbed his M16 and threw it over his shoulder and got shot right in the ass. It just knocked him down.

Later in the day [after air strikes and an infantry charge against the Viet Cong bunker line] things finally began to settle down. Tim Johnson was there in the hooch and we had been talking. He was getting ready to take a look out of the hole I had been firing from earlier in the day. I was about to tell him not to, when a sniper round hit him in the forehead, and he died. Later that night, when things were pretty much totally calm, John Howell was lighting a cigarette. From the flash of that cigarette being lit there was one fucking round fired. It went right between me and Howell, and we weren't sitting maybe 5 inches apart. That bullet went right between us. It was so close between us that when it went past I watched the flame on the match waver as the bullet went by.

WALTER RADOWENCHUK

Walter Radowenchuk was originally from Lakewood, Ohio, near Cleveland. The son of Ukrainian immigrants, Radowenchuk had a short stint in junior college before being drafted in the spring of 1966. Radowenchuk served in the 2nd Platoon of Charlie Company, 4th of the 47th with Bill Geier and Frank Schwan. Radowenchuk was wounded in action in the battle of June 19, 1967. After recuperating and returning home from Vietnam Radowenchuk went to work for the phone company until his retirement in 2003. Radowenchuk married his sweetheart Carol and helped raise two children.

I remember heading inland. What I could see ahead of me was a series of rice paddies. As I was walking I was close to a hooch, and there was an old Vietnamese man standing there looking at us. He was old, so I didn't really have much concern about him. Then we started heading across open rice paddies. We went maybe 200 meters and all of a sudden gunfire erupted on us. I was not close to any of the paddy dikes so I just hit the ground right there, just dropped. To my right was the river where our boats were, and while I was lying in the rice paddy, which was dry, I saw these small boats of ours [PABs – plastic assault boats], and I saw one of them literally blown out of the water. Okay. That made me feel real bad. Because I knew that we had run into something big.

To my immediate front the way I was facing was a tributary that went off of the river, and there were some hooches in front of it across that little tributary. The distance I would say was maybe 75 meters. I saw one guy running out of that hooch, and I fired at him. Then I went to reload a new magazine; I don't know if I hit the guy or not. I had an M16 with a grenade launcher on it. At that point I figured, "Hey, we've run into something big. These are Viet Cong." So I started firing grenades at that hooch I saw him coming out of. And I saw the grenades going through the sides of the hooch; it was made of straw or whatever. At that point all hell broke loose; I mean firing all over the place. I was getting ready to put a grenade into the launcher, when my hand felt like somebody slapped me on the wrist, and I see blood pouring

Barbara and Fred Kenney on their wedding day.

James Nall on operations in the Mekong Delta.

Pauline Laurent and Howard Querry pictured here before he was sent to Vietnam in 1968. (Courtesy of Pauline Laurent)

Antony Goodrich during a break on patrol.

Terry McBride and his M60 machine gun.

Frank Linster standing beside his helicopter, "Mr Lucky."

Alan Richards (left) with Ronnie Gann shown here on the right of the picture.

Larry Lukes (left) along with two of his friends from 3rd Platoon, Tim Fischer and Ron Vidovic.

Ernie Hartman on an operation in the Mekong Delta.

Carl Cortright aboard ship soon after his arrival in Vietnam.

Steve Hopper posing in front of Charlie Company's sign at their base area at Dong Tam.

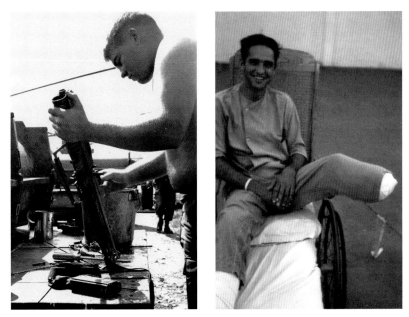

Top left: Kirby Spain cleaning his weapons between patrols.
Top right: Ron Vidovic posing in the hospital after losing his leg.

John Young during operations in 1967.

Top left: Frank Schwan aboard the troopship to Vietnam.
Top right: Richard Rubio aboard ship.

Elijah Taylor, 17 June 1967.

out of both sides of the wrist. I got a bullet right through my right wrist. It didn't hurt much. Didn't break no bones, but blood really came out.

Now I'm lying in a prone position when my left arm, with a lot of pain, just flies backwards. A round hit me in the upper left arm and went right through the bone. Right through the arm. Now that hurt. That really hurt. I thought about getting to the paddy dike, but things were really flying. Thought I was better off just in a prone position. A few minutes later I felt a stinging sensation in my left ankle. I got a round in my left ankle, which broke my ankle. Also a flesh wound in my calf and one through the side of my right foot. I was hit five times. It was so hard to tell time in an incident like that, but I would say I was hit five times say within maybe a minute. I yelled out, "I'm hit! I'm hit!" And Sergeant Searcy left his position and ran, kind of crouched down, to me. He started bandaging me up; he bandaged my wrist and my left upper arm. While he was doing this I heard him kind of go "Owwww! Oh!" He got hit too, in his leg.

We are out of action at this point. I see Phantom jets come in and smoke grenades in front of our position. I see bombs being dropped and palm trees flying up in the air. Time wise, I couldn't tell you how long that lasted. Seemed like it lasted forever to me. I heard .50-caliber machine guns going. At this point I'm lying on my back. I remember my helmet kept coming off my head as I'm lying there, and I hear these .50-caliber machine guns going at us and with my right hand I keep putting that helmet back on my head. Not that that would stop a .50-caliber round. After what seemed like an eternity of artillery and bombs, things seemed to quiet down a little bit. They got a helicopter in close to me, real close. I remember that Chaplain Windmiller came up to check on me. I don't know how much blood I lost; I don't think that I was all there. I just remember the commotion. I do remember the lieutenant yelling at me, "Radowenchuk, GET UP!" I yelled back, "I'm dyin'!" He didn't know how bad I was hit and later apologized. They placed me in the chopper. It had its rotors going, you know. As it was ready to take off we maybe lifted a couple of feet off the ground and BAM right back down on the skids. Something got hit. I grabbed my left arm to hold it, and I jumped out of the chopper. And right away I got on my back and attempted to kind of worm my way away from the chopper. I'm thinkin' that the VC are going to try and blow it up with an RPG or something. But I didn't get very far.

I'm lying on my back, and the tide has started to come in. I'm already lying in water, a couple inches of water in the rice paddy. As I'm lying on my back looking at things, I see one red cross-marked helicopter approximately 100 yards away from me go up in the air, loaded up with wounded I'm sure, and it got up quite high, maybe a couple hundred feet in the air. All of a sudden I see it coming down. I knew that it got hit, and it crashed. I thought to myself, "Oh, God. Can things get any worse?"

ELIJAH TAYLOR
Medic in 3rd Platoon of Charlie Company

On June 18, Lieutenant Hoskins and Sergeant Marr were going to meet with Captain Larson to get a briefing. When Sergeant Marr came back down to give us our briefing we were all looking around to see where we were going on the map. I started to look but thought, "Oh hell, I ain't lookin' at no damn map." At that time somebody had come up with the bright idea that one platoon would be on boats in the river [PABs, plastic assault boats with no armor, used in an experiment to make infantry more mobile in the watery Mekong Delta]. My platoon, 3rd Platoon, did that one time, and I didn't like it because it goes against everything the infantry trains you. You were supposed to stay at least 5 meters apart and not get crowded up. Then they put you in these little boats? And for me it was twofold because I can't swim and I'm out there in this doggone boat. So the operation was for the 3rd Platoon to be on those boats the next day – my platoon. And the 4th Platoon [the mortar platoon] was going to be ground pounding. By the next morning the operation was changed, and we switched platoons. They put the 4th Platoon on the boats.

I don't know what the reason was for it. And that 4th Platoon got wiped out that day. They got wiped out. My good buddy and mentor, Robert Cara, he was the head medic in our company. He had been my roommate at Fort Riley and had volunteered for the Army. He was on those boats that day and was killed. They never had a chance.

That morning they dropped us off, and I was telling Smitty, his name was James Smith, that this was June 19 and I was supposed to be home drinking red soda water and eating barbeque and celebrating. He said, "Why would you do that?" And I said, "Oh, that's right. You're from Cleveland. What it is in Texas is Juneteenth [a holiday marking the abolition of slavery in Texas in 1865]." As soon as I said that all hell broke loose. We got fire from everywhere out of tree lines and swamps. Man, we started returning fire, and our lieutenant began to call in artillery. Man, he could put that stuff right on the money, too. At that time we thought that we were the only platoon under attack, and we were pinned down. Then the call came in that 2nd Platoon was hit. Jace Johnston, the RTO, yelled, "The 2nd Platoon is hit, and the medic is down!" And I thought of Bill Geier, their medic, being hit, and heard that they were up there near a hooch I could see. I asked Jace Johnston, "That's about 200 meters, isn't it?" And he said, "Yeah, and that's where they are." And I started taking off stuff, and he said, "Man, what are you doing?" And I said, "I'm going to help the 2nd Platoon." And he said, "But you have to go across that open rice paddy." And I said, "Yeah, I know." By that time, Lieutenant Hoskins had gotten the information that I was going across, and he came over and said, "Doc, you know I can't order you to go across that rice paddy; it's too dangerous." I said, "Yeah, lieutenant, but the 2nd Platoon is down, Geier's down; I can make it across there." He said, "Okay."

I went out across, and I guess I got about 30 meters, and nothing was going on. Those buggers waited until I got out there in the middle of nowhere, and then just opened up on me like nobody's business. But I never did think about going back. I was just focused on getting up to that hooch. So what I would do was run for about 10 or 11 meters and get down. Then I would wait a little while; then I would get up and run again. Finally I got to a dike, and I could see those guys lying around just holding them off, you know. And I finally got there, and there was some guys wounded, man. There was really no hope for them. So I just prioritized, you know. Some guys were almost dead. Then I found Geier. He had been hit in the chest, with an entrance and exit wound. He had been shot while working on another man who was down. I was leaning over him, talking to him. Medics are trained not to really tell a guy the situation he is in. I was telling him, "Geier, we gonna get the chopper in and get you off to the hospital. Just stay loose; stay loose." As I leaned in I could see that he was fading, and I thought, "Oh, man." He had a stare on his face; couldn't move. But he looked like he understood what I was saying. But he couldn't respond to it. Finally he just drifted on off. Geier was such a nice person – had a baby face. Real quiet. He didn't do like a lot of soldiers. Some would want to go to a village and get 'em a woman. But Geier didn't do stuff like that. He was just a nice, likable fellow. A nice kid who had got caught up in the draft. He got killed doing his job.

Many of the others were lying in a daze like they couldn't believe it. All the time I was being exposed to a lot of fire, but I never really did think about that. I don't know how many men I patched up that day. While I was patching people up I hear a scream, and Bill Riley had somehow gotten up there and had been hit by a .50-caliber shell right in mid thigh. I ran out there in the rice paddy and started patching on him, and the wound was so deep that I had to take out my biggest field dressing. He was screaming, and I could barely stop the bleeding. Man, I used so many field dressings, but I finally got it tied off. He was still crying out in pain. They issue you five vials of morphine, and I stuck him in the shoulder with the morphine, and he quieted down. By that time someone was hollering, "Doc! You'd better get out of there, that's a .50-caliber shooting at you!" And I hadn't even thought of it. And I looked up, and those doggone .50-caliber shells were knocking dirt off of the dike, man, and I finally had to kind of drag Riley kind of up against that dike to get him to some kind of safety.

Later on we were still fighting and I told the lieutenant that we needed to get the medevac in there, and we were still under fire. We got a dust off in there and I put Forrest Ramos on there. He had an injured elbow, and I said, "Ramos, you goin' in on the chopper." He said, "Okay, Doc." Then we went back to fighting, and I heard a sputtering sound. I looked back and the pilot was trying to get the chopper back up, then all of a sudden it just crashes to the ground. You look back and it's like a movie. It came down on its side just like a bird that fell out of the sky. You can't believe it. You think "No! They didn't shoot that chopper down!" Then some of us started running over there to see who we can save. As I remember the skid of that Huey was right across Ramos' neck. Nobody survived that crash. Nobody. Then I thought about it; Ramos only had an elbow wound. He was of no more use to us – couldn't use his arm – but he had what we call a million-dollar wound. I thought about it for a long time; maybe if I hadn't put him on there he would have survived. That was the worst day we had. There were four medics in the company, and two of us survived that day.

On July 11, 1967 Charlie Company was involved in a battle in which the reconnaissance element was cut off and four men were killed in action.

FRANK SCHWAN

Frank Schwan was originally from a Hungarian neighborhood in Cleveland. After high school Schwan went to work in a factory and loved to hang around in pool halls. Schwan was drafted in the spring of 1966 and served in the 2nd Platoon of Charlie Company, 4th of the 47th Infantry with Bill Geier and Walter Radowenchuk. Schwan was wounded in action on July 11, 1967, and had to evade Viet Cong patrols the entire night. After the war Schwan worked for Ohio Bell until his retirement in 2000. Schwan now enjoys hunting and fishing, though the wounds he sustained in Vietnam still bother him from time to time.

On July 11, six of us were selected to go out and recon in front of the company. It was myself on the M60, Sergeant George Smith, Phil Ferro, Butch Eakins, Harold King, and a new replacement named Henry Hubbard. Typically when we were exposed in an open rice paddy, I knew that I was going to be one of the first ones shot because of the firepower that I had. So I tended to go behind someone. So if we were walking forward, I would be behind someone. We walked straight, and then we made a dogleg left, and that move exposed me, and as soon as it did, I got shot. As I walked, I got shot in the stomach and in the shoulder, and it spun me and literally flipped me. Now I was looking back in the direction we had come from. My gun went flying forward; I don't know where. I felt a little bit of stinging, but no immediate pain. My body didn't capture that pain right away. A short time after I started to wriggle, and I realized that someone was shooting at me, so I stopped moving. I heard some shots, and two guys were behind me behind a mud wall – a rice paddy dike, maybe 2 feet high. King and Hubbard were back behind me firing about 15 yards away. I yelled back, "Cover me! I'm coming back!" So they opened up fire, and I got up and ran and dove over the dike. Once I got there I looked to see what had happened. I saw the stomach shot and the shoulder shot, but I saw very little blood. I'm not sure what happened then for a while, because I passed out.

A little while later I came to, and King had gone forward to get my machine gun. There was still continuous enemy fire going on, but we have some cover now. But Smith, Ferro, and Eakins were exposed out in front of us somewhere, within just a few yards of an entire dug-in enemy company. I knew Eakins especially well because he had trained with me as part of the weapons squad. These guys who were shooting at us were in hardened bunkers. We didn't know who was alive and who was dead out there in front of us. Our first reaction, as we were trained, was to fire back and achieve fire superiority. At this point I think that they were still firing, but there wasn't much that they could do. With all this going on I promised myself that I would not die in this shit hole. I took great strength in that, and that is what probably brought me through it – the thought that I was not going to die in this shit hole.

COMBAT

Then I think that I passed out. Later I woke up again and King was diving over the dike. He dove over, and I passed out again. I woke up, and Hubbard was just looking at King. I turned over and noticed that King was lying still, and I told Hubbard to give him mouth-to-mouth. He did; he started to give him mouth-to-mouth, and opened up his shirt, and I saw that a bullet had gone right through his neck. It had come out just below his Adam's apple. I suspect that he died choking on his own blood. I thought about that for some time – if I hadn't passed out I could have helped. In my mind I thought that I could have helped him. But now I realize that we couldn't have opened up any kind of air passage, that I was in no shape to save him. I did what I could by throwing out smoke grenades to let our guys know where we were.

I passed out again, and when I woke up it was already getting dark. Hubbard and I could hear the enemy talking; there was a group of them. Obviously they were gonna come out. I told Hubbard, "Load up all you got, because they are coming over. They have got to know that there is somebody back here." I grabbed two grenades – interlocked the grenades. I put a finger in the pins of both grenades. If they were coming over the dike, they weren't going to keep us alive. And I certainly wasn't going to keep them alive. We were all gonna go someplace. But for whatever reason they held up; they just kept talking and talking. Then I told Hubbard that we had to get out of there. If we crawled along the dike and stayed low maybe we could make it to another dike and begin heading back toward our company. He was scared stiff, but he crawled away and I followed. I wasn't too happy about what had happened to me either. But I knew that if we were caught there they would kill us and strip us. That was the intent of the grenades. If they came over the wall I would just grab their feet and we'd all go to a happy place.

We probably crawled about 30 yards and found another paddy dike going back toward our company lines, which were hundreds of yards to our rear. Then it was dark enough where we were able to stand up and start walking. Then I started to pass out again. My bleeding was not external; it was internal. Periodically I would also have to stop and throw up blood. I knew what was happening.

I couldn't put a bandage over it; the greatest damage was internal. During all this, they [American forces] would shoot up flares, which would illuminate the entire area. Hubbard and I would have to dive down; we did that about three times. The third time I could not drop down anymore. Physically I was spent. I just kept on walking, with Hubbard supporting me on one side. Eventually we came to a mounded area with graves and bushes on it. I knew by walking much further we would run into our guys. We would hold up here and wait until morning to see where our guys were. It is nighttime; we had been in a firefight. I knew what I would do instinctively if I saw a shadow coming toward me. I was thinking that I didn't want to get shot by my own people. Maybe they have pulled out completely, but I suspect that our guys were nearby somewhere.

So we stayed there on that mound. I passed out I think a couple of times. I know that I threw up blood again. I told Hubbard to look out there toward our guys. It was starting to get a little light, so I said, "Look out there. Our guys gotta be there." Then I passed out again. I woke up; I don't know how much time had passed, and I look up. Hubbard is right over me, looking at me. I knew that he thought I was dying, which I was. But I wasn't that close to death. Then I crawled forward a little bit and saw our guys; I saw their helmets and stuff. I told Hubbard to get down, and I called out Mario Lopez' name. "Mario Lopez! This is Frank Schwan! Don't shoot!" With that they jumped right up. Then I said, "We're standing up! We're standing up!" Then they all came over. They took me back to the captain's headquarters, and I saw Jack Benedick [the platoon leader]. I talked with the company first sergeant for a little bit, who called in a helicopter dust off. I wound up sitting there by myself. Then a helicopter came in and I thought, "Oh, great!" But then they just dropped off supplies and took off. I couldn't believe it. Then another helicopter came in and took me to a Navy ship.

On October 6, Charlie Company was involved in its last major battle of the original draftees' tour of duty in Vietnam. Four men were killed, including Fred Kenney.

COMBAT

ALAN RICHARDS
Member of 4th Platoon of Charlie Company

On October 6, 1967 we were out on operation functioning as a rifle squad. Back in training we had joked, telling guys, "Spread out; one hand grenade would get you all." I remember walking through this rice paddy and approaching a tree line, and it seemed like we were bunched up, and I just motioned to everybody to spread out. No sooner than I had said that we were kind of walking offset, Steve [Hopper, Richards' good friend] and his platoon were off to my right in front of us going through this rice paddy. We were pretty much out in the middle. All of a sudden we started getting fired upon. I remember plopping down into the water, and I had picked up along the line an aluminum tubing backpack frame that made it easier to carry a lot of equipment – and I remember seeing the rounds hitting the water around me. And then it felt like someone had come up and kicked me as hard as they could in the shoulder. It flipped me over onto my back. My left arm was pretty much useless. But I remember looking down at the strap [of the backpack] and it had a quick release where the strap holding it up would break in half. And I remember thinking that "Oh, I finally get to use this." So I pulled the strap, and the backpack fell away. Then I was able to crawl back behind a dike, which wasn't much of a dike, more like just thick clumps of mud.

I remember a medic coming over to me and saying, "Where does it hurt?" I said, "My back." Later on I found out through x-rays that the bullet stopped right next to my spine. But my back was what was really killing me. My arm was kind of just flopping around. The bullet had hit me in the ball joint of the shoulder and shattered all that and then went into my back. I'm lucky on two counts. One, it could have gone forward and into my heart, but it went into my shoulder blade and stopped right next to my spine. That's what was giving me the pain, and when the medic came over there he cut the back of my shirt open because I was complaining about my back. The medic said, "I don't see anything." And I said, "It came in through the shoulder." He said,

"There is nothing in your back; the bullet has not come out and there is only a small hole in your shoulder where the bullet went in." The shirt was already cut in half, and I remember him tying the rest of it around my body and around my arm to immobilize my arm. Then Ronnie Gann [another member of Richards' platoon and a close friend] came over to see how I was. I looked over at him to tell him to keep his head down, because he kept sticking his head up to look and shoot, and right after I said that to him he ended up getting hit too. The bullet went in the top of his shoulder and missed his heart but punctured one of his lungs. I asked about him when I got to the hospital. I asked, "What happened to Gann?" and they told me that he was going to be all right; he was going to make it.

I remember crawling back. It seemed to me that I was wounded around lunchtime. All the while I could hear Steve Hopper yelling back and forth calling artillery in pretty much on top of himself. I remember lying there and gunships coming in over our heads and the medic trying to keep me awake so I didn't slump down into the water. I remember crawling back toward where the choppers would land, but the bullet in my back made that extremely hard to do. I really had a problem trying to crawl. After we had gone 50 or a hundred yards back I told the medic, "I'm gonna get up and just run back." But my arm was just flopping around because the bones were all broken, so he tied my shirt around me tighter to keep my arm from flopping around. Then we just got up and ran the rest of the way. I remember getting back to a certain point and not wanting to go any further because I wanted the medic to go back and get Ronnie Gann. I really didn't know about anybody else who was around me; who was hit and who wasn't hit. It seemed like once I got on the helicopter that there were quite a few bodies on the helicopter with me. I remember trying to fit in there because there was basically this hole in my shoulder and the medic had gotten a lot of the blood off of me. I'm not sure how seriously wounded people thought I was. I remember them putting me on that helicopter and sitting there in one of those canvas chairs. Every time somebody touched my back I winced from the pain.

COMBAT

STEVE HOPPER
Member of 3rd Platoon of Charlie Company

On that particular day our platoon was on point for the company, and my squad, 3rd Squad, was on point for the platoon. It was myself, Ybarra, a replacement who was my RTO. We had a new lieutenant in our platoon at that time, Davis. I had three new replacements, Horney, Burkhead, and Alldridge in my squad. I didn't know them [the replacements] very well. Burkhead and Alldridge were new; they had been with us for maybe a month. Burkhead and Alldridge were short timers. They had as I recall less than 30 days left in Vietnam before they were due to go home.

We had just left a tree line, and my squad was out in the open rice paddies. The rest of the platoon was kind of held up inside the tree line. We could hear a battle going on to our right. And as we got out into this rice paddy, we were asked to hold up, and I motioned for everybody to kneel down. We were waiting for orders, and we were told to take a right turn and go over and assist another company in our unit that was getting some heat. So I gave everybody directions in my squad and we made the right turn. Alldridge was out on point for my squad, and he went off and we all fell in behind him. We were scattered quite well in the rice paddy. We kept our spacing. The only guy close to me was Ybarra. We were headed toward another tree line and still out in the middle of a rice paddy. We had not moved but maybe 50 to 100 yards, and the enemy opened up on us. What bothers me looking back at it is that they were watching us the whole time we were in those rice paddies. They had bunkers dug into the dikes. They were well reinforced. They had phenomenal cover. You just could not see that they were out there at all.

Burkhead and Alldridge were across the dike and into another paddy. When they opened up on us, we all hit the ground. The guys who were around me all low-crawled through the rice paddy up against this dike. Fortunately we had the dike between ourselves and the enemy. Burkhead moved back toward me on the other side of the dike. We were taking fire. Horney was off to my left, but most of my squad was off to the right. My RTO was right there with me, and he got wounded in the initial opening burst of fire. So I pulled the radio off of him and strapped it onto my back, and I grabbed him and drug him up right beside me there at the dike. We started taking fire from the front of us and just off to my left there was another dike. And where those two dikes crossed, there was a Viet Cong bunker right there firing at me and everyone along the dike. So we tried to keep our fire focused on that bunker to keep that person down. This bunker had us dead to rights.

The gunfire was heavy; you couldn't get up. If you got up, you were shot. We were trying to keep this other bunker out of commission, where it couldn't fire. I could see the little hole in the dike that this guy was shooting out of. The VC had a couple of them strategically placed along the dikes, where he could shoot down one dike and down the other dike because he was at the intersection. Horney was off to my left, and we were yelling at each other, giving instructions as to what to do. One of us would cover for the other while the other was reloading. Burkhead was literally right across the dike from me, and I asked him, "Have you seen Alldridge?" And he said, "No, I haven't. He was out in front of me, and I saw him go down in the initial burst." So Burkhead said, "I'm gonna go out and check on him." So Burkhead left us for just a moment, and we were in some rice. We kept fire on this other bunker so he couldn't fire at us. We tried to lob grenades into that little hole, and they would just bounce off. This hole was no bigger than a fruit jar, and I was about 10 meters from that bunker.

I had called in a gunship to see if we could get this bunker taken out with rockets. He had us pinned down. And pretty soon this Viet Cong had thrown a grenade out at me. It landed 3 or 4 feet from me and splashed into the water. I literally just curled up into a ball, thinking, "Well, if it goes off it will get me; if it doesn't, then so be it." And it never went off. At that time the gunship arrived, and I popped a smoke grenade on the dike in front of me and gave instructions to this chopper pilot that the bunker was 10 meters to the west of that smoke grenade. I said, "The bunker is at the intersection of the dikes. Can you come in and put a rocket into that intersection?" He was talking back to me saying, "Roger," and he makes a big loop in the air and kind of came around, and the first time he came around he opened up with his machine guns and peppered the entire area, which is not what I wanted. I quickly got on the radio again and asked him to hold fire. I told him, "I don't want a machine gun; I want a rocket. One single rocket put into the intersection of those dikes!" Fortunately none of my guys were hit by the machine-gun fire, but it peppered all around us. You could see the rounds hitting the water all around us. Anyway, he said "10-4" and made another big loop around, and he came in and put a rocket exactly at the intersection of those dikes and took that bunker out.

About that time Burkhead came back and he said, "Sergeant Hopper, Alldridge is dead!" There was another bunker a little further down another dike out to the front of us across the dike from this intersection where I was. Burkhead raised his head to tell me this message and I was listening, had my head up as well. I heard a single shot, and Burkhead was killed. He was literally just a foot away from me when he was shot. They got him in the head, which was all that was showing when he raised up to talk to me. He just slumped down in the water. At that point I was mad. I kept a clip of tracers in my ammo pouch all the time – 20 rounds of tracers. I took my clip out and put in my tracers so I could see them, see where they're going. We got this other bunker to open fire on us again. We purposely moved, and I laid my M16 up on the dike, and when this guy started firing, this person who had just shot Burkhead and probably Alldridge as well, I opened up with my 20 rounds of tracers and pumped every round right in the hole that he was shooting out of. Took care of that bunker, but we weren't sure what else was out there.

At that point in time I started calling in artillery and walking it in toward us to take care of any remaining bunkers that were out there. At that point we decided that the safest way to get my guys back was to wait until darkness. It was getting late in the afternoon, so we waited until dark. I got everybody collected, and we started moving away from these bunkers and not knowing what we would run into. We didn't know if there was enemy down there or not. But we needed to get out of that paddy and move back to our unit. So I got my guys gathered up, and we started moving back. Then all of a sudden we took fire from directly behind us, which I didn't quite understand because our unit was behind us. But we continued on down until we came to another intersection of dikes, and it was a point where you were afraid even to raise your head because you didn't know what was there. But we got across that intersection of dikes, and then we started low-crawling in the water back toward our unit while staying next to a dike to have some cover.

We were crawling along this dike, and one or two guys were in front of me. I had my RTO still beside me, and there was an opening in the dike maybe 12 inches wide or so. And water was flowing from the rice paddy we had just left into this rice paddy we were in now. They used that hole for irrigation. I had the strangest feeling that if I got close to that break in the dike that I felt just, "Wow, somebody could see me." At that moment I heard a shot fired and something hit me in the face. From somewhere back from where we had just left, someone had fired at us. I thought I had been hit in the face. But actually the round had hit the dike and splattered mud into my face. At that point I grabbed my RTO and said, "Guys, let's get the hell out of here." We literally double-timed it; got up and ran back to our unit. We yelled at them that we were standing up and coming in. We ran back the final 30 or 40 yards and had cover again.

That's where I hooked up with [Platoon Sergeant] Joe Marr. He and some of his guys had been pinned down. He asked me if I'd seen Lieutenant Davis [a new replacement platoon leader]. We got the wounded guys out of there and got them moved further behind the unit where there was cover and some first aid. I was there with Joe Marr and I told him that I hadn't seen Lieutenant Davis. Nobody knew where Lieutenant Davis was. I was still calling in artillery and walking it toward us. I walked it in pretty close, to the point where I got hit in the shoulder with a shell fragment. Joe Marr had been hit in the hand earlier. They brought another platoon up, and it now held the dike where we had been, and our platoon pulled back and got some rest that night.

I remember that night that we kept illumination going all night long through artillery. We still were not sure if we had gotten all of the enemy. Daybreak came, and the area was quiet. The enemy had left. We found Lieutenant Davis. He was literally just behind me [where he had been the previous day], which is not where he should have been as our platoon leader. He had fallen in right behind my squad. He was in the middle of this rice paddy when the battle had begun. He was shot in the leg, which had severed the artery, and he just basically bled to death. No one could get to him, and no one knew he was there. So we lost Lieutenant Davis that day as well. He was from Tennessee.

RICHARD RUBIO

Originally from Canoga Park, California where his father worked as a foreman on a local ranch. Rubio was a high school classmate of Fred Kenney. Drafted along with Kenney and several others in the spring of 1967, Rubio served in the 3rd Platoon of Charlie Company, 4th of the 47th. Rubio was the platoon member nearest to the spot where Fred Kenney was killed. After the war Rubio returned home to California and worked for Schlitz Brewing Company, married, and helped raise three children. After his retirement Rubio taught golf at the El Caballero Country Club.

Fred Kenney was blond and made Robert Redford look ugly. He was an exceptionally good-looking guy, and a real nice guy. He was quiet and friendly. Everybody liked him. He didn't want to be a sergeant, but one of us had to do it, and they picked him. We told him, "Better you than us!" Kenney was athletic, was between a surfer and a greaser is what we would have called them in those days. I knew Fred for most of my school days; he was a year older than me. I knew all of the older kids at Canoga High because of my older brothers. I knew his sister too; she was one of the best-looking girls in school. I knew his wife; she went to Canoga High too. We were so close, like a band of brothers. The girls thought Fred was maybe even too perfect, the way he looked and the way he dressed.

Kenney's son was born while we were on the ship to Vietnam. After we got there he showed us all pictures of little Freddie that he got in the mail.

On July 11 we are walking along, walking point, and we keep noticing these Nipa palms stuck in the ground in fields in rows, like scarecrows. And I think to myself, "I've seen these before. I've seen these before." But I couldn't think of where. They were markings for the killing zone. The VC would set up their machine guns and everything, and these Nipa palm fronds were like the sidelines of a football field. Anything inside those fronds was in the killing zone. I had just begun to figure out that we were on the wrong side of the killing zone when Fred Kenney said, "Okay. It is my time to walk point today." And he grabs me and pushes me behind him. Fred Kenney was my sergeant, and I was his RTO at the time. We used to tease each other, everybody in the squad, by saying, "It is my turn to watch you today." He told me that and stepped in front of me.

We could hear some firing in the distance and figured that we could outflank them. Fred turned around and walked toward some Nipa palms on a small plateau with some houses on it. He no sooner turned around and started walking forward and BOOM. He got it right then and there. He was dead instantly. Probably shot through the heart. I started screaming, "Kenney! Kenney! No! No! No! No!" I couldn't get to him because there was shooting everywhere like crazy. There were VC on both sides of us.

Then I had to start yelling at the guys behind me. There was a rookie behind me, and I told him to get down. We tried digging some cover in the wet mud, because we were exposed, and most of our guys were back further still in some trees. I yelled at Terry McBride to open up with his machine gun and had other guys fire their M79s [grenade launchers] at 90 degrees because they are like 30 yards behind me, and I'm only 10 yards from the enemy. Then the tide started coming into the rice paddy, and there was this sampan out there. I told McBride to send the sampan to me so we can use it for cover. McBride and some other guys shoved the sampan towards me. Then I told McBride to open up with everything he had, and the kid and I got behind the sampan and made it back to McBride and the rest of the platoon.

Then I see this VC running with a machine gun. I tried to shoot him, but my M16 jammed. One of our guys had been hit, so I pick up his rifle, and I pulled the trigger. Just as I pulled the trigger it blew up. The barrel looked like something out of a cartoon where it splits open like a flower at the end. I lost my hearing for a while. Apparently the barrel had been filled up with mud. I can't believe that I lived after that thing blew up.

We were trying to regroup and go get Kenney. It had gotten dark. The guys were tapping me on the shoulder; there were like five or six of us. And we are crawling out to go and get Kenney. But it was so dark. The guys didn't know that I couldn't hear. We couldn't find him, and the enemy was still there, so we decided to pull back. I didn't know until later that the next day, Tom Conroy and some others went out to find Fred's body. I had lost a lot of friends that day. There were guys from Canoga High all across the company. I lost a lot of friends that day. I had to accept the fact that I wasn't going home. The only way to get through it is accept the fact that you are not getting home. Otherwise worry is going to kill you. If you accept the fact that you are going to die, all you can do then is live.

ERNIE HARTMAN
Member of 1st Platoon of Charlie Company

I was a replacement in the unit. It was kind of hard to break into the circles that the older guys had formed. I was just trying to learn how not to die and how not to get other guys killed. Then came July 4, one of my first real missions with the unit. After patrolling with the company, our squad was sent to backtrack to set a night ambush. We were walking through a deserted village toward our ambush site in the late afternoon. We were supposed to let the company know if anybody was coming in at them. We were headed back through this village that we had already gone through that day, and nobody was there. But to our surprise two Viet Cong come running out of a hooch there. They were surprised too. Our two point guys and the Viet Cong stood staring at each other for a few seconds, and then our point guys started firing. They chased them down toward the end of town. One of our point guys shot a Viet Cong in the calf. One Viet Cong went left, and the other went right. One was hit, but the other got away.

This is a horror that I've had my whole life. The wounded guy didn't have a weapon, but the squad leader said, "Kill him." The point man who had shot him didn't want to do it. I didn't want to do it. I had never even seen a battle to this point, or even heard a shot being fired in anger. Now this. The machine gunner walked up and unloaded on the Viet Cong at point-blank range. All my life I'll live with that; I should have stopped it. But it all happened in a few seconds. The squad leader later explained that we were so far from our company with night closing in. The other Viet Cong had gotten away and had no doubt alerted other units to our presence. He thought we had to kill him to save ourselves. I'm from a little town of about 600; I couldn't fathom doing something like that. It didn't fit with my morals. I don't know if I had many, but that killing sure as hell wasn't one of them. Keep in mind, this is July 4, and the company had been through one hell of a battle on June 19. They had so much hate built up in them after that battle. I didn't have it. I didn't have that hatred yet.

It was on July 11 that I started to fit in. We had a big firefight that day. I was on the M60, and when the firing started, me and my ammo bearer tried to hide behind a sapling maybe 6 inches wide. There were bullets flying all over the place. It was my baptism by fire. After the battle we had to bag up bodies, and then the realization set in. They [the Viet Cong] are here to try and kill me, and I am here to try and kill them.

It was the July 29 that changed me; after that day killing wouldn't have bothered me. We had set up a perimeter along a stream that ran like an "L." It was in the morning; some guys were getting coffee and I was shaving. And a spray of bullets come flying in. Benny Bridges got hit in the head, Jo Jo [Joel Segaster], who I was right beside, got hit in the gut, and I got some serious shrapnel wounds in my legs and back. I know that I've been hit, and our squad leader runs over and gets my machine gun and starts shooting across the stream into the foliage – really shooting at nothing, because you couldn't see anything over there. The main pain I felt was in my leg, but after things calmed down I noticed that my nuts were kind of hurting. The doc let me know, though, that everything seemed okay. A piece of shrapnel had just nicked me down there. Then they called in a medevac for us, and Jo Jo kept saying, "I'm going home. I'm going home." He was hurting, but he was happy. Bridges, though, I think died there on the chopper with us.

I had been in Vietnam about five weeks, and still had 11 months to go yet.

In July 1969 US Marines and South Vietnamese forces launched a multi-battalion operation to clear the Que Son mountains in the I Corps area of South Vietnam, resulting in several running battles in the rugged highlands.

ANTHONY GOODRICH
Member of Mike Company, 3rd Battalion, 5th Marines

Operation *Durham Peak* – this is where I got into my first firefight. I remember we were running patrols from our little ridgeline to a ridgeline that was higher than us. It was a pretty good trail that had been well used where we had our position. We found some spider holes and some tunnels up there also. We knew that the enemy was close. One day we were on a patrol. I should probably tell you my lieutenant's name was Lieutenant Williams – the only platoon commander's name I remember from Vietnam because he was so good. We were on patrol one day going up to this mountain, actually with the mountain ridge that kind of overlooked all the other mountains. Highest point from where we were at. We were on patrol one day; we stopped. The lieutenant told us to stop, and we were going to take a break. One of our platoon members, a Native American guy from

Arizona, saw a line of Vietnamese about 200 meters from us going up this denuded hill. It was just flat, and there was nothing growing. There was 15 or 20 of them humping up the side of this mountain. Lieutenant had us all get on line, and we opened fire. We actually ambushed these guys. It was pretty amazing. We fired everything. We fired LAWs [light anti-armor weapons] at them, bloopers [grenade launchers], machine-gun fire, and M16 and M14 fire. Everybody was firing on line. Probably 20 of us, 25 of us.

I remember feeding ammo into the gun for my machine gunner and picking out targets for him. I'd say "20 meters to the left," and he'd go right over there. He was a great gunner. A great gunner. The enemy was running around on the hill. They had no idea where the fire was coming from. You could see them getting hit. You could see them actually getting blown apart. We had a guy with a LAW who actually took this guy. You could actually see him fall apart, arms and legs going different directions. We got no return fire. These guys had no clue what was going on. After all this was over we called the air strike in. They came and dropped napalm and 250-pound bombs.

We had to go check out the area. I remember the first thing was the smell of the napalm and the smell of the burnt flesh. That always stuck in my mind. We found, I want to say, three bodies, and they were shot to hell. I mean there were big gaps, big holes in them. One guy had no face. His face was missing. We found no weapons, but backpacks with rice, some medical supplies. Lots of blood trails. Lots of blood trails everywhere. We knew that they were going to a place that we were going to have to go to. I think we found some documents too on a couple of these guys, and the lieutenant had them. Came back to our position, gave all the stuff to the skipper of the company. There were some intelligence guys there that radioed back what we had found. The next day the skipper decided to send two platoon patrols down the same trail, up the same ridge. This was probably mid-morning. This is a two-platoon patrol. They sent us over. We were the lead platoon. I remember walking through the area where we had ambushed these guys and you could still smell things there.

COMBAT

Then we started getting sniper fire. The first time I'd ever had rounds going over my head. They made a very distinct sound. I remember everybody of course jumps off the side of the trail facing outward and calls for guns up. My gunner gets up; I'm right behind him. We run right to the front of the column. I'm feeding belts into the gun. He's doing it off hand, with the sling over his shoulder. We're just chewing up the jungle in front of us. I thought it was great. I thought it was just fascinating and just fun as hell. I realized I was paying too much attention to what was going on in front of me instead of paying attention to the rounds I was feeding into the machine gun, and we ran out. The machine gunner smacked me. Screamed at me as he opened up the breach of the gun said, "Goddamn it, I told you." As I pulled another belt off my shoulder, which I should have done anyway, I realized that we were being shot at. I remember rounds hitting around us. I remember hearing rounds go by my head. I remember him screaming at me. It was that moment that I realized that somebody was trying to kill me. I realized that this was real; this was not training. This was the real thing. I remember I pissed my pants that day.

Anyway, I got the belt into the gun. They were still shooting at us. To this day I have no idea why they didn't hit us. I remember seeing rounds hit all around us and going by us and whizzing right by my ear. We got up and moved forward and they disappeared. The enemy disappeared. The gunner was pissed off at me, as he should be. "You know you don't be paying attention to what's going on there. Your job is to make sure this gun does not quit." I remember firing my .45 after I put that second belt in there. He said, "You did the right thing with the bushes there, you did the right thing." As I was feeding the gun, I was firing my .45 pistol into the brush around us. That scared me. I knew then that I was going to have to change my thought pattern if I was going to get through the war. I had to concentrate on what I was doing. He kind of congratulated me, said I did a great job. "When we moved, you moved right with me. I appreciate that. Just make sure you concentrate on your job with the gun. That's all you have to do. Don't worry about anything else." I learned another lesson that day. Thank God that wasn't a fatal one for anybody in the platoon. I remember shaking like hell. In fact, I did that after every firefight. I remember getting sick and throwing up. I knew that it was real. I knew that people were going to die even though nobody died that day.

Went back to the defensive position that night. The next day I don't know whether it was two platoons or the whole company went on the patrol. We knew that something was going to happen, so we went back up that hill again. We were the lead platoon again. We topped this ridge and everything exploded. Everything blew up. I remember being knocked down, knocked out. Knocked into a bomb crater. There was automatic weapons fire, and RPG fire. I even think they were dropping mortars in on us. We were ambushed badly. The 2nd Platoon, which was behind us, were in the middle of the kill zone. I remember waking up, my head was ringing, I couldn't hear. All I remember is the light, bright lights. Lots of dust, lots of smoke. Being scared shitless. My gunner, I had no idea wherever he was. He got knocked off the trail also. I remember just being scared. I remember hearing screaming. When my hearing started coming back hearing screaming, and I had no idea what to do. I didn't know what to do. When I looked down the hill, I saw this Marine, big black guy, machine gunner from the 2nd Platoon, running up the hill with a gun, with a machine gun. Firing on both sides of the trail. That's when I saw guys in pith helmets. They were shooting at him. He got up there, killed I want to say six or seven North Vietnamese, and he got shot and killed 20 yards in front of me. He basically broke the ambush up single-handedly, this guy. His name was L. A. Hayes. Larry Hayes. I live today because of him. I'm sure they would have killed all of us.

After Hayes got killed we swept the area, and the enemy, of course, had disappeared like they usually do. The thing that sticks out in my mind is that I lost something that day. I was so damn pissed off. I was so angry about his death and I wasn't able to do anything about it. I still feel bad about it. I still feel kind of guilty because I didn't do anything. I was so scared that I had no clue what was going on. I remember we had several KIAs and several WIAs. I remember the choppers came in – we blew an LZ at the top of this mountain to get everybody out that had been hit. I can't forget how bloody the LZ was. It was just drenched in blood. I lost my humanity or something that day. I don't know what happened. I got numbed. I numbed my feelings. My anger and fear from that day on is what carried me through Vietnam. That's how I survived it. We weren't ever able to mourn the deaths that I saw there. That was one of the things that bothered me for a long, long time. Somebody would get killed. Put them in a body bag and then you'd forget about it because you had to go do the next thing you had to do. So, I guess I lost my innocence that day or something. Something that's always stuck in my mind. That was a big change in my life that day.

The North Vietnamese and Viet Cong often struck at US and South Vietnamese fire support bases, stationary and often isolated emplacements housing an array of artillery. The attacks sometimes involved only mortar fire, but also often included infantry assaults by specialist sapper units, as in the case of a North Vietnamese assault on Fire Support Base Buff in August of 1968.

GARY FRANKLIN
Member of the 198th Light Infantry Brigade

We had been warned and we were on 100 percent alert that there was a buildup of NVA and Viet Cong in the whole area, and they had captured some people, and we knew sometime during the week that they were going to try to hit Bin Sanh. Bin Sanh was a fairly sizeable village on Highway 1 and the ARVNs [South Vietnamese soldiers] had kind of a regional headquarters there. LZ Dottie was there close, a big firebase, and Buff was a fairly good-sized firebase. We had 105 Howitzers, our own 81mm mortars, and four deuce [4.2-inch] mortars, and it wasn't too big a firebase at the time. We had 3rd Platoon and 2nd Platoon there. The captain and 1st Platoon were over on Dottie. So, we were on 100 percent alert. It happened to be that I was on a bunker next to the corner bunker. I was on bunker 13 and we had a flood-lamp unit that they had flown out. This thing was an Army jeep with a generator in the back and a big flood lamp that looked kind of like a large, huge television. It was a flood lamp that could generate a million-candlelight power, and supposedly this guy told us when they backed up there beside our bunker, they got a little behind our bunker and beside it, and he said, "They won't shoot at this because it will blind them. This thing puts out so much light!"

Well, about 2:30 that morning they suddenly hit LZ Dottie over there and Dottie was maybe 3 miles away. It was right on Highway 1. Boy, it was taking a pounding. They were taking incoming rockets and RPGs. We had the radio; we were listening to them, and we should have been paying more attention to our own perimeter. We figured we might get hit, but we thought we were ready, and we were watching Dottie. About 2:30 they hit us with mortars and started mortaring Buff real heavy and the guy popped in the jeep, cranked up the generator, and he turned that spotlight on. It was on about three seconds and somebody had good enough vision to hit it because they hit it with an RPG and just blew the whole back out of the jeep. I think some of the shrapnel I got back in my shoulder came off that jeep. But they just blew the back end out of that thing.

We had four people in our bunker. They blew that thing and we were just taking heavy mortars. We were on the radio, and everybody was yelling for illumination because we couldn't see a thing. The first thing you want to do is get on top of the bunker because normally by the time the mortars hit, the NVA were already inside the wire. They would crawl through the wire or something. What they done that night, they took a bunch of metal stakes and they laid them on the wire and they pushed the wire down and somebody had crawled in there and checked it for trip flares already. They were already inside the wire, and, as soon as the mortars hit, they were past the bunkers on our side. They got inside there and were throwing grenades up in the mortar pit, which kept the mortar guys from getting out and getting us illumination.

COMBAT

They blew the bunker number 14 there; they threw about a 40-pound satchel charge in it and detonated it. Calentine and the other guy were both inside the bunker. It killed both of them. Our platoon medic, Doc Schwan, grabbed his medical stuff, and he was in bunker 15. He grabbed his medical bag. He should have taken his M16 with him, but he went running because he thought he could get over there and help the guys, Calentine and his buddy. Well, just when he got there he realized there was someone standing in the middle of the bunker in all the rubble, and the bunker was blown completely in except for about half the front wall. And it turned out that it wasn't one of our guys that was standing in the middle of the bunker, it was an NVA and had an AK47, and he shot Doc in the stomach and hit both femoral arteries. He made it back to bunker 15, and they got down in the bunker, got flashlights out, got his medical kit, but when he saw where he was hit he said, "Guys, I'll make it about a minute and a half and I'm going to bleed to death." And he did. There was a pool of blood. There was about 5 gallons of blood over there in the bottom of that bunker. I can't imagine a human having that much blood, but he bled to death in about a minute and a half. He just said, "Somebody hold my hand," and in about a minute and a half, he was gone.

We fought for I guess about 20 minutes, and the ones we didn't kill coming in, we killed coming back out. Fortunately, those guys had been at the mortar pit. I think there was two Viet Cong or North Vietnamese; it's hard to tell because they came through the wire stripped down to just their underwear so they could feel everything. So, they didn't have their uniforms on and [we] really couldn't tell if they were NVA or Viet Cong. But, they were from the 403rd Sapper Battalion. I've got one of their little handmade cigarette lighters, which was probably beat out of one of our airplanes, I imagine. It's a little handmade aluminum lighter. They just had grenades up there and they threw all the grenades and they tried to run back out and we killed them going out.

I think we had two mortars actually hit our bunker, but one of them was when Fint got blew unconscious. We built us a little fighting position in the front right corner of the bunker and we sandbagged it; we double sandbagged it. It was big enough one person could get in there, and we had all our grenades strung around on top of it, and a nice little fighting position. Well, it saved our hide, but not because we got in there to fight. One of the first mortar rounds I think hit inside that fighting position and it blew the sandbags off and blew all the grenades out of the way and hurt Fint pretty bad, but it probably saved the other two of us. One of the guys had a 60mm mortar; it was either a mortar or a good-sized grenade, went off right between his legs. It turned out he bled to death on the way in. I think he was conscious when we got him on the dust off, but that was about 30 minutes after he got hit, and he was dead on arrival when we got back to Chu Lai at the hospital. We got them out of there about 3:30 and then the other guy from the flood lamp and I stayed there until about 6:30 the next morning after sun up because we were low ranking and we weren't hit that bad. We weren't bleeding enough to where it was a serious problem or anything so we just stayed there and defended the bunker. It was nearly out of personnel. I think they had two or three other wounded really bad too in some of the other bunkers there on Buff. It was the first time that we got overrun or something and the first time things got really serious for me.

Helicopter pilots in Vietnam dealt with their own unique perils of aerial combat, and also sometimes had to face enemy assaults on their bases.

FRANK LINSTER
Member of the 188th Assault Helicopter Company

The SF guys captured some documents, and part of it was an [enemy] attack plan. When they figured it out that it was our base camp [that was going to be attacked] we went on 100 percent alert. I mean, if you weren't flying you were in the bunker line getting ready. I don't care if you were an officer or if you were an

NCO or enlisted, you were out there doing something; everybody was getting ready. I just happened to be staff duty officer that night, and I had my radio, and I was talking to the bunkers and talking back to the base and the gunships, when they hit. The other guys ran out to the flight line, got in their gunships, and some of the guys were flying with their helmet and their thongs and shorts. That's all they had on because that's all they could grab before the attack came. I'm not sure; I think we had six gunships up there during that attack that night, and I would try to talk to them because I've got a .50-caliber shooting at us and I need them guys to take him out – and the chatter on the radio, everybody wants to talk.

It took me a long time to finally get the attention of one of the gun crews and direct him to where that .50 was shooting from. He was sitting right in a hooch right on the edge of the village. I mean, I could sit there and watch him. But, the trench line behind the bunkers was deep, and being only 5 foot 9 I couldn't see out of the darn thing. So, I crawled out of the bunker and got behind a tree, a big old rubber tree, a Michelin rubber tree, so that I could see what was going on, and that way I could better help direct my bunkers where I need them to concentrate their fire. Besides just the guys coming, and they pumped up flares and stuff like that for us so we had them [the Viet Cong attackers] silhouetted so they showed up really easy, I was also trying to keep the bunker guys shooting on their line of fire to get interlocking fire from the bunkers and trying to get everybody to shoot where you were supposed to be shooting. Don't worry about the guy next door to you. He's taking care of his business.

The VC didn't get that close because we got a starlight scope, which, when you take it and shoot it at night, the least little bit of light lights up everything in green and so we seen them coming. We let them get within 50 feet before we hit a couple of flares, I mean, they lit up the show real good. That's when the [Viet Cong] .50 opened up. I seen him right away, and the fire was coming over the top of our heads. Well, .50 tracers at night looked like a basketball coming at you. I needed to get him taken out before he did some real damage. He wasn't shooting at my bunkers; he was shooting between the bunkers, and I thought for a while he was definitely shooting at me, but how could he see me unless he had a starlight scope, too? But, he definitely had the tree I was hiding behind. He made a lot of holes in that tree.

We finally got them. The guns did a great job, and then we had some defensive fires. They were shooting within 50 meters, 150 feet, of the bunker lines. We were ducking so we wouldn't get hit by our own shrapnel because they would have called me up and they would say and I would holler on the radio, "Duck!" and everybody would duck, the artillery would hit, give it a couple of seconds and then get back up on them guns. Our guys, our door gunners, were shooting very close to our bunker. I bet they were shooting within 10 feet of the bunker line because some of the VC got that close as they were coming in because, I mean, wave after wave they were dying, and by the time the sun come up they had [dragged] most of their dead away so we got very little intelligence from them. We didn't find anything on the people's bodies, the few that were left, to identify what unit they were. A lot of times you can find a cigarette lighter or a letter from home or something on their person, but the sappers, those guys are pretty darn good about not bringing any information with them. They were good fighters – there was no doubt about it – but they were coming regardless of whether we knew they were coming or not.

They fired 60mm mortars at us. Right after the battle we did a sweep and we found one 60mm mortar that had landed in our compound that hadn't gone off. A young private had only been in country a couple of days reached down and said, "Hey, I found it!" You should have seen everybody run, and all of a sudden now realizes what he's got – he's got a live 60mm mortar in his hand – and he's just statue of liberty! So, he stood there until the EOD [explosive ordnance disposal] team come. I don't know who the kid was, but if he didn't mess his britches he had good, good control over his bowels. I mean, just the reaction because we were walking literally shoulder to shoulder and he said, "I found it! I found it!" and everybody just gone, like leprosy. You never seen a bunch of tired guys move so fast in your life. Things like that, now it's funny. At the time, everybody just knew this guy was going to disintegrate with the least little movement, whatever it took. That thing was still alive as all get out, but the EOD team picked it up and took it out to the bunker line and blew it and got all the way out there.

A few weeks later we were in our helicopters supporting a unit that was making a sweep to make sure that no Viet Cong were coming through to re-infiltrate a pacified village. We came in there in the morning at first light and put them [US troops] right on the ocean [near the village] and started pushing back. What we did was we took the gunships and put them on the backside of the village to keep anybody from sneaking out the back. And to sneak out the back, it was 8 miles to the first hiding place. That was a long run. A bunch of people, 28 guys, came out the back of the village heading off and we tried to use the gunships to stop them. As long as we were putting direct fire down near them, they would stop running, but as soon as we'd go pass by them to make our turn, they'd take off again. We played games with them for ten or 15 minutes probably before the village chief finally got upset, and all of a sudden he comes on the radio and says, "Kill them." The next gunship rolls and gives a three-second burst out of a mini gun, and they were all down. They went in and searched them and found out every one of them was NVA.

One of the toughest things I ever had to do in Nam was when I was flying a mission; I was in the southern area of operations, and one of my guys had been shot down, and it was just at dusk. Well, the medevac had come in and picked up guys and taken them to the hospital. We knew there were six people on the airplane, and we knew that the medevac had taken four to the hospital, and my guys called me up. Since I was the closest, my job was to go to the hospital and identify how many of those four were ours. So, when I got there two of them were ours; two were infantry guys that were part of the kick-out because what they were doing is that they were supporting this infantry battalion or infantry company, it was on top of a mountain, and they were kicking out supplies on top of the mountain. They had come under fire, so my warrant was sitting on the ground down in the valley waiting on the firefight to get over with. The firefight was over so he came up to kick off the last load, it was just at sunset, and somebody shot out his engine and he's coming off the mountain getting down in the bottom. Well, they had been spraying Agent Orange in our area at that time, and as he flared at the bottom he hit a tree where the foliage was all gone. He didn't see it. He ran into the side and knocked off his tail boom and crashed into the bottom and exploded in fire because he had almost a full load of fuel on.

The two guys that we lost were the gunner and the pilot; 19 years old, both of them 19 years old. When the fire was brought down and they got in there, the pilot still had the controls in his hands. He never quit flying it, and the gunner was draped over him trying to get him out of his seat when they both got killed by the flame from the helicopter. When I got in there, the copilot, they were just taking the battle dressing off his leg because he had got thrown through the window, and his left leg had hit the radio console coming out because he hit that hard. His seat had literally been torn out of the aircraft, and when they opened up the bandage I could see the wound, and, I was no doctor, but I knew he was going to lose his leg, which he did, and then one of the kick-out guys had got burnt real bad, and he had inhaled a bunch of fire in his lungs, and they had just done a tracheotomy on him, and he passed on that night, too. The crew chief that was in the aircraft, he ended up with a broken ankle, broken nose, and a dislocated shoulder, and he said the only reason that he survived the fire is that as the fire was whipping up he jumped, and that's probably where he broke his ankle and stuff. Because it was during the rainy season he had his wet weather gear on over the top of his flight suit, and he had his visor down so his nose got burnt and his chin and stuff got burnt. Because it was cold, he had his collar and everything all up and buttoned tight around his neck so none of his body was burned, but some of the rubber actually melted into his flight suit. He says, "I probably dislocated my shoulder when I hit the ground." He says, "I'm not sure when the hell I broke my ankle." But, he was back flying in less than a month. They had him back in the air flying again.

COMBAT

I look at what we, as a group, did, not just our company but aviators as a group. One, we were young and dumb, and didn't know any better, right? But we did whatever the job took. Whatever it took to get the job done was what we tried to accomplish. My experience with my people is that I didn't have any shirkers. I didn't have anybody that said, "I am not going to do it" or "I don't want to do it." When we had a mission, we went. Nobody ever said, "I can't do that today" or "I don't want to do that today."

―――――――――――――

Those who saw combat in Vietnam sing the praises of chopper pilots, especially medevac pilots, who braved the hell of battle to rescue the wounded and dying, and never seemed to say no – no matter how hopeless the situation. It was during the 1970 invasion of Cambodia that James Moran's unit received the call to aid South Vietnamese soldiers in desperate trouble.

JAMES MORAN

Jim Moran was from the Worcester, Massachusetts area and attended the University of Connecticut. Uncomfortable with the discord on college campuses, Moran volunteered for the draft in 1968. Moran served as an AH-1 Cobra pilot with C Battery, 2nd of the 20th Aerial Rocket Artillery, 1st Cavalry Division in Quan Loi, Vietnam during 1970 and 1971.

Basically what happened, during the Cambodian operation an ARVN [Army of the Republic of Vietnam] airborne unit, and I believe it was a company-size unit, established contact with North Vietnamese troops northeast of Kontum, Republic of Vietnam. That contact was initiated on May 23 [1970] and a medical evacuation had taken place on the 23rd and the LZ was "cold," in other words, there was no ground fire. On May 24, at about 1600 hours, a medevac was scrambled through Quan Loi; it was Medevac Two. It was crewed by Steve Madika, who was the aircraft commander, and First Lieutenant Leroy Carburot, who was the pilot/copilot. Along with that two AH-1Gs [Cobra gunships] were scrambled from C Battery, 2nd of the 20th ARA [Aerial Rocket Artillery] at Quan Loi, and those aircraft were crewed by First Lieutenant George Alexander, aircraft commander; pilot was WO1 [Warrant Officer] Jim Moran. The second aircraft was crewed by CWO [Chief Warrant Officer] Paul Garrity, the aircraft commander, and WO1 Jimmy L. Nabors in the front seat. We dispatched to the area, and as we approached we made contact with the American advisors on the ground, and they reported that the LZ was cold although they had eight wounded ARVN troopers on the ground. I don't know how you got a cold LZ with eight wounded troopers but that's how it was. But we took their word for it.

Standard procedure was the medevac would set up on approach to the LZ; one Cobra would go low with him to act as a screen and give him close support as he was going in, and one Cobra would stay high, covering the two birds that were going into the LZ. Med Two approached on a southeasterly heading, trying to keep the sun at his back. Alexander and myself went down with him. As we approached the LZ, we could see troops on the ground. We didn't get any fire, but as Med Two decelerated all hell broke loose, and we could see tracers in the daylight, which was unusual. We started to break across his nose and we saw him get hit. When he went down, Madika was hit in the chest armor by two rounds and he took a round in his left thigh. Carburot noticed that, he tried to recover the aircraft, not realizing that the engine was disintegrating and the tail boom had severed. Because of the rotor RPM that was still left, the aircraft rose off the ground a little bit, but it rotated on the axis of the rotor system because he'd lost tail rotor control obviously, with a severed tailbone. The aircraft landed hard, rolled over, the fuel cells ruptured and it caught fire. As that was happening Alexander was breaking left around the front of him. We saw the fire coming out of the southeasterly side of the LZ and he broke really hard right to avoid the fire; we could see it, and as we looked down we could see bunkers.

COMBAT

Apparently what had happened was this ARVN company had stumbled into an NVA bunker complex. We were later told that those bunkers were concrete reinforced, which counts for the fact that we shot a whole lot of rockets at it and really didn't do much damage to them. We went back to help – Garrity was screaming for us to get the hell out of the way so that he could put some rockets down on the bunkers where most of the fire was coming from. Alexander and I went back to altitude and we set up our daisy chain with the American advisor on the ground putting down suppressive fires, trying to knock out some of these bunkers. At about that time, a Huey from B Company, 229th, its call sign Killer Spade Four, came on the scene, had heard what was going on and volunteered to make an attempt to go in and pick up the downed crew. He got the short final [about to land] and he took heavy fire, disabled his aircraft, but he was able to fly it out a short distance away, land, and another aircraft from the 229th picked him and his crew up and evacuated them. They kind of, as it were, flew off into the sunset and we never heard from them again. After he left, we were getting low on ammunition but Medevac One – commanded by Captain Henry Tuell also from the 15th Medical Battalion – came in. Alexander and I went with him and tried to insert him into the LZ and that was a no go. His aircraft took heavy fire, as did we, but we had the advantage of having a little air speed and being able to maneuver, where the medevac was just a sitting duck decelerating into the LZ. Tuell did not crash. He made it out of there heavily damaged.

While all of this was going on, we were getting low on fuel and low on bullets. We scrambled another section of Cobras out of Quan Loi. They tried to get another medevac in that was piloted by First Lieutenant Tom Reed; that aircraft was damaged and the fuel cells were pierced. They landed a short distance away and they were picked up by another aircraft and evacuated. A fourth attempt was made by CWO Ray Zepp, Medevac Two-Three to get his aircraft in, but he was shot down, managed to get it away from the LZ, but his aircraft was disabled and he was also picked up. By that time it was getting a little dark; we had one aircraft already destroyed, three down and two damaged. Tuell's aircraft and the

Cobra that I was in, we took hits in the tail boom and rotor system. When we got it back they changed the rotor blades and put duct tape over the bullet holes. That was how you repaired sheet metal real quick. We could not get anything in there at night; it would have been suicide to try to go back in at night.

The following day we put together a planned rescue attempt that involved several medevac choppers, which had to be borrowed from other units because Charlie Company – which was supplying all of these medevac choppers on the first day – had run out of airplanes. They just didn't have anything that would fly. Mac Cookson led two heavy fire teams of three Cobras each up to the LZ, and we did a very heavy rocket prep before attempting to get aircraft in for the rescue. Several of those aircraft were disabled but all the crews were rescued. The final bird in was the command and control ship and they evacuated the rest of Madika's crew. We put the whole thing to bed on the 25th.

[During the fighting on the 24th] we were anywhere from, at various times, 50 to 200 feet above ground level. Air speed going into the LZ probably no more than 50 knots. We were decelerating with the medevac to shield him as he went in. We would normally slow down with him, we tried to time it; as he made his landing, we would break across his front at low speed to shield him and then we would take up a low-level orbit, using the turret weapons, the mini-guns which I did fire ineffectively, just trying to make some noise. We didn't know how many bad guys were down there, but they were all over the place. Somebody said later that artillery was impacting in the area and we're saying, "I don't remember any artillery," and I don't know that it would do any good because the NVA were in the perimeter; it was just people all over the place. The ARVN on the ground were fighting for their lives. During the night they provided security for Madika and Carburot and Louis Rocco and the other surviving crewmember of Medevac Two. The gunner, a kid named Taylor, was killed in the crash when the aircraft rolled over on him. I had nothing but absolute respect for medevac crews. Those guys never said no and they never quit. They would go in the worst damn weather in the middle of night, hot LZ they just went. They went; they never said no. They just kept feeding people into that thing. The bird in front of them would go down; they'd say, "Okay, my turn." Gutsy guys, really gutsy guys.

You've heard the cliché, after a while you weren't fighting for mom, apple pie, country, or any of that; you were fighting for one another and it was just a dedication amongst the helicopter crews anyway. If one of your pals went down, you did everything to get him. We didn't care about the machines – the Army had tons of machines – we cared about the people, so we'd just go get them and you developed a rapport. We became very, very close with the medevac crews. We had many, many aircraft shot up shielding those guys and we would literally just stick ourselves between them and the bad guys because they were defenseless. They got a medic and maybe the crew chief hanging out the door on a hoist trying to lug some poor grunt up through the jungle on a jungle penetrator or a rigid litter if he was seriously injured and everybody in the world could see them. The little people in the bushes with the AK, Uncle Ho put a big floral ribbon on their chest if they whacked a helicopter; that was a big deal for them.

_____

For the wives of men in Vietnam, the stories of their husbands' final days in combat were often only pieced together from letters or learned from friends long after the fact.

PAULINE LAURENT
Wife of Howard Querry

Howard left in March, right around the 1st of March, 1968. He was Company A, 3rd Battalion, 39th Infantry, 9th Infantry Division. He wrote that he went to this French fort called Fort Courage, and it was near Saigon, and it was surrounded by a moat, and he said that as long as they were at that old French fort, Fort Courage, that he felt safe there. He said that what they would do is they would go out during the day on these reconnaissance missions, whatever that means. They would go out and I guess look for the enemy. And search around and if they found them, shoot them and then they'd come back to the French fort at night. But once he wrote to me that they were leaving the fort for an extended period of time. It wasn't just going to be a day trip; they were leaving for several days to go to Saigon. So, one of his last letters he wrote, you know, "We're leaving the French fort and I don't know if I'll be able to write you. You know, I'll write you when I come back. I don't know how long we're going to be there, but it's going to be more than a day trip." And that's the weekend that he died. It was Mother's Day weekend.

BARBARA JOHNS
Wife of Jack Geoghegan

[When I wrote to my husband Jack in Vietnam] a lot of it was about Cammie and what Cammie was doing and how she was growing and changing and our hopes for the future, of where we might go when he came back from Vietnam. We thought we'd go back to Tanzania, but not necessarily. But we had hopes of going back into that world, into a third world. I remember [in his letters] that he said it was a beautiful country and he wanted to bring me there when the war was over. I think he may have even had hopes of some time when the war was over that there would be a lot that needed to be done and he probably would have seen himself in some role that way, going back to Vietnam in that role, which was really more the essence of Jack, was doing for people. Helping people, not killing people.

I do know that the men in his command were extremely important to him and he cared deeply about each one. On board ship he wrote, "Everyone here is a little edgy, but this will end the moment we land, and I only hope that none of my men are killed. I know that they will fight like hell and that we are a well-knit team. God bless them all. It certainly seems odd that these men who are going to fight for the US will find it difficult to get a job back home when they come back because they lack education."

COMBAT

In what was probably Jack's last letter to his parents, he wrote on November 7, "We have been on the defensive perimeter for almost two weeks and have been actively patrolling for that time. The men are becoming more professional every day. Replacements have already arrived for the men who went home sick or those leaving the Army for good. As each one goes home, I feel very good that he has made it safely." And then, "Each day here increases one's love of the United States and the desire for security. Even Grand Central Station seems a paradise right now. How I will enjoy a quiet ride in Connecticut when I return, with no one shooting at me. I know that my life will never be the same after I return from here. Even in Africa, we didn't realize how many comforts we had compared to here. Death is so close that the small things make life worthwhile – a cup of coffee, a drink of water. Please do not get me wrong. I'm not complaining, only thanking God for the opportunity to learn what is really important and to see what honor can be like. It will make me a much better man. We learn each day." And that was in a letter to his parents, so that tells you what kind of a person he was. One week and a day later after he wrote that letter, Jack and all but three of his men died in the Ia Drang Valley. I will never know if Jack killed anyone but I will always, always, always be grateful to know that he died as he lived, going to the aid of one of his men, a soldier named Willy Godbolt. As you know, their names are next to each other on the Vietnam Memorial. I can't help but repeat the words of that Catholic Relief Services worker, that Jack would be incapable of deserting a dangerous situation in order to take care of Jack. And several months later, Mom Geoghegan made the ultimate act in forgiveness, and quietly had a Mass said for whoever the North Vietnamese soldier was who fired the shot that killed her son; God would know who he was.

6 LOSS

There are 58,178 names etched into the black granite of the Vietnam Veterans Memorial. The vast majority of those lost in Vietnam were young men, in the prime of their lives with everything to live for – 30,096 of those killed were ages 18–21. While mines, booby traps, grenades, and illness all took a toll on American soldiers in Vietnam, the greatest losses by far were caused by small-arms fire, accounting for a total of 18,518 American dead. Utilizing the racial characterizations of the time, which usually included Hispanics as part of the Caucasian population, the death toll broke down as follows along race lines: 50,120 Caucasian, 7,264 African-American, 252 Malayan, 226 American Indian, 116 Mongolian, and the remainder unknown. Of the total number of US dead in the war, 17,215 were married, leaving behind widows and young families.

Early in the war, the next of kin received news of a loved one's death via telegram, but later casualty notification teams were established across the country to deliver the painful news in person. Normally at least two military officials, clad in their dress uniforms and with at least one of higher rank than the deceased, would arrive with the solemn tidings that the family's loved one had been killed in action in the Republic of Vietnam. As often as they could, the military officials would remain on hand until other adult family members arrived to assist the mother, father, or wife in their time of need.

At the heart of war is tragedy. Parents bury their children; young wives become widows; younger siblings lose their idols; children lose fathers – fathers who will become but distant memories. For so many families life was shattered by a simple glance out of a living room window only to notice two immaculately clad military men walking up the driveway. Processing the information was painful, sometimes so painful that families and young lives never recovered from the shock and loss. Children fled upstairs to weep in their rooms, mothers collapsed into the arms of the notification officials, fathers stoically attempted to hide their feelings. War had transformed the joy of life into grief over a future never to come.

But life went on. Normally within 24 hours a casualty assistance officer would arrive to begin the labor of dealing with insurance benefits, delivery of the body, and the details of the funeral. Family members could choose to handle all of the details themselves, but most funerals for American soldiers killed in Vietnam had a military element, usually including a military honor guard, a 21-gun salute, the playing of Taps, and the handing of the folded flag that had adorned the casket to the next of kin. After the solemn ritual, and as the crush of relatives and well wishers departed, the parents, siblings, wives, and children – those who had loved the slain most dearly – had to try to move on with their lives. Even though their world would never again be full and complete, they had to try to live.

If you should ever find yourself at the Vietnam Veterans Memorial in Washington, D.C., take time to find the names of these young men and to remember those they left behind.

LOSS

Geoghegan, John (Jack); Panel 3E, Line 56. Killed in action, November 15, 1965

Geier, William (Bill); Panel 22E, Line 12. Killed in action, June 19, 1967

Kenney, Elmer (Fred); Panel 23E, Line 52. Killed in action, July 11, 1967

Querry, Howard; Panel 58E, Line 13. Killed in action, May 10, 1968

BARBARA JOHNS
Wife of Jack Geoghegan

[When the telegram arrived concerning Jack's death] I was not home; I was with Jack's aunt in New Rochelle, New York, about an hour away [from her in-laws' home in Connecticut]. And I wanted to be with her because her husband had died two years to the day, actually, before Jack, which I, at that time, didn't know. And his mother had to call me on the telephone to tell me that the telegram had come. I can remember just where I was standing, and I just sank down to the floor when my mother-in-law told me what was in the telegram. And then she said to me, "We're so glad that he married you." That was so beautiful. That was just the kind of person she was. Oh, it was unreal, absolutely unreal. I just couldn't believe it. Of course, that's the same reaction everybody has, I think, when you receive news like that. And we talked for a little while, and Jack's aunt came. She was my mother-in-law's sister, actually, and she came over to me when she saw my reaction to the phone call, and I had to tell her and she put her arms around me because she adored Jack, too. Everybody did. And then when I got off the phone I remember walking through the dining room and looking out the window and seeing cars going by and thinking, "The world is still here." It was a strange, strange reaction. And I went upstairs where Cammie was asleep, and she was at that point five months old. And I picked her up and I held her for several minutes and thought about how Jack had said that when he came back, we need to give Cammie a little brother or sister, but now it would just be the two of us. It was a very, extremely sad moment. Unreal.

I said to her, "It's just the two of us now." She was only five months old. At that age, babies don't wake up very easily, so I quietly put her back in her crib, and she didn't wake up from my holding her. I just patted her and told her I would try to make up for her loss, that I would be both parents to her. And I told her we would be near Mimi and Gigi and they would always be there to help us, and we would help them, too. And that's what happened, really. Cammie was a bright little baby and always happy and smiling, and she really is the one who held us all together.

He was killed on November 15, and it was two weeks later when his body came home. My brother at the time was a Marine, and he was stationed in Hawaii. The bodies were sent through Hawaii, and he accompanied Jack's body home from Hawaii, which was a wonderful thing that he did. And he was with us for several days through the funeral, my brother was. He had been in Vietnam himself, twice. Jack's body went right to the funeral home. They let us know, and then we went over to see him.

I was with Jack's parents. We each individually went. Oh, gosh, I remember his father. It was so sad. It was a hermetically sealed casket and there was a glass top to it so his body was under a glass top. And his father just kept – his hand just kept stroking the glass like he was trying to get through it to touch Jack's body. Oh, it was one of the saddest things I've ever seen. He never – Jack's father actually lived for 18 years after that. It was amazing. He was a whole different person.

It was just – unreal. I'd look at him and think – of course he looked like he was asleep and I would think what a strong, wonderful, energetic person he was in life and it was so unbelievable to see him there knowing that it was over, that he would never, never be with us again except in spirit, memory, thought. It was a very powerful feeling. It's why I didn't think he would be killed in Vietnam, because he had so much to do on this earth, that God wouldn't take him. I really believed that, which made the shock even greater when he was killed.

We talked about it and decided to have the funeral in Pelham, New York, which is where Jack grew up. The funeral was in St Catherine's Church in Pelham, New York, and there were hundreds and hundreds of people there. It was just astonishing. And there was an honor guard from Pennsylvania Military College that came up to be there. The commandant of cadets was there from Pennsylvania Military College. It was a wonderful, wonderful tribute to Jack, the presence of all those people.

JAMES GEIER

Brother of Bill Geier, who served in 2nd Platoon of Charlie Company

I was so proud of my brother for serving. I was 13 years old and liked to watch *Combat* on television; it never crossed my mind that anything bad could happen to Bill. The television shows never did present the reality of particularly this kind of a war. My dad had served in the Military Police in World War II. He met my mother while he was serving in the military. If my parents were worried about Bill being drafted they hid it well. They probably felt that it was their obligation to support the war. So they just supported Bill as best they could when he was drafted. Bill was a great kid; ideal. He was a blessing to our mom and dad. He was a good son, period.

After the end of Bill's training in December 1966, he came home for a short leave before shipping out to Vietnam. We were all there in Maywood [Illinois]; all of our relatives and friends were there. We had a party in the basement; we played music, our favorite 45s. There was dancing, a conga line. It was just a celebration of having Bill there. Bill put on his uniform and showed it to everybody. We still have that photo.

That day in July 1967 I answered the door and there were two military personnel standing there. It was pretty devastating. There were two well-dressed officers on the front porch of our house in Maywood. I got mom and then went upstairs crying, bawling once I had established what was taking place. My mom had to call my dad back from work. The military handled that as well as you can. The news set my dad back for a number of years. I don't know that he ever really shook it. He and Bill had been so close. He was depressed for a number of years. It didn't get to the point where he couldn't function. He still carried out his obligations to the family, but he lost a lot of vigor there for a period of years. My mom had raised us all Catholic, and we had a good foundational basis of faith. That is what carried my mom through. In fact my dad strengthened his religious foundation too following that.

It was hard to read my dad's demeanor. In some ways I thought he was angry. Whether it was the war itself or the government side of it, I don't know. He never really did share that. Or was it just depression that he had to reconcile with, because it was his first-born? And they had shared a significant bond. We all did. We were a close-knit family, and we still are. For dad religion took hold more after that; he would sit down and say grace to himself. You could feel a sadness in dad. But it didn't affect how he dealt with the family; he probably held people closer in a lot of ways after losing Bill. But there was this persona of sadness about him. But he did come out of it. Just like anybody going through mourning or bereavement, he had to reconcile with himself. Mom had a stronger faith initially, and she tried to portray that to him, and she accomplished that – to put it in God's hands for a higher purpose.

Bill is in a cemetery in one of the northern suburbs of Chicago. They had a military funeral, with the 21-gun salute and the flag. I remember that well. Bill is buried next to my father. The whole extended family was there. They all loved him and took it pretty hard.

It takes so long to heal. It took the guys from Charlie Company over a decade to begin to get together and heal. They are still pulling guys in. These guys are in their 60s and are just now getting together to share their stories. They are completely broken when they begin to tell their stories, when they begin to talk. That's the kind of healing it takes – a lifetime of healing. The family feels the same way. You never shake it, but at the same time you welcome the association with the guys who were there.

LOSS

It means a lot to know that these guys were so supportive of Bill and respected him and held him in high regard. It was at the reunions that we found out the circumstances of Bill's death. He had wanted to be a medic, which spoke to his character, and went through the extra training and became a medic. He died while he was trying to save another man's life. I was proud of him. That's quite a deal.

BERNICE GEIER
Mother of Bill Geier

Bill was born May 1, 1946, the oldest of our four children. He has one sister, Jackie, and two brothers, Bob and Jim. His dad worked in the printing business as a pressman operating a four-color press. I was a homemaker. Bill was a quiet, loving, easy-going and very thoughtful person. On Mother's Day in 1967 [while Bill was deployed to Vietnam] he sent me fresh flowers from Hawaii. (Today the box that held the flowers contains all of the letters he wrote.) His letters never mentioned how rough life was in Vietnam.

His dad was discharged from the Army in fall of 1945. We lived for 18 years on the northwest side of Chicago. Housing was a scarcity after World War II. We began family life in a small, four-room flat behind a shoemaker's shop. The only drawback was no hot water. Our family grew – Jackie was born in 1948 and Bob in 1951 – but the flat didn't expand. On Bob's second birthday, we moved to a first-floor flat in the same building. That was a blessing – six very large rooms and hot water too. Jim was born in 1953. The neighborhood was well cared for, school was within walking distance, and families were in the middle-income bracket. The neighborhood had enough children to keep my children entertained.

Bill attended public grade school. His grades were excellent. When he was in 7th and 8th grade he took the job of crossing guard. I remember watching him as he guided children across the intersection near our house. His goal was to be an architect.

VIETNAM

After graduating from grade school, he enrolled at Lane Tech. He was active in school programs and a member in several clubs. I remember that he built a good size scale-model house that occupied a spot on the floor of his room. He graduated from Lane in January 1964. After his graduation from high school we moved to Maywood, a suburb of Chicago. We finally bought our first home. He attended two years of Triton College before he was drafted into the Army. He worked part time at Sears while going to college. I remember when he worked at Sears, he would sometimes come home with a bag of JuJu fruits, and we would share time together enjoying the goodies.

Transportation in suburbs was not as good as in the city. Bill never obtained a driver's license. I drove him to his classes. Bill played Little League until he grew past the age allowed. Then he coached with his dad a Little League team that his two brothers played on. Football and softball games were other pastimes he enjoyed. These were parks or empty lot games with friends. He was a Chicago Bears fan like his dad.

He loved the outdoors. We camped as a family on summer vacations in Wisconsin and Michigan. First camp-out was in an old Army tent. We upgraded to bigger and better tents as the years passed. When he left for Vietnam we made plans for a vacation to Colorado in 1968. We made that trip in 1968 – he came along in memory. We bought a 14-foot Shasta travel trailer. He would have loved seeing the beauty of the West. Still have the camper. My first grandson and his family travel the road in our vintage trailer.

The day the sad news came started out so beautiful. It had rained before dawn, and there was the clean fresh smell of the spring shower in the air. I happened to look out the window and saw two Army men coming to the door. I knew before the knock on the door what message they carried.

With God's help and the aid of our extended family we slowly started to accept the crisis in our lives. We all had times of sadness, but after a while we began to live again. I know Bill would have wanted us to go forward.

He's our angel.

LOSS

BARBARA HILL
Wife of Fred Kenney

My mom was taking me down to San Francisco to see my grandfather. We got there and they were crying, and I knew that something was wrong. They had gotten a telegram that he was missing in action. So we had this horrible drive home. I still remember that horrible drive and the wait. It was awful. It was the most awful thing; you can't imagine. [We had only been married a year and a half, and] little Freddie was only five months old. He was just a little guy.

We went back home, and we waited. It was the next day that two officers came to the door. We had a funeral for Fred in Canoga Park, and the military was there. There was a 21-gun salute, and then they gave me the folded flag. There were a lot of people in attendance, and afterward we all went over to the nearby VA.

I just couldn't stay in Cottonwood [California] anymore, so I moved in with Fred's sister Mary in a trailer in Paradise Cove. Eventually I moved into a condo in Woodland Hills – my sister, myself, and the baby. A lot of my friends had husbands who were going to Vietnam, and they were getting married. I just remember that it was the most horrible, horrible time. I was young, alone, and had this baby. I didn't know what to do. My friend Bonnie was having a party for Don Hill [a boy Barbara had once dated in high school]. He had told other friends that when he got back from his own tour in Vietnam that he was going to marry me and take care of us. And that is pretty much what he did. I was 22 and so alone. I was lonely and scared and just wanted to be normal.

Don was back, and we started dating. It wasn't like I didn't know him, and he was really good with Freddie. He really wanted to get married, so we gave it a whirl. I wanted some normalcy, like everybody else seemed to have. It seemed like all of my friends were married, and everybody else was part of a couple, so I did it. We kept Fred's picture up on the wall forever. When Freddie was four, and I thought he could understand it, we told him about his father. He was very upset, but he knew about his father since he was a little guy. Don was his dad. He calls Don dad, because Don was his dad. Don was good with him.

Don and I got divorced in 1986; I was single again, without a job – with five kids. But I lucked out. A friend of ours who had been in the service, Ronnie Olson, hired me, and I had a wonderful job working with him for almost 22 years. We worked together at First American Title. I got lucky. It has worked out. Freddie is happily married and has two babies who are the cutest things ever and a teenager. He is happy and well adjusted. Freddie is very proud of his father. He once saw pictures of his dad surfing and said, "Wow! I didn't know that he was a surfer!" Freddie is a surfer too. He talks to all of the Kenney relatives, especially on Facebook. Freddie is just good friends with all of them. They are all kind of keeping connected, and I think that is really nice.

One day Tom Conroy, from Fred's unit, called my son. It wasn't that hard. We aren't that far from where Fred used to live, only ten minutes away. Freddie has the same name as his father, and one day they just called him, hoping that he was related to the Fred Kenney who they had known. One day in 2008, Freddie calls me and tells me that these guys have called from Charlie Company. He was kind of afraid to tell me because he thought I was going to be upset. He said that they all want to talk to you. Can I give them your number? I said "sure," and I'm not kidding, later that day I was talking with three of them. Tom Conroy [who had retrieved Fred Kenney's body from the battlefield the day after his death], Bill Reynolds, and Stan Cockerell. I learned the details of how Fred was lost. I had thought that I had known, but I really didn't. Tom Conroy had written it all down. I hadn't known the complete details. It was bad. Tom began writing poems about Fred, and began to send them to me. He asked me if I minded if he sent the poems to me. They were nice poems. They were so nice.

I then went to the Charlie Company reunion in Washington, D.C. in 2008. It was so nice. I couldn't believe how happy they all were to meet me and talk. It seemed like it made them feel better after they talked to me. It was awesome. They told me about how they nicknamed Fred "Coolwig" because of his wavy hair. It was all good stuff. I also went to a company reunion in Las Vegas in

2010. They showed all of the pictures back when the guys were young. I really like going. I feel good when I go. I think that the reunions have probably offered closure.

Fred Kenney was such a good man. He had been the man of the house for his family [after his father had passed away]. It was a big family – Mary Lou, Sandy, the twins [Fred and Susan], Ruthie, Tommy, Charles, and Gordon. As the oldest boy, Fred had to help take charge. He was such a great guy. You know, we were young. We never had any fights. He was so nice to me. You just can't believe how nice he was. I'll never find anybody that nice to me again. It was love at first sight.

PAULINE LAURENT
Wife of Howard Querry

I was living with my parents back in Prairie Du Rocher, Illinois because Howard decided that since I was pregnant, that would be a good place for me to be. So, he kind of persuaded me. He was very persuasive, you know, like he persuaded me to marry him.

Well, it actually began the weekend of Mother's Day. Mother's Day was on Sunday and I think it was, I don't know, sometime that weekend when I picked up the paper. I really made a habit of not reading the paper because the paper was full of the news of the war, and I already knew my husband was in the war. I didn't really want to read about it because it just increased my anxiety. So I pretty much ignored the paper. And the same way with television; my father was an avid TV watcher, so I always saw the fighting because my father had the TV on. You know, the evening news was on every night. But what happened was I somehow picked up the Sunday paper and literally found this article. It wasn't on the front page or anything; it was kind of way in the back pages of the newspaper, and it was like I was drawn; some force was drawing me to this article, and I read about it, and it was about a battle in Vietnam. And it was about my husband's unit. And when I read it, I had this realization that my husband was dead, and it was kind of like an intuitive thing. It was like I didn't know how I knew it, but I just knew it, and I just started sobbing. I remember I was sitting outside in the backyard under the sycamore tree and my mother came out and said, "What is the matter?" And I said, "Howard is dead, I know it." And I was sobbing and crying and she said, "Don't be silly. How do you know it?" And I showed her the article, and she read the article, and then she just went back in the kitchen and then it was business as usual. You know, that's how my family was. It's just, "Okay, what's next? What's the next thing to do?" And then that whole weekend, I was suffering from really bad anxiety. By that time, I was seven months pregnant.

I couldn't sleep because intuitively I knew that he was dead, and the baby was just turning around and moving a lot, and I was really scared because I thought that I was going to have the baby early, and I was trying to like calm myself down because I didn't want the baby to come early. But I knew that he was dead, so it was a very, very traumatic few days. And I wrote him a letter every day during this time, and I just recently reread those letters, and I was just trying to tell him the trauma that I was going through. "I'm so worried, they're fighting in Saigon. You said you were leaving the French fort, I'm sure you're there." I didn't really say, "I read about a battle and I think you're dead." I just kept writing the letters because I was refusing to accept this feeling that I had that he was dead, and the only defense I had against this feeling was write him another letter. So I was writing like two or three letters a day during that weekend.

Well, he died on May 10, and then on May 15, five days later, my mother had just gotten home from work from the grocery store, and she was fixing dinner, and I was standing in the family room looking out the front windows, and my father was watching the evening news. I saw this green Army car pull up in front of the house, and my heart started racing and pounding. I knew that they were coming to tell me that he was dead. And I told my mother that there was an Army car out in the front and then the dog – Howard had gotten this dog before he went to Vietnam – the dog started barking. I took the dog and put the dog in the basement and went to the front door. It took these guys a long time to get out of the car and come to the front door. It was like they just kept sitting in the car, and sitting in the car, and sitting in the car. Finally, they came to the door, and I went to the door and they said, "We're looking for Pauline Querry." And I said, "That's me." And then they just looked at me and they saw that I was pregnant. And I don't think I invited them in. I think I just started saying to them, "Is he dead or wounded? Is he dead or wounded?" And they didn't answer me. And finally, probably my mother invited them in, and then they kind of read this thing to me. They didn't really speak it, they read it like it was a script and they said you know, "We regret to inform you that your husband has been fatally wounded" or "mortally wounded." They didn't say "Dead," and I was in such a state of trauma, that I didn't hear the word "Dead," so I kept hanging on to the hope that maybe he's injured, and I kept saying, "Is he injured or is he dead? Is he injured or is he dead?" And they wouldn't give me a straight answer. It was just so frustrating for me. Finally my mother said to me, "Honey, he's dead."

Then I went into this foggy place of non-reality. I can just remember bits and pieces of words like "medals," and "funeral," and "arrangements" and you know, just words. I remember just sitting there trying to maintain some degree of sanity when I wanted to just explode myself in emotion. [I just tried to] hold it together while these guys were still there. So, they delivered all the information they needed to deliver, kind of like they were delivering a script to me, and then they got up and left, and it was then that I went into my bedroom. I shut the door and I said, "Just leave me alone." And I remember throwing myself on the bed, and of course then the baby really started kicking and squirming. I felt like my life had just blown up. Like literally, somebody had just thrown a grenade into the middle of my life, and I felt like I couldn't breathe. I did not know how I was going to survive.

Then I remember at some point, I came out of my room and my mother had invited all these relatives over. So I had to walk out and be with all these relatives at a time when I really just wanted to be alone. My brothers and sisters that lived close by, my aunts and uncles, it's like they all came over to my house. So when I walked out of that room, I had to be strong again. My mother and father gave me no permission to be emotional because neither one of them had permission to be emotional. So I had to walk out and be the stoic war widow the minute I walked out of that room, and I spent about 25 years being the stoic war widow. It cost me a lot. When Howard's body came back from Vietnam, we could not open the coffin. And I was not told why. I was just told that I could not open the coffin. We were told that it was non-viewable, which means, "Don't look at the body." So, I remember my brother at the time, my youngest brother said to me, "If you want, I will open the coffin and identify Howard's body if you want me to." He had been in the Marine Corps and I think he felt it was his duty to do it. And I said, "You don't have to do that." But because I didn't see Howard's dead body, I hung onto some ray of hope that possibly it could've been a mistake. So, I went to the funeral. I went to the cemetery; we put the coffin in the ground, and I didn't know that I was doing this, but in retrospect, I pretended he was still alive. And so, everything that reminded me of Vietnam, I couldn't be with. The box that came back with all of his things, I put those things in cardboard boxes, stuck them away in the bottom of the closet, and never looked at them.

7 A WORLD OF HURT

Any Vietnam War movie from *Forrest Gump* to *We Were Soldiers* tells the story – an American has been wounded in battle. A medic rushes over and administers first aid, while a call goes out for a medical evacuation. Within minutes a helicopter lands amid the hail of enemy weapon fire to retrieve the wounded man. As the helicopter takes off, a hospital a short flight away prepares to receive and treat the casualty. This scene is almost the quintessential image of the entire conflict.

In the brutal, small-unit fighting that typified the Vietnam War, speed was the key to saving the lives of young men who suffered the nearly infinite variety of horrific wounds that are the byproduct of battle, including gunshot wounds, shrapnel wounds, shattered limbs, traumatic amputations, and punctured lungs. In many cases it was the UH-1 Iroquois, or "Huey," helicopter that made all the difference. Helicopter medical evacuations revolutionized military medicine in Vietnam. Unlike previous wars, where often hours separated the moment of wounding from in-hospital care, most injured US personnel in Vietnam made it to triage centers and modern medical facilities in about an hour. In some cases, fortunate soldiers reached hospitals in less than 20 minutes. It was the Army Medical Corps' prodigious use of helicopters as air ambulances that made possible this quick transfer from battlefield to operating room table and saved the lives of thousands of American troops.

Over 150,000 of the roughly 300,000 American servicemen wounded in Vietnam required hospital care. During World War II, 4 percent of wounded troops died after arriving at a hospital, but, due in the main to the speed of transport, casualties reaching medical facilities during the Vietnam War suffered a fatality rate of only 1 percent. Medical treatment took place at various installations in South Vietnam, Japan, the Philippines, and the United States. The United States Army established its first hospital at Nha Trang, South Vietnam, in 1965. Three years later, in 1968, the United States Army operated a network of 19 hospitals across South Vietnam, providing 5,283 beds and some of the best medical care available anywhere in the world. Since the war in Vietnam lacked static lines between friend and foe, military hospitals were strategically placed throughout South Vietnam and on US Navy hospital ships offshore. These facilities included field and surgical hospitals as well as evacuation and convalescent centers. By 1969, 16,000 physicians and 15,000 nurses of the Army Medical Corps served in South Vietnam.

To handle war wounded, the American military employed a five-tiered medical system. At the first level were the medics and corpsmen serving alongside US Army troops and Marines in the field. Tasked with stabilizing a wounded soldier while awaiting medical evacuation, medics performed emergency tracheotomies, stopped excessive blood loss, provided morphine for pain relief, and made temporary splints for damaged limbs. In a very real sense, medics did whatever they could to save the lives of their patients. Once on board a helicopter, a wounded soldier was usually taken to a divisional clearing station. At this second level of medical care, a team of physicians and nurses provided patients with blood transfusions, antibiotics, and tetanus antitoxin. Mobile surgical hospitals provided the third level of medical care. Here surgeons were best suited to helping servicemen with severe hemorrhaging and blocked airways. The world-class American military medical facilities in Japan and the Philippines were the fourth level of medical care. At these hospitals, specialists treated soldiers suffering from major ailments, both physical and psychiatric. The US military expected that soldiers treated at this stage would return to Vietnam once they had recuperated. Major military hospitals in the United States, ranging from the Letterman Army Hospital in San Francisco to Walter Reed Army Medical Center in Washington, D.C., comprised the fifth tier of medical care. Soldiers reaching this level of care were typically badly wounded and were recovering from major surgeries that severely limited their mobility or bodily functions and were not expected to return to Vietnam. Hospitals at this level cared for 11,584 patients between 1965 and 1969 and offered a range of rehabilitation services.

Even amid the massive military medical infrastructure, the shock first of getting wounded and then the long and often painful road to recovery was an intensely individual, and often lonely, experience, where surviving the actual wound – whether the loss of a limb, or the perforation of the colon – was merely the first step. The experiences of solders in the medical system often varied in accordance with the severity of their wounds. Some were only in the hospital for a few days of rest, air conditioning, and good food before returning to duty. Critically wounded soldiers, though, often spent months healing from multiple surgeries and lying in hospital beds undergoing agonizing rehabilitation – recovering from broken backs, severed spines, lost limbs, or ghastly burns. Just as their bodies were torn and battered, so too were many soldiers' minds. How should a 20-year-old react to waking in a hospital bed without arms? How do you write to your parents and tell them that their beloved son will never walk again? It was often the case that wounded soldiers only saw familiar faces again when they reached home – the faces of their parents and family members. It was then that true healing could begin.

VIETNAM

GARY FRANKLIN
Member of the 198th Light Infantry Brigade

[After the August attack on Firebase Buff] if you were hurt real bad they sent you to Japan or the United States. If you were hurt a little bit they sewed you up, cleaned your wounds, sent you over to 91st Evacuation Hospital, and you stayed about a week and a half there as kind of recuperation. I got in there, and when I got in there I was thinking I was hurt pretty bad. I got in there and we had 14 guys there in triage being prepped, and what they were doing with most of them, they put us on hold. They checked us over real quick and said, "Sit down in that bed and we'll call you when we get to you." Most of them were trying to get them strong enough for surgery, and out of the 14 there I think nine were unconscious, and they lost about five before they could even get them in surgery. Sometime there I got to thinking, "Well maybe I ain't hurt at all! This is not bad!" Those guys were hurt. They were really torn up pretty bad. They [the communist forces] hit about nearly every one of the major firebases in Americal Division that night, so they had wounded from all over. I found out then that the surgery and everything is not like *M*A*S*H* on TV. They don't pick out every little piece of shrapnel and everything. They find what really might do some future damage and what's hurt real bad – cut artery, cut vein, a piece of shrapnel near your heart, piece of shrapnel near your spinal column. Anything else they leave in place. It's already hot and cauterized, and if they don't think it's going to hurt you much they just leave it. They didn't really have time to mess with it, really. They had people hurt ten times worse than you were, so they were rushing through people there just as fast as they could. I wouldn't say the medical care wasn't good; those guys were mostly young, drafted doctors, and by the time they came home they were probably super surgeons. They were really good, and I think they were really conscientious about what they did. They just had their hands full so much that they didn't have time to take the time to do anything special. They patched you up, and away you went.

A WORLD OF HURT

[In the 91st Evacuation Hospital] I got chewed out a lot! Over there they were senior medics, and those guys were pretty experienced. What we found out, I didn't know it when I got there, I knew that officers only had to spend six months in the field and just plain old grunts spent a year, but they had such a hard time keeping officers alive. They were losing so many officers – it was such a tough job – that they only had to spend six months in the field, and it was the same way with medics. They spent six months out in the field, and if they lived that long they got to rotate back to a job back in Chu Lai, either working in surgery or working over there at 91st Evac or something like that. Those guys were pretty experienced. I knew they were busy. They always had somebody they needed to take care of, so I kept getting up and going and getting a book or something. They deburred my wounds, which is they just cut the skin on the outside and cleaned it up, because shrapnel makes a real jagged, torn wound. So they deburred my wounds and then they wait about three or four days to see if you get infection. Vietnam was notorious for infection. So, if you didn't get infection, they sewed you up. If you did get infection, they sent you to Japan. I didn't get any infection, so they sewed me up over there at 91st Evac. During that first three or four days I kept getting up and going and getting me a book or something to do because I got so bored and mainly I was just real stiff and sore, and it would break my wound open and it'd start bleeding again. Then I'd get the bed messed up and then I'd get chewed out. After about the second day I gave up and I'd just call when I want something because I realized that I wasn't saving them any trouble. They were spending more trouble changing my bandages and cleaning my bed up than anything else, so I'd just call and, "Can you go get me a book?" I got chewed out a bunch over there. That was pretty entertaining, too. At least I got out of the field and got hot food for a while. Once I was there, and I never got wounded that bad again. I didn't really want to. Once in there is enough!

KIRBY SPAIN
Member of 1st Platoon of Charlie Company

[After being wounded by a booby trap in the same April 1967 incident that had killed Lieutenant Black.] They pulled me in and done x-rays. Well, they said they could see shrapnel in my stomach. I'm telling this doctor, "No, you seen something else." Because the grenade went off behind me, off to my right rear. This piece came along, and it just sliced open a wound right there on my stomach. Grazed me, I guess you would call it. I had a piece embedded in my arm because I was holding my rifle up. So my right arm was bent and a piece went right into my forearm. And there was a piece that hit me in the back and got within a quarter of an inch of my backbone. [But the doctor] decides since there is shrapnel that they are going to cut me open and do an exploratory. Otherwise, I would probably have been back to the unit in a couple days. So they cut me open, and I got a scar about a foot long right down the middle of my stomach. From what that doctor said, they got out all my intestines and held them up to the light and checked for holes, shrapnel, and stuff. Then they put me back together. But I told this doctor, "What you are looking at is probably my breakfast." And he said, "What did you have?" I said, "I had a can of beefsteak with potatoes and gravy." It came out of our C rations, and it was quite tasty. I had gotten a chunk of C-4 from the engineers the day before. Had my little stove going after rolling up a ball of C-4 and lighting it. Stove was made of a C-ration can top, and I set my main course on top of the stove to heat it up. When the surgery was over with, I don't know how long I was out, but I hurt a whole lot more than before. The doctor came over, said I was right. I said, "How's that?" He said, "We did not find any shrapnel in your stomach." I said, "What did you find?" He said, "Chunks of potatoes." I said, "Well, okay."

The doctor, the one that had operated on me, he came around every day about 5 o'clock and gave me two cold beers. I hate to say this, but I figured out the first day or two they would only give you morphine every four hours. If you complained between those four hours, they would give you those Darvon pills. I would save them up under my pillow and have at least four of those when beer time came around. I would pop my four Darvon pills with my beer. It was like taking a trip without leaving the farm.

Several more of the guys started coming in, and one of my buddies was over there in the middle of ward. He had been running during a firefight and got shot, and the bullet went in his index finger on his right hand and came out, it never hit a bone. But it did cut his finger – there were two holes in there. For a 30-caliber round that was something else for it to do, because usually there is a little hole going in and then it blows everything off when it comes out. They sent him up to the hospital and all he was doing was waiting for breakfast, lunch, and supper. He started cursing, "I have not been up here two days and I have already gained about 15 pounds!" He said, "Man, this is great!" But they sent him back out to the unit.

One guy, Danny Bailey, was hurt so bad that they were going to send him to Japan. [Bailey had been wounded by a booby trap, which had nearly blown off his leg.] Now Bailey was not the brightest star in the sky. But he was tough, and he would do any damn thing you told him to. He got kind of tired lying in bed, and I mean he was wounded bad. It messed a bunch of muscles and stuff up in his legs and his back. He got to getting up in the hospital ward in Long Binh, and the doctors saw how much better he was getting that when they released him they sent him back to the unit at Dong Tam. He was slotted to go to Japan, and on his own effort Bailey had rehabbed himself, and they sent him back to the field. Of course he was on crutches and could not do anything when he got down there. But about a month later he heard that his buddies were in a battle [on June 19] and in trouble and he put down his crutches, went and got his field gear, and came out with the ammo chopper. That sounds like him.

I got to where I could get up and walk around a little bit. I was in the hospital for three weeks. After about a week and a half, I got to where I could get to the mess hall. I would go there, go outside, and over to the latrine. I thought I was doing pretty good, which I guess I was. I would go around from one hospital bay to the next. Best I can remember it was the first air conditioning I had been in since leaving Fort Riley. The first time I got cooled off was in that hospital ward. I would go from one room to the next checking to see if any of the guys I knew had come in, and there were several. Other than getting to visit them – tried to get their spirits up a little bit – my favorite part about that whole deal up there in the hospital is when Chuck Conners, he played *The Rifleman*, came through one day. I got to shake hands with him; he sat down there on the edge of the bed and we talked for a little while. I did not realize he was as big as he was. Next week I was there, Henry Fonda came through. Then there was a guy the last week I was there, he was a game warden down there in Florida and he had that show *Flipper*. I kept looking around for Jane Fonda but I never did see her.

[When I was discharged from the] 24th Evac in Long Binh I was standing there waiting, and they said I was to report to Bear Cat. I said, "How am I meant to get back to Bear Cat?" They just looked at me, did not say anything, and gave me my web gear, field gear, and my rifle. I got to looking and I said, "I want the rest of my ammo." The one sergeant standing there said that was it, and I said, "No it is not. I had two more 20-round magazines." They went back there and dug around and gave me my two magazines. So I had my full load of ammunition. A lieutenant who was also being discharged said, "Come on; we will hitchhike." We hitchhiked all the way back. They dropped us off at the end of the road. The last mile and a half, I had to walk to get back to Bear Cat. I thought, "This is really something."

DON TRCKA
Member of 3rd Platoon of Charlie Company

[After being wounded in the battle on May 15] they flew me to Bear Cat and I was completely out. When I woke up, I had two Purple Hearts on my pillow. They said the general had stopped by. I do not recall who the general was. I was out, so he just laid them on my pillow. After I saw these two Purple Hearts, I put my hand on my stomach and I had a big patch on it – I am talking about with gauze and everything. I said, "What the hell happened to me?" They told me I had a colostomy. They told me that in World War II people died from [wounds like mine] because they could not evac them quick enough. Plus, I had the arm, which they did not sew up. It was just open all the way; you could almost see the bone. Of course they had it wrapped, but not stitched up.

[With a colostomy] they take your intestines away from your colon, I think. You do not use your colon; you use the side where the pack was.

From Bear Cat they moved me to Saigon. They told me later that they did not want to sew up my arm because they did not want to get infection in it. So they left it open. Then they transported me to Saigon, where I stayed one day. The next day they flew me to Camp Zama, Japan, to the Army base there. I stayed in Japan for at least 30 days. But I still had the colostomy. I took a lot of pain medications because, other than the colostomy, I had wired sutures – eight of them – and they were like the big paper clips. I had those in my stomach.

The Army had called my dad and mother and told them I was wounded. They did not tell them how bad I was wounded, but just to know I was wounded and on my way to Japan. I had not called my mom or dad for a week or so because I was still in so much pain with all those wired sutures and colostomy. I did not know how to explain that to them. I eventually called them; talked to my dad, and then I talked to my mom. Of course they all prayed for me at the church, which they had told that I was wounded in Vietnam but was okay. My dad said, "You got hit in the arm?" I said, "Yeah dad, I got hit in the arm but I also got it in the stomach." He said, "The stomach?" See, the Army did not tell him that. They just told him I was hit. I told him what I had and he said, "Son, you did okay." I said, "I think I am coming home." So I stayed in Japan, and they finally sewed up my arm in the sick bay. I sat in a chair and watched them sew up my arm. There was a gentleman next to me from the Marines. He had lost both his legs by stepping on a mine. He was there for a long time. Of course he was still taking pain medication, so I said to him, "I need more pain medication." I was not only taking mine, I was taking some of his because I was in pain. I had sent him a letter telling him where I was, how I was doing, and hoped he was okay. When I got back to the States, at Fort Sam Houston, I got his letter back. It said on it, "Receiver deceased, return to sender." I got that letter back because he was dead.

When I first got hit, I said to myself, "You cannot die." That is when I saw that picture [of my girlfriend taped to my rifle butt] and said, "You are not going to die." The doctors took real good care of me. They did everything they were supposed to do because I made it. When I left after more than 30 days, I flew to Long Beach, California. In the cargo aircraft they flew you in from Japan to California, I laid down the entire time. I had pain medication going through me from an IV. When we got to Long Beach, they opened the back and said, "Don, we are going to carry you off." I said, "You are not, I am walking off this plane." I walked off. Of course when I hit the bottom, I went back on the bed. But I walked off that plane; I was not going to let them carry me.

I stayed there in the California hospital for about two days and then went to the hospital in San Antonio. When I got there, I called my dad and said, "Dad, I am at Sam Houston, San Antonio." My aunt and uncle lived in San Antonio. He said, "Can I have them come see you?" I said, "Yeah, dad." He said that he, mom, and Beverly [Don's girlfriend] would come up. So they came up the next day and I remember going to the restroom and my dad followed me because I had to change the dressing on the colostomy. He said, "Son, you did okay; I am proud of you."

When my parents left, Bev stayed back. I was sick; I was throwing up and was not feeling good. She told me I looked like crap, and I know she cried. I had to cough, so I would not get pneumonia. The guy said if I did not cough, he would "put the snake down you." I did not want the snake. It was a tube that they put in you so you could cough. They called it the snake. I said you are not putting that snake down me, even though it hurt to cough because of the sutures. The next day I was better. She was amazed I could change in 24 hours. Then they took out the sutures, which was a big relief. I mean it was just like someone opened up your stomach and said now is the time to get the relief. About a week later I went into surgery and everything was put back together. I stayed there another two weeks. A captain came in and said, "Son, where would you want to be stationed?" They were giving me the option of going to any place I wanted and I said, "Fort Hood, Texas" because that was about three hours from home.

CARL CORTRIGHT
Member of 1st Platoon of Charlie Company

[After being shot through the spine on May 15, 1967] I did not stay in the hospital; they stabilized me and gave me some blood. They were going to medevac me to a specialist to operate on my back/spinal cord. They gave me morphine, and I was feeling better. They x-rayed me, gave me morphine, and I was feeling drowsy. At the second hospital they stabilized me first for four or five hours before operating on me. They were busy with other cases or something; I did not know what the heck was going on. After four or five hours they woke me to give me something to put me under. They told me to count backwards from 100; after 91 I was out. I finally woke up after all this, hearing noises like in a movie, strange whispering noises getting louder and louder. I opened my eyes and I was facing the floor. I said, "Where the hell am I?" Then everything hit, "Oh shit, I was wounded." I was so weak I could hardly move. The first thing I said was that I wanted water. I had been out for a number of hours. After the surgery they wheeled me into a ward and said they could not give me any water to drink for three days. I dropped my mouth and said, "Three days?!" A colonel came out a few days later and gave me a Purple Heart. The guys that were wounded were moving around and joking a little bit. I asked the doctor, after having been there for about a week, "When will I start walking again?" He said, "It does not look very good, son." But the staff said I could be walking around again; I just have to try harder. Well that is not necessarily so. The staff were always trying every day to get you to move your feet. Even later, when I was in San Francisco, they would say, "Okay, let us see you move that toe." Mentally I am trying to get my brain going. After about two or three months of this, I said, "You know, I have heard that it does not happen within two to four weeks because the swelling around the spinal cord can make temporary paralysis, but after that you should start to get something back." After three or four weeks and you do not, that was what got me. It was hard being paralyzed and weird without feeling below the hips.

The first hospital they sent me to, the first person by my side was a chaplain holding my hand. At the second hospital a chaplain asked me if I contacted my parents. What the chaplains do is send a message to your parents. It was routine: "Your son has been wounded; do not be too concerned about him or anything." Of course your parents are. The chaplain asked if I wrote anything to my parents yet, and I shook my head no. He asked if I could write, and I said not very good. I was so damn weak since I had lost a lot of blood. He sat me down and wrote a note. He helped me write to my parents. I wrote about a page saying that I was wounded but okay. They had no idea how bad I really was yet.

I only flew from Vietnam to Japan for one night. The next morning they got me another big Air Force transport from Japan to Travis Air Force Base northeast of San Francisco. That is when I called my parents. My parents saw me the next day, and my dad freaked out more than my mother did. They saw me laid out on this stryker frame [a rigid bed used for paralysis patients]. It isn't much wider than an ironing board; it is only about 6½ feet long. Very narrow, and it is not much more comfortable. Every two hours, they flip you on your stomach and two hours later onto your back. Twenty-four hours, day after day. My parents asked, "How do you sleep?" I said, "What do you mean? I can't sleep." My parents were just shocked to see their son lying there on this little stryker frame.

Being on the stryker frame was like a ferris wheel. It was lousy. You go back up then back again on your stomach. This went on for about three weeks until I said I can't sleep at night. The doctor finally left me lying on my back all night so I could sleep a little better. I spent two months in Letterman Hospital in the San Francisco area. Next they told me they were sending me down to Long Beach VA [hospital]. Now at that point, I had no idea what my future was going to be. I thought I was going to spend the rest of my life in bed. Nobody told me anything. Nobody came around and said anything about getting out of bed or rehabilitation. Nobody told me anything. So I thought life was going to be my damn bed. Went down to Long Beach, [a hospital with] five wings of 50 guys each, all with spinal cord injuries. The next day this young nurse comes in with a wheelchair and said, "All right, out of that bed." I said, "Me out of bed?" I was like 100 pounds; I just could not eat. I needed help; that is how weak I was. They got me in a wheelchair after two or three days, and I was gone out of there. I could not leave the hospital, but I would be down the aisles. I found my will again. It gave me some more will again and independence. I had been stuck in that damn bed for ten weeks. I got a little more independent, and I got some leave. I would leave for the day, take off and go out to eat somewhere. Eventually I would leave the hospital but come down sick again. So I had to be readmitted. I came down sick with infection. They retired me in October 1967; I had been in the military service for exactly one year.

WALTER RADOWENCHUK
Member of 2nd Platoon of Charlie Company

[After being wounded in the battle of June 19] I remember they took me out of the chopper; I was on a stretcher, and they took me into an operating room. I was all wet, and I started getting cold. I was soaking wet from the water in the rice paddy. They started to cut my boots off, and my clothing – taking my shirt and everything off. Here is the funny part. I remember saying to someone, "When are they going to operate on me?" And I had already been operated on and come out of the anesthesia.

The care was excellent. That was one thing I never complained about the US Army. I always felt that they gave us good equipment and they provided well for us. I think I spent two weeks in that hospital. I had a patch on my eye from the rotor wash blowing in my eye. I remember during my two-week stay that Floyd Patterson was one of the personalities visiting the troops. He came to my bed and I was introduced to him. I remember him shaking my hand. I had a cast from my elbow to my right wrist, full-arm cast on my right arm, cast on my left ankle, bandages on my right foot and left calf. I noticed they were photographing other troopers shaking hands with Floyd Patterson, but they never took a picture of Floyd Patterson and me because I do not think I looked too good with casts all over and a patch on my eye. They never photographed me because I think those photos were supposed to go back to your hometown newspaper.

They flew me out of there to a hospital in Japan. The wounds were too severe to stay in country, so they shipped me out to Japan. I was there for approximately a month. From there I made my first call to my parents. I do not remember if they had been alerted, notified. I remember calling on a phone to my parents that I was in Japan and had been wounded. My mom, she was relieved that I was out of Vietnam, and that I would be coming home alive.

After a month in Japan, they flew me out of there to Elmendorf, Alaska. We stopped there for a short period of time; then they flew me to Fort Meade, Maryland. I could hear screams from guys that were getting their wounds in the chest or whatever, cleaned. I felt I was blessed, always thought I was very fortunate. To this day I still believe the good Lord saved me. Anyway, I was in Fort Meade for a few days, I think, and then they put me on a bus and bussed me to Valley Forge Hospital in Pennsylvania. I was in Valley Forge for maybe one or two weeks before they gave me a 30-day convalescent leave. So I got on a plane and flew home, grabbed a taxi. I did not even call my parents, just flew in to Hopkins Airport near Cleveland and hopped in a taxi. Pulled in front of my parents' house, I knocked on the door, and boy were they glad to see me. Especially my mom. I was in khakis, had a cast on my left arm, and a cast on my left foot and a big bandage on my right wrist. But boy was she happy to see me.

A WORLD OF HURT

FRANK SCHWAN
Member of 2nd Platoon of Charlie Company

[After his nightlong ordeal in the fighting on July 11, 1967.] The other helicopter came in and took me to a Navy ship – a rescue or a hospital ship, whatever you want to call it. Landed there, saw one of the corpsmen there. He looked at my wounds, and they were just oozing out body liquids rather than blood. He said, "I could put bandages on there; let me at least give you a shower and get you cleaned-up." He did; stripped my clothes off, gave me a shower, and cleaned me up a little bit. I came out of there and saw a few of the other guys that got hurt; Jackson was one of them. He got shot in the neck and he was there. There were a few other guys sitting there. I was flown from there to a regular hospital. We arrived and a major, a nurse, asked questions and looked at where I got shot. You could see I got shot in the stomach and the shoulder. She asked me, "Well, when were you shot?" This might have been two or three o'clock in the afternoon. I said I was shot at one o'clock. She said "okay," but I said, "That was yesterday." She said, "He is next!" Off I went to the surgery room to be repaired. I think I stayed awake and told them something like, "I'm not going to die in this shit hole. Whatever dissecting you are going to do, be gentle about it. Make small stitches because I'm not going to go anywhere; I'm going to be here." What they did was exploratory. The just opened me up, leafed through all the things, took out things, patched up whatever had to be patched up. That was the end of my career in Vietnam.

I was in the hospital with a stomach wound. The rounds went through the front, through the back. Shoulder the same way. Probably an AK47. What that does when you shot it, it tends to rise and that is exactly what happened. The first shot was in the stomach and the second shot was up. I wrote one letter home to my brother and explained to him what had happened to me. I asked him to talk to our parents and explain that I was injured but okay.

They told me they gave me 27 pints of blood. What that told me was I was still bleeding internally. They had drained my wounded left side and were giving me pints of blood. I was in good shape then, excellent shape, which really helped. Then I was informed I had to go into surgery, again. They claimed a stress ulcer, but what I think happened was my intestines were nicked and continued to bleed; they overlooked it. Does not matter – I survived. They put a drainage tube on my back, and they in turn said, "We cannot do a whole lot for you here." I was on a liquid diet for a while, so I lost quite a bit of weight. I was then told I was going to be shipped to Okinawa, Japan for recovery. They also did a procedure on my right shoulder, so they cut into that. Not sure why, but maybe things were not working too well.

The nurses were excellent. I do not recall any of their names, but I remember one of their faces. They gave us excellent care and gave us anything we wanted. Best nurses around. I remember getting pictures from home that were glued together. One of the nurses steamed them apart on her own time. I was put on a transport plane and they put a clamp on the tube on my back. When I arrived at the new hospital in Japan, the surgeon, a major, asked me some questions. He asked me about the tube and I said, "I was instructed to tell you that it is not a chest tube; it is below that for drainage." He said, "Son, whoever put that there missed it by one rib." Meaning it was too high. He said, "If the clamp would have fallen off on the trip over to Japan, your lung would have collapsed and you would have probably died on that plane."

When you think back about it, it is very possible he [the surgeon] would have had five to ten surgeries that day. They were stacking up, so what you do is the best you can with the time you have. So that is what probably happened to me.

Something that will stay with me for a long time was when I wound up eating at the cafeteria. I had my tray and was going in line. I walked into this guy; I looked up and it was a friend of mine who lived a block away from my home. I believe he was in the 4th Division and injured. He drove a tank, not a tank but one of those tracks. He was injured on his nose and forehead and was there for recuperation. We obviously celebrated. We drank that night and probably the next day, too. We laughed and joked. I asked him where he was going from here and he said, "Nowhere; I'm staying here. They found out I know how to play basketball." He played high school basketball for a pretty good team. He was 6'3" or 6'4", thin, and wound up playing basketball for the Army base. Not a bad gig at all. For me, short recuperation. I had probably 60-some days left before my tour would expire and the major said, "Son, you are not going back. You are going home. I will keep you here until you recoup enough, and then we will ship you home." That is what turned out to be. Had he been a strict officer, I could have been shipped back to Vietnam in bad shape, physically bad shape. I was probably 100-some pounds then and gaining some weight, but I was not able to do much with the injury and the stitches. I was uncomfortable for a while. The shoulder was okay; the injury was not as bad there. I shipped home, stayed there for a while, and then showed up at Fort Knox.

[Me being wounded really worried my parents.] You only know how parents are when you become a parent yourself and experience some of the hardships and anguish your children go through. They were helpless to do anything knowing that their son got injured somewhere thousands of miles away, and they couldn't do anything for him. Very helpless feeling. My dad mentioned once that whatever it took, he was going to come to Vietnam. But he learned that traveling to that country was virtually impossible, and he couldn't have done much to help anyway.

ALAN RICHARDS
Member of 4th Platoon of Charlie Company

[After being wounded on October 6, 1967] I remember kind of sitting there because I had this hole in my shoulder and that the medic had tried to patch this up. There wasn't a lot of blood all over me. So I'm not sure how severely injured people thought I was. I remember them putting me on the helicopter and sitting in one of those canvas chairs. Every time somebody put their hand on my back, I'd wince from the pain. Matter of fact when we got into the hospital, I remember sitting on the examining table and sitting for a long time. Again, the people coming in probably looked worse than I was. I remember at one point the doctor coming over and touching my back and me wincing in pain. He said, "What's the matter?" I said, "Well, the bullet is still in there." It was like all of a sudden a red light went off all over the place. He got me into the operating room. Went from there to Long Binh. I was in the hospital in Long Binh for a while. They had left my back open because the wound was infected. Supposedly the VC, the Viet Cong, would soak the bullets in something poisonous so that you would get infected. So they ended up taking part of my shoulder blade out, and half my back was laid open. I laid in Long Binh for I don't know how many days with that just open and draining. That wasn't so painful as much as when they finally decided to stitch it all back together again. I remember waking up and asking for something for pain. That was probably the only time because I was in shock when I got shot. That is the only time I can actually remember asking for painkillers for anything. That was probably the worst pain I've been in in all my life. Obviously I got over that and wound up in Japan for a week or so.

They attempted to fly you to a hospital as close to home as possible [and they flew me to] Great Lakes Hospital outside of Chicago. I was en route to go there but something was wrong with the plane and we ended up in Alaska. After being in Vietnam getting to Alaska for like their first snowfall [was great]. We actually had to stay overnight as they fixed the plane. It was just beautiful. We were on the sixth floor of the hospital; we had the view going through the wilderness-type areas with snow on the ground and moose walking across the lawn of the hospital. It was just incredible, guys literally getting down and kissing the ground. I literally saw that. Just being happy with finally being back in the real world.

I was ambulatory. I had a full-body cast on, from my waist up to my neck. My right arm stuck out of the cast; everything else was in the cast, waist up. Secured my arm and my shoulder. Basically my bones from my arm to my shoulder were all shattered. Then from there I went down to the Great Lakes Naval Hospital. I was one of the very few Army guys in the Navy hospital. Quite a few Marines who I became friends with. At that time, it was a fairly new hospital. Now what would happen was the guys who didn't need to be in a hospital bed all day long would be sent over to the old hospital. There would be two or three guys to a room over there. You would be given little duties during the day. I was a runner for the Army detachment that was there, and I also became one of the sergeants-at-arms for that building. That old building just happened to be next door to a training center for the WAVES [Women Accepted for Voluntary Emergency Service]. It wasn't all bad. We shared the cafeteria together.

I don't remember if it was the first day or not, but it was soon after I was there my sister and one of my older brothers started coming down to visit me. The Great Lakes Naval Hospital was about a two-hour drive, if that, so it wasn't real bad. So once I got feeling a little bit better, there was a train that went from the Great Lakes area out to Milwaukee. A lot of the Navy guys who were training down at Great Lakes Naval Base would go up to Milwaukee on weekend passes. Seems to me we were supposed to stay within a certain mile radius. My hometown was a little bit out of that. I stretched the truth a little bit and said, "Oh yeah, it's within the radius."

RON VIDOVIC

Member of 3rd Platoon of Charlie Company

[After losing his leg to a Viet Cong mine] I was still conscious [at the hospital before surgery], but I was really, really rummy. They got me there to the hospital and the first thing I did was – these nurses come out to the helicopter. I said, "By golly, I guess we do have some good-looking people around." This was the first time I seen women around in a long time. Seemed like I was flirting with them; well I was. I was pretty much all drugged out. They started questioning me how all this happened. They gave me a shot, sort of like a truth serum. They questioned how this happened because – this is the strangest thing – they said that some people would actually shoot themselves to get out of Vietnam. By giving them these shots, the truth came out. There was this other guy in the hospital with me. He had thrown a hand grenade out in back of him when he was walking; it blew up and he got peppered with it. There were some instances like that that were happening over there. He got patched up. They [nurses and doctors] were rough on him in there in the hospital.

I knew myself that I was going to lose my left leg. There was no way they were going to put that thing back on. They operated on me right away and got that stuff taken care of. When I woke up the next day, there was a nurse sitting beside the bed trying to tell me what happened. My left leg was gone below the knee. My right leg was in a big cast. They almost took it, but they kept it there to see how it was going to work out – to see if it would heal and if I could have a movable foot. It did work out, thank goodness.

It was awfully horrible in that hospital because they did not have much of that nerve medicine to keep all the pain down. They could just give morphine and just keep knocking you out. They would knock you out for a while, then bring you back in and loosen the pain down a little bit. There were a lot of spasm pain; the one nurse would make a big ice pack and wrap my leg stump in it. That would work wonders, better than the morphine half the time. I was there for probably about a week, in the hospital, and the guys would come by and see me before I got ready to get out of there. Hoskins [my platoon leader] came out to see me that one day. He brought me a carton of cigarettes. He was going to come out and see me again, but they had already flown me out. They flew me out of there to Saigon.

I had seen some of the other guys in there that were so much worse. This one guy actually died in the ward. They were working on him half the night, and he was in really bad condition. He ended up dying as they were working on him that night. You see some of them with their heads all wrapped up, looking horrible, and I just felt very fortunate just to be alive. It was really a horrible thing to see and a sad situation. This one guy that was across from me – that did that to himself with the grenade – the next day, they were in there right away and they had him up out of that bed and he was walking. He was whining and complaining. He said, "It hurts, it hurts!" They did not care at all that it was hurting. He was getting up there and walking; he was going back out.

A WORLD OF HURT

I tried to make the best of it. One of the nurses said, "You know, they have these legs you can put on and you will be able to walk this way." I tried to believe them and get on with it. I knew I was going to be able to walk again. I just felt so fortunate, but it hurt like hell. The only way you could try to turn anything around was to joke about it a little bit. McBride and some of the other guys came to the hospital when I was in there. The hospital had some sort of USO show with girls from Australia. I was so constipated and had to go to the bathroom so bad. I could not get up or anything. So a couple of them guys picked me up and put me on the potty so I could go. I went, and it was one the stinkiest, most horrible things you ever seen in your life. They got that pan moved out of the way and after that that USO girl came in there who had sung in the show. It stunk like heck, and McBride and those guys were laughing. It did help out a lot. Glad to be alive.

I was only there for a few days. Then I went to Saigon for a while. The only thing I did not like there was when they did an inspection of me and did not give me morphine in my leg before taking some more shrapnel out. Boy, that just about tore my head off. After that there, everything else was just excellent care, giving me enough shots and keeping my wounds clean. Yeah, they had pretty nurses too. They were a good thing to see over there. You get tired of seeing guys all the time.

The Army sent my mom notification when I got hurt over there. When I was getting out of Saigon and getting ready to go to Japan is when they sent her the letter. She thought I was already back in the States. She thought I was in California because all your mail goes through California then to your house. So she thought I was in California. She was going to come down to California and see me at that post office. My brother told her, "No, he is not there. He is still overseas somewhere." She was all upset. They sent that telegram off when I was probably in Saigon. That was where a general came in there and gave me a purple heart.

I pulled in there [Japan] and they were taking me into this one little ward and all of a sudden Bill Riley [who had been in Vidovic's company but who had been wounded and evacuated two months prior] was in there. Well, he was over in Japan still. He was in a body cast because his leg had nearly been blown off. Body cast all the way from his belly button to the tip of his toes. They came wheeling me into the one ward in Japan and he says, "Vidovic, what are you doing here?" So we just started rattling on about each other. That is how he told me he had to lose part of his leg – shortened his leg. The next afternoon, though, they flew him back to the States. I stayed there for maybe a couple days or something. Then they took me out of there and flew me to California for overnight. That is when they notified my mom and told her that they were bringing me to Madigan [Army Medical Center at Fort Lewis, Washington], which was only about 6 miles away from my home.

When I got admitted is when I think I finally notified my mom and brother. They came out and saw me. I could not walk or move around very well. The one leg was pretty much all casted, and my other one was off. The staff put all us amputees in the same ward. So everybody in that ward I was at, maybe 40 or some people, had arms or legs off, or both. When I got there, too, I felt like I did not have an awfully lot wrong with me compared to some of the guys that had both legs off at the groin. Lucky to even be alive, I felt like I was. Nasty-looking mess in there.

When your mom sees it, they think they got to end up taking care of you. They think you're an itty-bitty baby again. You got to let them know that it is just a part of life and get back to work walking. I was in the hospital for nine months. The craziest thing was when I got there, the next day I asked them if I could go home. They were joking with me and said, "Buddy, if you can get up and walk, you can go home." So the first guy came in, they just got done changing our bedding, and I was sitting there. This guy next to me had crutches and I had never walked on my other leg, the one with the cast on it, for 30 days. I was 6 foot and down to about 125 pounds. So I was skin and bones, no muscle after everything there. So I said to the guy, "Hey, could I borrow your crutches for a minute?" He said, "Why?" I said, "They said if I could walk I could go home." I said, "I walked on crutches before, no big deal." So I got that crutch and got onto that leg, and there was no way that was going to hold me. So I fell on the floor and fell on the end of my stump they had cut off. It snapped the bone about 3 inches up. For it to be a good amputee stump you cannot have a cracked stump. So the staff came running in there; I was bleeding all over the place. The guy had just changed my bedding and there was blood all over it. They finally got it [the stump] all wrapped up and everything. Then a nurse came in there. She said, "If you ever try to stand up like that again, I'll cut your other leg off." She was mad. I told her, "Well, they said if I could walk I could go home." She said, "You ain't never going home if you do that again." End up having to cut another 3 inches off it. They had to cut the part off that was all cracked. They cut that off, and I did not try to get up anymore. I shut up and listened to them.

Had a pretty good time in that hospital. My buddies all came out to see me. We had some pretty wild times in there. So my brother and Jerry and them came out to see me this one Friday night. They partied with me for a while. They would allow you to have about three beers a day when you were bedridden. They parked their car outside and brought in the same beer they were serving in the hospital. I could have three beers, but I [already] had a couple that day and another one that night. What they were doing, my buddy Jerry and my brother, was going out to the car and bringing a couple of the same type back in. So we had a whole pile of them. We started getting a little noisy. The staff knew something was going on after I got sick like a dog and barfed.

In this ward you had curtains dividing us off. Probably about four of us sitting in one square and another four at another section. I was there for about nine months to get rehabilitated, learning how to walk. They got me a prosthetic leg quite a few months after I got there. They had to wait before they did a prosthetic because my leg was cracked. That took a long time to heal. They did not get me to walk on one for quite a few months. I spent a good month and a half of trying to get the muscle built back up and walking in between bars to get where I could really start to walk where it felt okay and was not going to fall downstairs or anything. It took a while to get the muscle back.

VIETNAM

When I got ready to walk it seemed to take a long time to figure out how to move one foot in front of the other. Felt like walking like a little baby all over again. It was weird learning to walk like that again. After I got it down, it was pretty good then to learn how to do stairs. I spent the last two months waiting to get my discharge. I was in the hospital, but I was not doing duty in no barracks or anything. I was just walking around the hospital, cleaning the areas, dumping ashtrays – doing duty like that for rehabilitation and strengthening everything. I walked out of that hospital on the two-year anniversary of having been drafted.

8 CHANGING ATTITUDES

The young civilians turned soldiers had arrived in Vietnam as green as grass. Some had been drafted and as a result had a chip on their shoulders; others saw military service as a kind of violent grand adventure; some joined because they needed the money; others truly believed in a national crusade to save South Vietnam and the world from the threat of communism. None of the new soldiers, though, had known what to expect. They had not understood the brutal realities of war and combat. A very few soldiers had arrived in Vietnam believing that they would never return home, having had a sort of premonition of their own deaths. But 19- and 20-year-olds don't tend to think fatalistically. Many more had understood that they might get wounded in Vietnam, perhaps a picturesque bullet wound in the shoulder while firing from the hip before being given an obligatory smoke by one of their buddies and being whisked away to recuperation

– wounds as experienced in the World War II movies of their youths. Most, as is so common among the young and vibrant, had arrived in Vietnam believing implicitly in their immortality. Effectively unable to conceive of the possibility of their own violent deaths, these young soldiers had arrived in Vietnam certain that they would make it home physically and mentally unscarred. Life – marriage, children, success – was going to continue once their year of service had come to an end.

But for many the reality of war intervened, changing everything. Death had come, and they had meted out death to others. Perhaps the most frightening thing of all about war was its shocking randomness, its unpredictability. The very best of soldiers, the brave men who did everything right, might suddenly get blown to bits before your very eyes, their bodies little more than unidentifiable chunks of meat. Those with the most to live for, young husbands and fathers, might die on their last day in the field when they were so close to going home to reclaim their lives. Poor soldiers, ones who could hardly tie their bootlaces without supervision, might survive the entire year without a scratch. War decided who would die and who would survive, and good soldiers – dedicated young men – were powerless to alter that fact. Powerlessness in the face of the destructive and deadly nature of modern combat came as a shock to many of the young American soldiers who had arrived in Vietnam, leaving them to grapple with questions of their own mortality at an age when most civilians were wondering what girl to date or what party to attend.

The powerful and eternal questions broached by the ongoing, brutal drumbeat of war led to marked changes in the viewpoints and attitudes of many American soldiers as their Vietnam service slowly unfolded. Perhaps making the changes even more pronounced, US soldiers in Vietnam were not immune to the protests and discord that rocked the American home front. The young men who America sent to fight its distant war were all too well aware that many in their country did not support them or their war. For some soldiers combat simply made them meaner; they became killers, often seeking vengeance for their fallen friends. Others simply fixated on survival, certainly their own and perhaps that of their closest circle of friends. They had lost so many brothers to war that they were not sure that they could bear to lose any more. They had lost so many brothers to war that they refused to make new friends – it hurt too much to lose them. They focused their main energy on survival, on reaching that magical day when they would board the freedom bird for home. Nothing else mattered. Many who had once believed in the cause of the war began to wonder whether the whole thing was worth it. Was Vietnam – dirty, smelly Vietnam – worth the sacrifice of so many young American lives? Was an ephemeral struggle against communism worth your best friend never getting the chance to go home and see his child? For some the sacrifice of war meant that the United States had to redouble its efforts to achieve victory. How could the country possibly even consider pulling out of Vietnam with the job undone? That would waste the blood sacrifice paid by so many. Vietnam was now sacred ground, a war that had to be won at all costs.

The brutality of battle in a war that dragged on and on – a war with no end in sight, just more battles – was a heavy spiritual and emotional weight for the hundreds of thousands of young Americans who experienced the sharp end of war in Vietnam. Although soldiers dealt with the experience of war in myriad ways, that experience left no American combat soldier unscathed.

STEVE HUNTSMAN

Member of 1st Platoon of Charlie Company

I don't remember much about the helicopter ride [from the battle of May 15 when he had been wounded along with Pete Jarczewski, Charlie Nelson, and Carl Cortright]. But I do remember being glad to get out of that battle. I was glad to get out of that battle. The helicopter took us to the hospital at Bien Hoa. It wasn't all that bad. They just cleaned it up and patched it up. I was in the hospital about two weeks. After a couple of days I could get up and walk. There was even a little movie theater for the guys who were able. I went to visit Charlie Nelson; he was in another ward. I remember going over to see him, and he had a cast on. I asked him, "Charlie, are you sorry that you volunteered to go out into the field now?" He said, "No, not really." And I asked him if he wanted to go back out. He said, "Hell yes! I have to go out there and get even with those little bastards!" The chaplain came around to see everybody and wrote to our parents.

[After recuperation] I went back to the unit and ran another patrol before we went back to Dong Tam [the divisional base area. While there an officer offered each man a chance to reenlist for two more years of service, which would result in a posting to a non-combat position.] I hated the Army, and I hated being shot at worse than that. But I'd just got a letter from my brother-in-law. He was telling me about all these people protesting the war and marching against it and all that kind of shit. He said, "Do whatever you have to do to be safe, because this war is not popular, and there is no reason for you to die because of an unpopular war." That made my decision a little easier. I made the decision to reenlist, but it was very emotional. The emotions are still very close to the surface to this day. Reenlisting was a very hard thing to do. I can't explain it, other than it seemed like the right thing to do because my brother-in-law said it is not worth dying for.

That month pretty much changed my life forever. We were all good friends, and reenlisting leaves a feeling of guilt, but I was not the only one who did it. I think the thing that made it easier for me was what my brother-in-law wrote in the letter. He just flat said it is not worth dying for. It is unpopular; everybody is protesting. And I thought to myself, "Yeah. Why do I have to go through all this crap when nobody wants it?" There is an old saying, "When old men cannot agree, they send their young sons to die for them." That has been the most true thing in my life since. If old men can't agree, why can't they just go themselves? Don't send somebody else to do your dirty work. It is a hard thing for me in several different ways.

CHANGING ATTITUDES

MIKE LETHCOE
Member of 2nd Platoon of Alpha Company

[After the battle of June 19 in which Alpha Company suffered nearly 90 percent casualties] they pulled us back for several days while we got replacements in. It just broke my unit really bad because all these replacements were mostly draftees who were coming from all the basic training places across the country. They didn't have near the training that we had. They didn't have near the esprit de corps or the will to fight. They were young kids who didn't want to be there. They didn't want to listen. You tried to teach them to stay alive, but they wouldn't listen to you. You would take them out in the field, and they couldn't maintain a formation. They wanted to cluster up, which is a deadly thing to do. It was a bad scene. We'd go out on patrols, and I was extremely worried about safety because of all the green troops that we had with us. They gave us fairly light duties while we were trying to break in these new troops. But the unit, my platoon, never was the same. Our platoon sergeant, Sergeant Hill, did not go out on that patrol on the 19th. His assistant had gone. He got killed right off. So Sergeant Hill went out on these later patrols. They gave us fairly easy duty; we didn't run into anything heavy again for a while.

Our morale was way low. You had lost all these people killed and wounded, and they're gone. You don't know what happened to them. People who are wounded would go back into the hospitals and were gone. You would never hear from them. The wondering. Did this man live? We knew who was dead, but we had a lot of people who were wounded that disappeared. And we didn't know if they had lived through their wounds, if they had recovered, or what. That was tough. And then getting in all these green people that did not want to be there, wouldn't listen to anything. Our morale was real bad for a long time. By then you didn't want to get close to people. The writing was on the wall. If it hit the fan again you knew you were gonna lose a lot of those people. "I will not conform" was the watchword, like they could make somebody suffer or something by not conforming. And all they did was get themselves killed and other people killed. I reenlisted not long after that to get away from the outfit.

We went into a village one day, came out of these woods near the village, and we scared up a Viet Cong. He jumped up and dropped his weapon while he was running back to the village. I told one of these new guys, "Shoot him! Get him! Get him!" These two guys, they shot, and one of them turned to the other after he got away and said, "Were you trying to hit him?" And the other said, "Well no, I wasn't trying to hit him." We moved into this village and they set up an ambush by the time we got there, and we had to fight our way in. Things like that were hard to take. I was carrying a shotgun. They decided that they were going to try some shotguns there in the delta, so they gave a couple of shotguns out. So I didn't have the range to shoot the man; he was 200 yards off. These other two troops just fired rounds but didn't try to hit the man. He ran back into the village and told them we were coming. My thoughts were that Alpha Company wasn't the place to be if you wanted to live for a long time, so I reenlisted for Vung Tau.

LARRY LUKES
Member of 3rd Platoon of Charlie Company

[On June 20, Charlie Company had to police up the numerous dead of Alpha Company's battlefield of June 19.] I couldn't believe it. They had just waited until they were out in the middle of that open rice paddy before they opened up on them. There wasn't anywhere for them to go. We had a detail where we would drag them down to the river and give them to other people who would have them shipped out. I was in a detail going through the VC bunkers and cleaning them out. I was one of the lucky ones; I didn't have to go down and police up all the bodies. There were quite a few dead Viet Cong lying around. I never did count them, but there were a lot of them there. It was gruesome in that heat; you know, you really get cold. To this day I don't go to funerals.

I just cannot stand to go to funerals. I went to my mom's and my dad's, and it really just bothered me a lot to see them.

In a battle like June 19, you lose so many of your friends, and your buddies are all dead. I didn't even cry when my mom and dad died. Emotionally you get cold. Death is death. We're all going to die. The old saying is "It is better him than me." And that is a sad thing to say, but that is basically exactly how everybody felt. You develop a closeness to death, and I don't know if that is good or if it is bad. It was pretty quiet on the ship the next day. Everybody had their own losses, their own memories. It affected everybody. I think that we were probably closer – probably closer than we ever were before. And you always wondered who was going to be next. We had four or five new replacements come in, and nobody wanted to be friends with them. Nobody wanted to talk to them. I think that was a lot of it. You just didn't want that feeling. You just knew that they were going to get wounded or killed. June 19 made the unit better, more aware of what could happen. It is something that I don't think I would ever want my son or anybody close to me ever to have to go through. I don't think that it made me more religious – I always did believe in God – but it did make me more aware. I went to the chaplain's memorial services. That was a sad, sad day. We were there to survive and keep each other alive.

JOHN YOUNG

Member of 1st Platoon of Charlie Company

[On returning to the barracks ships after the battle of June 19.] The battalion was only about one-third or two-thirds the number that had gone out three days before. The ammi barge that floated alongside – there in front of me was a pile of web gear from Alpha Company [that had been nearly wiped out on June 19], from all those bodies that we had policed up. It was the web gear from those men: helmets, pistol belts, ammo pouches. Must have been piled 3 feet high and maybe 10 feet across in a circular pile. All of it black with clotted, coagulated blood. Stinky, muddy, bloody.

That was the first thing that we all saw – that big pile of bloody web gear. We were so few coming back. So many less than when we went out. The battalion's morale at that point was at an all-time low, no matter how the numbers might have been reported, and I remember that within a day or two the *Stars and Stripes* had a story about it where they said that we had killed 250 VC; we had 44 KIA and in the three figures wounded. But I don't recall a final figure on friendly losses for the battle. Maybe there were as many as 80 men killed in the battalion that day.

There weren't many conversations. It was as if what was left of the battalion was in a state of shock, just in disbelief that we could have lost so many men in such a short period of time. We were just stunned. I don't remember us talking among ourselves about that battle, even though obviously there would have been nothing else to talk about. What I do remember is that I, myself, was really very shaken. I was regular army; I was doing what I had enlisted to do. All these months I'd been very gung ho about being a squad leader and the fact that we were fighting this war in Vietnam for good reasons. Supportive of the whole effort – unquestioningly supportive. Then June 19 happened, and, my God, we lost so many men, and I was shaken because this was the first time that the real cost of it all was driven home to me. When you lose men one or two at a time over a period of months I guess it doesn't seem so bad. Then you lose a whole bunch of people in one afternoon and you just get hit like with a hammer: "Wow; this is really an expensive thing we are in." I thought, "Well, you asked for this. You enlisted. You asked to come to Vietnam. So what, are you losing your courage now that young men died and you yourself could have gotten killed? Are you losing your guts now? You can't face it? You can't handle it?" On a number of levels I was really very shaken.

Although I was not then religious and I am still not religious, I knew that the chaplain was on our ship. I knew that if nothing else he would be an intelligent man capable of carrying on a conversation and capable of understanding. So I sought him out and talked to him. I was just thinking out loud as I was talking to him. The only thing I really remember telling him was, "Chaplain,

I am just really tired of seeing ugly things happen to good men."
I don't know what else I said to him, and I don't remember
anything he said to me. We talked maybe 20 or 30 minutes. The
next thing I remember must have been the following day; I was
going through what I guess is a very human sort of development.
Now we have had two full days of being back on the ship, of
having showers, hot meals, and a bunk to sleep in. By this day I
remember being up on the outer deck of the ship just looking at
the river and the countryside. I remember actually sort of arguing
with myself, saying, "It couldn't have been that bad." On one side
of my memory June 19 is very fresh, and all those guys who had
gotten killed and how frightened I was – how miserable it was and
the ugliness of it all. Here I am three days later with a few good
hot meals under my belt and a couple good nights' sleep, and I'm
already thinking in my mind, "It couldn't have been that bad.
I could do it again. It wasn't that bad." I was already beginning to
recover from it, thinking that if I lived through it, it couldn't have
been that bad. Already beginning to bounce back from the actual
shock of the experience itself.

By the time I came home from Vietnam, I was a thoroughgoing,
abusive drinker, drinking seven days a week and getting drunk
seven days a week. And I can pin it down to almost the day
in Vietnam when that started, and it would have been very soon
after June 19. I drank after June 19 in order to be able to sleep. The
battalion was never the same after June 19. At the battalion level
we were two-thirds different. Of the battalion that had arrived in
January, two-thirds of those guys are gone. Almost overnight it is
a totally different battalion. Even within my company the
casualties were something like 30 percent; Charlie Company's
casualties must have been roughly one man out of three on June
19. So the whole battalion had changed. The attitudes of those of
us who had survived – maybe I shouldn't speak for anyone else –
my attitude after June 19 was changed. I just decided that it was
the most important thing I could do – I was a pretty good squad
leader, I felt – I thought for me, from here on out the most
important mission I have is to keep my men safe or, at the very
least, keep them alive. Everything else was going to be secondary

to that. In the past I had been serious about carrying out the mission that was given to me – ambushes and things. They would give me a grid coordinate [on the map] to go to and set up an ambush. I would be offensive. But the rest of the tour after June 19 I did exactly what they told me to do and no more. When I went out on an ambush after June 19, I went out and found a place from which I could defend myself. I didn't go off with an offensive idea in mind looking to kill somebody. I went out looking for a piece of ground where I could put down and be safe and hoped not to see anybody all night long.

After June 19 everyone had changed. It may seem counterintuitive, but there wasn't a great deal of discussion among us, the survivors. We might refer to it vaguely, but I don't recall that we sat down and talked about it much. The losses were really very painful, and you don't want to keep bringing up a subject that is so painful to talk about. So there wasn't a great deal of talk, but everybody's attitude was different. For me the biggest change was on operations I played a different role; I just wanted to keep my people safe. We got a lot of replacements in after June 19. When we had gotten replacements in during the first half of the year, I treated them just the way I had done to my men originally. I was very interested in learning everything about them I could, stuff right out of the field manual: get to know your men; get to know everything about them. Where they're from, what their hometown is, what their education is. What is their girlfriend's name? Are they from a farm? All that kind of stuff. So that you establish some sort of personal relationship with them so you know things about them that enable you to be a more effective leader. Well, I didn't do any more of that. I'd get a replacement in, and I didn't want to know anything more about him than what it says on his name tape and what weapon you think he can handle. Now we've all learned the lesson that it is not a good idea to have buddies, or to get close to people, because we had all learned the lesson about how painful it is to lose them. From this point on when replacements came in, I didn't learn anything more about them than I absolutely had to. Generally just their last name and their weapon specialty. In future operations after June 19, when you are out on an operation and you had a little piece of work that was a little more dangerous than average, like running a recon of a tree line, I tried to be fair about that. That is the only reasonable way to run it. Those recons were so routine; we had to do them so often. It involves sending three men out in front of the company a couple hundred yards to recon a tree line. Most of the time the enemy would not be there; but if they were, the lives of the recon unit were forfeit. When the turn came around to my squad to run recons, I would take myself and two men and run the first recon. I would take my turn at it. I didn't feel that I could point to three men and say "go do that," unless they had seen me do it too. But often in such situations it was the replacements who got the shitty end of the stick.

TERRY MCBRIDE
Member of 3rd Platoon of Charlie Company

[In a battle on July 11, 1967, Fred Kenney, a well-liked member of McBride and Larry Lukes' platoon, had been hit and presumably killed in an ambush. In danger of being overrun, the platoon had to pull back and form a defensive night position without having retrieved Kenney's body.] The platoon pulled back and spent the night in the company position. I was telling everybody that we ought to lead a team out there at least; lead a couple of guys out there to recover the body. You knew that they [the Viet Cong] were gonna come out and see what he's got on him. But they wouldn't let us do it. There were lights out there [on the battlefield] that night, candles or something. The enemy was searching the bodies. [When they reached Kenney's body the next day] his shirt was even unbuttoned. His web gear was gone. I remember when his kid was born; it was on the boat when we were going over [to Vietnam]. That's when he had found out that he had had a boy. Kenney was a cool guy. He was top notch. Just top notch. One of the better kiddos we had. I talked to his kid on the phone [years later]. He was proud that for somebody that he never knew that everybody remembered who he was and kept him in our hearts.

The unit was kind of pissed off. We burned down a hooch up there near where Kenney was at. It hurt. That one definitely shook everybody up. It really got everybody's attention. It cut the edge when they started messing with the dead, you know what I mean? It is not a good thing to do. It definitely got mean after that. Meaner. After this I made sure that the ones I found dead were dead, let's put it that way. This war changed me a lot. I got a little meaner. Actually I got a lot meaner. I guess I was mean when I went there, but it just never surfaced. I don't think that's something that just happens. It is like whatever you gotta do to draw juice from that's what you are gonna do, you know? And that's what it takes. I had a lot of that. A whole lot.

RON VIDOVIC
Member of 3rd Platoon of Charlie Company

After the battle of July 11, everything changed. You could see the personalities changing in everybody. They were just scared if they were going to be the next victim or what. They didn't take life for granted. They figured that if you can kill these guys off [the Viet Cong] maybe we can get out of here. You can only take so much before you snap over there like that. I had respect for some of the people still [the Vietnamese]. But you couldn't trust nobody. I was never raised that way, and the other guys who went over there were not raised that way either. But you see your buddies get taken out, it makes you into hardened soldiers. We weren't civilians anymore, that's for sure. [After July] we were based at Dong Tam. McBride, Fischer, and all us guys we got to do some security guarding around a little village there, probably six or seven hooches. We would walk that strip back and forth each night. During the day we would stay there [in bunkers], and they would bring our lunch out to us. They had a couple of little kids there, one we nicknamed "loudmouth." The kids would come and sit with us on our bunkers during the day and watch us and talk to us. They would bring in some pineapple. We would get a pineapple from them and give them some of our C rations. We would do that often in exchange for some of the food and bread that they would bring. Me, McBride, Riley, and Fischer got put out there for about a week or two weeks. It was a real great time out there.

I would walk around out there bare-footed and leave my boots in the area where we would sleep at night, and somebody stole my boots from me once. But they did give them back before we got ready to leave – after we told the little kids that we didn't want nothing to do with them anymore because they were robbing and cheating us, and they brought my boots right back to me and we were on good terms again. One day a big old rat came running out of one of these jugs [that the Vietnamese kept near their hooches], and Fischer was going to shoot it. And the little kids jumped up yelling, "NO! NO! NO!" Because they ate them over there they did. They had traps and everything out there where they could catch them. They didn't want Tim to shoot it, because it would blow it all apart. One time Fischer was trying to get some coconuts out of a tree and started shooting at them too to get them out of there. Maybe he could knock a couple down and get the juice out of them. These little kids warned us about not going off into the back part of the woods in back of their village because it was all booby-trapped. So we never wandered off over there. We just stayed in the front part and walked security back and forth.

That was an enjoyable time, you know. We became human again. There wasn't much stress on us or anything. You felt welcome, and you felt good about what you were doing again instead of feeling like you were turned against the whole world. This was after a couple of big fights my unit had been in where we had lost a lot of guys. Sometimes you have good times, and sometimes you have bad times.

STEVE HOPPER
Member of 3rd Platoon of Charlie Company

[After being involved in a firefight on October 6, 1967 in which his squad lost two men] it hits you like a ton of bricks, so to speak. It is almost overwhelming when you learn that one of the guys in your squad is killed. And then the guy who went out and verified that and reported back to me got killed as well. We had numbers assigned to everyone in our platoon, and we would call in the KIAs by number instead of a name. I remember calling in the fact that I had lost two of my guys. One of your guys getting shot and dying right there within a couple of feet of you, it shakes you up, you know. I felt responsible. While we were taking fire during all of this, he [Danny Burkhead] did have some cover out there in the rice. When he chose to raise his head to tell me what he had found [regarding the death of Gale Alldridge, another member of Hopper's squad], they took him out. That was hard to believe that that happened. Now I'd just lost two guys in my squad. As you watch things take place in Vietnam and back in the United States, you saw a lot of the rioting and the American public against what we were doing – we always had each other. That was one of our strengths; we knew each other so well. Even though they were replacements, you get to know them in a very short time. We had each other.

When you lose somebody it hurts. And at a point too you know that you are out there and responsible for these guys and their lives. You are trying to provide leadership all the time, while knowing that you are on your own because there is no way help can come in, so we called in help through artillery and through helicopters, which helped and got us to the point after dark so I could get my guys out of there. But you reach a point where you get mad. You get angry with the circumstances for happening that you obviously never anticipated. You took your guys out that morning and wanted to bring them all back that night. We had each other. That is what it was all about, looking out after one another. I thought a lot about it. Burkhead and Alldridge were scheduled to go home in 30 days. They almost made it. They almost made it. We didn't get them there. Circumstances like that happen, and you want to take control of everything you can, but you don't have total control.

[The next morning after the battle] for whatever reason, of course I had been wounded, they kept me in the back. They sent another platoon, 1st or 2nd Platoon in our company, out there to where we had been the day before. They were the ones that went out and found the bodies. At that point we knew Alldridge and Burkhead were out there, but we didn't know where Davis was [the platoon leader who had died in the same battle]. So we found them the next morning. The other thing that bothered me was that Burkhead had been there ten or 11 months as a truck driver. He was a truck driver. That was his last job prior to being assigned to our company. It made me question what we were doing. Here we took a person who had been in country for almost 11 months as a truck driver and all of a sudden put him into the infantry at the very end of his tour. It would have been one thing being transferred from an infantry group right into our group having had that recent experience. But Burkhead did not have that. That puts another element of doubt into your mind as to whether you did everything you could do to protect him and get him home. Why did the military do that? Why did we take a truck driver for 11 months and put him in the infantry for his last 60 days in Vietnam?

When you lost lives and you lost buddies – you lost a best friend – sometimes the guys were frustrated, and I guess you had to take that frustration out. Knowing that there was a 99 percent chance that those people in that village had a part in it. At least you felt that way. After a battle like that there are a lot of different anxieties felt. I remember writing home to both Alldridge's and Burkhead's parents. As their squad leader I sent a letter home to both of their parents letting them know what had happened that day. I apologized for the fact that we didn't get them home and keep them alive. It is a pretty solemn moment. You just went through what you went through and now you are a part of death in terms of taking other people's lives. And you are also a part of death in watching some of your own comrades get killed. You become accustomed to death. As you travel to Vietnam and try to figure out what you are made up of, you wonder whether or not you can take another person's life. But that is probably what you are going to end up doing. You quickly come to grips with that, that it is either you or them. And they are thinking the same thing. Someone has to lose, and you just pray to God that it won't be yourself.

VIETNAM

ANTHONY GOODRICH
Member of Mike Company, 3rd Battalion, 5th Marines

After Operation *Durham Peak* I had experienced my first dead Marines around me, and also dead enemy, and that kind of changed the way I thought about the war. Well, first of all I knew it was serious, I knew that I might get killed there, and I knew that I had to do things that I thought I would never be able to do to survive in Vietnam. So I made a decision that, after that first firefight and that first ambush that I survived, to do whatever was necessary to get through the war, so I basically cut my emotions off, and anger and fear drove me through the rest of my tour in Vietnam. I consider myself pretty lucky; I didn't get wounded in my tour there. I've done a little research on my company over the years, and out of my whole company, there was about 70 percent casualties when I was in Vietnam; that's either wounded or killed. It was mostly wounded from incoming or from booby traps, and booby traps were the big killer of the Marines that I served with.

We'd come in out of the bush, and they would have memorial services where they'd turn the rifle upside down with the bayonet, stick in the ground, and put a helmet on it. I guess at the time they didn't really mean anything, because it was usually weeks, if not months after these men had been killed and taken away in body bags. It was something that we all had to do, but it was very uncomfortable for me in the respect that it wasn't really a way to mourn these men, but it was a way for the Marine Corps, I guess, to mourn them. But I found it to be kind of ghoulish; I know that sounds weird, but I found it to be kind of ghoulish and kind of silly, and I know most of the Marines also felt the same way. And it was many years after the war that I was able to go to the Wall; there I was able to mourn these men.

My emotions were cut off because I couldn't dwell too much on the deaths at the time because we had jobs to do. We had other missions to go on, and if men did that it would really destroy their combat effectiveness for one thing. And I'd say that it was a way for the Marine Corps, I think, to think they were doing something for us, and at the time it didn't mean anything.

CHANGING ATTITUDES

There's an old Vietnam saying, "don't mean nothing," and that's basically what we said to each other when we were watching these rituals that would occur.

We had to continue with our missions, and we couldn't dwell too much on KIAs. I think that the best thing that we did was as quick as we could get a medevac in and get these guys out of there, especially the KIAs. Sometimes we had to spend nights with the bodies, and that was just a little bit too eerie for me. And our leaders, they just told us basically to forget it. We have to do something tomorrow; we've got to do something next week, so we've got to keep your concentration on what you need to do to get the job done. And I think that was probably the best advice at that time. Later we talked a little bit about it, talked about how good the people were. Most of the time it was some goofy black humor thing. It was just, we talked about how good the people were; we never talked about ourselves. It's funny, we never talked about are we going to be the next one to get it. It was, I hate to say this, I used to think, "It's better them than me," no matter who it was. We knew that these men that had died, died so we could stay alive, and that was a big burden, and it's a big burden even to this day, for me to realize that these men sacrificed themselves for me and that's really, really, what it was all about over there. That I had to trust the Marines around me, the ones that kept me alive, and the ones that died were the ones who kept us all alive. We tried to laugh about the person that was killed. There was a strange ritual when somebody would get killed. We would go through his gear and see what he had that we could take. I got an M14 off a dead Marine. I wanted that M14, and I just took it off the dead body. I figured, hey, he can't use it anymore. Well, we go through his backpack – if he had any C rations, if he had any extra ammo, anything that we would need, we would take it out of his pack and put it in our own pack, and maybe that was our way of honoring them. I know that sounds strange, but I think that they understood that they would do the same thing if something happened to us, and I think we all coped that way. We tried to forget about, I guess forget about them, even though we never did. It was just a matter of forgetting and getting on with business.

After *Durham Peak*, I got to the bottom of that hill after the end of that operation, just thinking that I still had 11 months to do. It was the first time somebody gave me a calendar. I started marking days off on the calendar. Well, I think that my illusions about the romanticism of war kind of got destroyed pretty quickly. My trust in the government kind of went away real quickly. We didn't sit around and discuss the politics of the war. We just knew we were stuck, and we knew, when I was there in '69 and '70, we knew that we weren't there to win. We used to sit there and say, "What the fuck are we doing, if we're not there to win?" We weren't taking ground, and if we did we'd give it right back to the enemy. It was basically a war of survival, not of anything else but just trying to stay alive, and it was frustrating in that sense. I think because we knew that nobody wanted to be the last person killed there. And it was just a matter of watching out for your buddy and trying to stay alive so you could get your tour over with and get the hell out of there. [There was a feeling that] "We're here as fodder basically, so the politicians in Paris can do their flapping of their mouths at the peace talks while we sit here and get killed." Nothing was being accomplished. I mean the war was over; it was coming to an end. We just didn't understand why we all weren't pulled out at once.

9 FREEDOM BIRD

Almost every member of the US military in South Vietnam looked forward to their DEROS, or Date Eligible for Return from Overseas. As a soldier's tour drew to a close, he often became fixated on returning home – on making it out of Vietnam alive to reclaim his life – resulting in a case of what soldiers referred to as "short timers' fever." Soldiers often kept a DEROS calendar, marking off the days until their return to "the world." As the days counted down, the anticipation of leaving Vietnam mounted and got especially bad for "single digit midgets" or those with fewer than ten days remaining in country. The last months in country found soldiers playing a waiting game. No one wanted to get wounded or worse, killed, in the twilight of their tours. After cheating death for nearly a year, could their luck run out so close to home? Yet fate was unkind to some soldiers. While some were transferred to the relative safety of rear-area assignments for their last days in country, others remained in the field on operations. For these unlucky men combat continued, and getting wounded and dying remained real, horrifying possibilities.

For over three million service men and women, "24 hours and a wakeup" – their last day in Vietnam – did indeed arrive. They had survived and would see their homes and families again. They had triumphed. But, as much as arriving in South Vietnam had once shocked many American soldiers, leaving that war-torn nation provided its own, often unexpected, psychic jolt. Combat soldiers had lived a life of hyper-alertness, adrenaline, and fear for nearly 12 months. They had lived among their brothers, the closest friends of their lives, in a world in which their actions truly mattered. The presence of death had made many men feel so alive, so vital. And now they were leaving. For many Americans, completing their tour left them with powerfully mixed emotions. On one hand soldiers were elated at the prospect of returning home, but they were also uneasy about the fates of those they were going to leave behind in Vietnam. They were leaving behind men they loved. Would their buddies survive? Would they ever see them again?

While the process of military out-processing at bases dotted across South Vietnam seemed maddeningly long to many, the trip back to the world was disorienting in its rapidity. Boarding civilian or military jetliners, soldiers cheered and shouted as their flights left South Vietnamese airspace. Just hours later they cheered again as the flights touched down on American soil. Their war and their time in Vietnam was over so abruptly. They had been in the field on operations and facing death often only days before, and now they were filing off of an airplane in the United States. There had been no time to decompress.

While there were as many coming home stories as there were veterans of Vietnam, for many the short journey from the airplane, from the world of men who understood Vietnam, and through the terminal and into the civilian world was sobering. Unlike their World War II-era fathers and uncles, Vietnam veterans were not returning to a country in the celebratory throes of victory; they were instead returning to a country riven by their war.

FREEDOM BIRD

Most men and women who served in South Vietnam were well aware of the escalating controversy and roiling war protests on the home front. But few understood the reality of what faced them upon their return home to a nation that many struggled to recognize. For some veterans the walk off of the freedom bird meant being met by crowds of antiwar protesters yelling, "baby killer," "rapist," and worse. Some veterans ignored the crowds, ready to get home and see the people who mattered. Others charged forward to fight and had to be held back. Some stood in shock wondering how their own generation could hate them so. For other veterans the return home was less confrontational, but equally unnerving. They weren't met with jeers and hurled epithets; they were met with apathy. Some were actively ignored, like nobody wanted to look at them or talk with them. Others were simply unnoticed as civilians walked past to go about their daily lives. It was a subtle and unexpected transformation that shocked many veterans. Only days before they had mattered; only days before they had been making life or death decisions among the best friends they would ever have. Now they walked among people who didn't know or care about their experiences, about their war. Now they were just people to rush past in an airport.

GARY FRANKLIN
Member of the 198th Light Infantry Brigade

I left the platoon with my squad leader Billy Chenault [out in the bush]. They were a pretty experienced platoon. 3rd Platoon was a bunch of veteran people, and I thought, "They're all going to be okay." I didn't feel quite so guilty about going home and just leaving them there. But I got a letter from Billy Chenault on the 23rd, a week after I came home. They were working around those rice paddies and all down there south of Chu Lai. On the 19th they were riding back to the night perimeter with H Troop [a tank unit with which they were working]. They'd been out taking the hills or something, and they were supposed to go set up the night perimeter somewhere else. Our platoon jumped on a couple of tracks [tanks] and just rode with them, and they just turned into this night perimeter. There was the lid from an ammunition can lying there on the ground, which they all thought was pretty curious. So the track commander, he yells to the driver, "Check that out!" Well, he climbs up out of that hatch, you know, the driver's hatch, and jumped off the track and jumped right on top of it, and it was a pressure-released device on top of what they thought was a gallon of explosives. It killed him and wounded the rest of the platoon. The only one left out there was Billy Chenault, and he lost his hearing I think in one ear completely for about a month and a half or so, and Billy had 82 days left I think, and I don't think Billy ever went back out either. So within two weeks the whole platoon was wiped out.

The same day, in a separate incident, Captain Manchester, he got shot through the butt with a .50 caliber. When I heard that, I figured it tore his legs off. Usually a .50 takes a limb. If you survived it, it takes something off. But Jerry Collins was still over there, and he jumped in the jeep and saw him when he came out of surgery. It went right through his butt, missed his hipbones, and just tore his butt up real bad. So within two weeks there, everybody I knew including the captain was hit; everybody was gone within two weeks.

JAMES NALL
Member of 1st Platoon of Charlie Company

After the battle of June 19, we had killed so many and lost so many that I was scared. Some will tell you that they got used to that. I never got used to that. It seemed like suicide. You get to a point where you get to be a vicious person. You don't care about the enemy's life. We lost so many of our guys that some didn't care about life anymore. Whatever they told me to do, I did it. I wanted to survive. The ones who did survive, we all met up on the same day to fly home. We started greeting each other. We were all on the same plane, Pan American. Everybody was screaming and hollering when that plane took off. I will never forget that day. I said, "Piss on Vietnam!" One song that always reminds me of Vietnam, Smitty used to play it on his record player, was the Players', "He'll Be Back."

We came into Travis Air Force Base. Then I flew into San Francisco. There were a lot of protestors there. We didn't get any happy greeting. It was like they were punishing us. I didn't feel too good. At first I thought I would feel pretty good about being part of the military and being proud that I had fought in Vietnam. But they didn't care. I stayed in Los Angeles for a week, and then I went on back to Alabama. Shoot, were they all glad to see me. You know a lot of guys in my hometown got killed – guys I had gone to high school with – but they were in different units.

At first they sent me to a training company at Fort Ord for my last three months of service. And then Martin Luther King, Jr. got killed. Then they had us working on riot training. But then I got out and I went back to work for the post office, where I had been working before I got drafted. That was one of the good things, that I didn't have to look for a job. I ended up working there for 34 years.

TERRY MCBRIDE
Member of 3rd Platoon of Charlie Company

I went home on January 9 or 10, whatever it was. We had a New Year's party, and it was pretty good. Got to see a few of the guys from the old outfit and everything. We were at Camp Alpha at Saigon. I got together with a bunch of the old guys there, and we partied pretty hard. Everyone was gathering to go home, well everyone that was left anyway.

We flew into San Francisco; we were supposed to go to Travis Air Force Base, but it was socked in with fog, so we ended up landing in San Francisco. We ran into a bunch of hippies and got spit on. It was interesting, anyway. Then we went to Oakland and were processed out from there as far as getting out of our fatigues and khakis and getting into greens. After that I went down to my mom's house down in California.

The protestors were the last thing on my mind. But it did not sit well with me, let's put it that way. It was pretty demoralizing in a lot of ways. The trouble with protestors was real brief when we were going from San Francisco to Oakland because we were all still a unit. It was when I left Oakland to fly down to my mom's that I flew alone, and I really got it. I was pretty much by myself. It was way different anyway. People yelled "woman killer" and "baby killer" and all that shit. They were not really pushing and shoving, but they got around you in a circle or at least tried to.

One of my cousins picked me up from the airport and drove me to my mom's house. I had two weeks off before I had to go back to serve my last few weeks in the Army. I was pretty shut down and hung out with a couple of my old friends and that was basically it: my old buddy Frank and a couple of my cousins. I was told to shut up about my time in Vietnam. They just did not want to hear about it. After I got back to my duty station, my cousin was killed in Vietnam on February 26, 1968. He lived 8 miles from where I was born and raised. We were pretty much raised together, but we went to rival schools. They did not have his service until May. I do not think they found his body until March. He was up in Khe Sanh; he was a Marine. That was a hard slap for me.

LARRY LUKES
Member of 3rd Platoon of Charlie Company

We flew home through the west coast and got treated like crap. We even had rotten eggs thrown at us. They made us put civilian clothes on because when we came in in our old khakis they were throwing crap at us. So they made us get civilian clothes put on to leave. Being treated this way demoralized me probably more than anything. To think that is how people treated us when we come home. They called us baby killers and woman rapers and every name you can think of. They were hollering at us, screaming, and throwing stuff at us. People talk about drug problems in Vietnam; I think probably more guys went to drugs and alcohol after they came home than they did when they were over there because of the way they were treated.

So that is how I flew home. I left there and had to land in Denver. I got 30 days at home, and I was stationed out at Fort Carson, Colorado. My wife was so happy. My mom and dad, her mom and dad, my brothers and sisters were all at the airport and everyone when I got home. I had a heck of a big party and everything else. My dad took me down to the VFW in order to buy me a drink. Over in Vietnam we could not get anything like 7-Up, Squirt, or anything. All we could get was grape and orange soda. So I drank scotch and root beer or scotch and grape soda. I got to the VFW bar and the bartender asked, "What are you going to have, soldier?" and I said, "scotch and root beer." He said, "What, are you sick?!" The guys at the VFW treated me well. Matter of fact a couple of the older guys gave me a lifetime membership to the VFW. They and my family treated me great. But for a good ten years you did not dare put Vietnam on a job application; they would not even hire you or talk to you.

STEVE HOPPER
Member of 3rd Platoon of Charlie Company

Before the end of my tour, I was rotated out of Charlie Company. You're happy to be rotated out of combat, but you lost contact with guys you had been with for a year and a half. You really got to know them as brothers. They were part of your family. We had each other, and then all of a sudden we didn't. Like Alan Richards. We had been on R&R together, and we had been wounded on the same day twice. Here was a guy I had gotten to know so well, was a very, very dear friend, and he was gone. He was plucked out of the unit because of his wound. All of a sudden he is out of your life. He was there the day before, and all of a sudden he is gone. And you just lose contact. You had to mentally prepare yourself for that; that one day you could be sitting there having lunch with your buddy, and the very next day one of you could be gone. And maybe never see them again.

VIETNAM

In January I was working with the Military Police at an ammo dump, and I get my paperwork to rotate home. I went to a processing center and turn in my rifle and gear, and I was told to wait around; at seven o'clock there will be some busses here to take you to the airport. So I walked over to a club they had there at the processing center, and here are a bunch of my buddies who I had been separated from all processing home at the same time. We waited, and waited, and waited on this bus to take us to the airport. Finally, around 11:30 that evening, they call us out and tell us that the busses are on their way. We get on the busses – there were like two or three busses – and a person in charge stepped on and said, "It is not unusual as we make this trip to the airport to receive sniper fire. So we will have a jeep with a machine gun at both ends of this convoy." You are sitting there thinking to yourself, "Oh dear; I've made it this far. Will I make it the next couple of miles to the airport?"

Well, we did. It was almost midnight when we got to the airport. We got off of the busses and sat down on the tarmac. There was no terminal. In came a commercial jet. It pulled up beside us there, and shut its engines off. They drove the steps up to the door, open the door up, and a whole planeload of replacement troops stepped off of the plane. Brand new guys, just coming into country. It is something that I'll never forget because we sat there on the tarmac. Here we were; we'd just been through a year of Nam. As you looked around our group you could see the wear and tear on their faces and on their bodies. And these young guys stepped off the plane. I say young; they were probably the same age we were. I was 20 years old at the time. As they walked by our group sitting on the ground, I don't think there was hardly a word spoken other than "good luck." And they said, "Congratulations on making it through." You didn't need to say anything; you could just look in each other's eyes and wonder how many of them were going to make it back. And they were looking at us, and you knew what they were thinking: "My God. Those guys are going home. How lucky they are." They got on the busses, we got on the plane, and the next thing you know we are in the air.

FREEDOM BIRD

When we landed, somewhere on the west coast, the seatbelt rule kind of went out the window. As soon as that plane touched down there were guys jumping up and down and hugging each other. It was a very, very exciting moment being back home. We got in at midnight, and the airport was quiet and empty. They took us out and put us on busses and drove us to a processing center. We were up all night getting fitted for new uniforms and things of that nature. I don't think that anyone went to sleep; we were just hyped up, running on adrenaline. It was so strange – at seven o'clock that next morning they made an announcement that our uniforms were ready. We went and got our uniforms on, said our goodbyes, and off we went. It was like, "I'll see you next week." That is the way the goodbyes were handled. It was so strange. Here are guys you have been with for so long. You stepped out the door, said goodbye to them, never to see some of them again ever. I remember going to the airport and thinking to myself, "Gee. I didn't get his parents' names or phone number." Some I didn't even recall their first names because we all went by last names. "Wow, was he from Kansas City, Kansas or Kansas City, Missouri?" All of a sudden you start asking yourself these questions that you wished you would have asked a year earlier. It all of a sudden hit home that you may never see these guys again.

At the airport I had called Jennifer's [his fiancée's] mother. I told her, "Joan, this is Steve. I'm home," and then I told her when I would be landing in St Louis. She told me that Jennifer would be there to pick me up. Well our flight kept getting delayed, and I called, but Jennifer had already left. I landed in St Louis, and we walked down the steps. I remember stepping off of the plane, and it was bitter, bitter cold. I walked in the terminal, and I heard a scream. It was Jennifer standing there. As I look back on it, it was strange. I was kind of out of touch with things I guess. I walked up and gave her a hug and a kiss, and then, very businesslike, said, "Let's go get my luggage." She kind of followed, and we held hands. I was just not thinking the way I normally would. Here was a person I knew so well but didn't know them anymore. I guess that I just didn't know what to say. I was like,

"Where are you parked?" I acted like I had just seen her the day before, like I had never been away from her.

We went out and got in the car. I forget what I had with me, maybe a duffel bag, and I threw it in the car. We headed for her home in Greenfield, Illinois where her parents lived. I was just awestruck by the ride leaving the airport. All the lights; there were just simply lights everywhere. For the last 12 months it had been such a dark time in my life, and it was so dark at night. Then all of a sudden the lights. I didn't know what to think; I didn't have a lot to say. Then we got to her parents' home. My mother and father were there, and several of my brothers and sisters that were local. We just all had a fantastic reunion, getting caught up with each other, just seeing each other. At dinner my dad said, "Well, Bill [Steve's brother who was also in the Army] is getting ready to make a little trip." I said, "Bill, where are you going? You getting transferred to a different post?" He said, "I'm going to Vietnam on Monday."

Jennifer and I got married during my 30-day leave, and then a honeymoon, and then I had about 60 days left to serve at Fort Leonard Wood, Missouri. So I reported into my unit down there, and I was a drill instructor. I was going to train new recruits for Vietnam. I remember reporting in, and our first sergeant called me down one morning and said, "Sergeant Hopper. Tomorrow morning at 5:30 there will be some trucks pull up in front of our barracks. You get in the front truck, and they will go and pick up our next company of recruits. You need to get them loaded up and get them back to the barracks here." So I got in the front truck, and of course it was dark. We drove around the base and the trucks pull up and stop. I look around and I'm at the same place I had been nearly two years earlier when I had gotten drafted and sent to Fort Leonard Wood. I look around and there are the same posts that I had been lined up behind. But now I was on the other side of the post. I was no longer the recruit; I was the leader. I jumped out of the trucks and right into the middle of their asses the way they had once done me. I spent the next couple of months training those guys for their service in Vietnam.

FREEDOM BIRD

MIKE LETHCOE
Member of 2nd Platoon of Alpha Company

By the end of my tour in Vietnam I was an adrenaline addict. At first I extended my tour for another six months and served with a crash rescue unit. I was trained as an aircraft firefighter. If anybody crashed, we would go and put the fire out. If a plane went down we would go and secure the site while medics worked on anyone who was hurt in the wreck. Working with us were a lot of burnt-out Vietnam guys who were just staying there. I extended again to stay there, but by then they had decided that you couldn't stay in Vietnam any more than two years. I'd already been there almost three, so they made me come home. I came home in 1969. There were protestors in the airport when I came in. I didn't like it at all. I had a bit of a confrontation with a hippie in the airport. Someone called me a baby killer, and I didn't take that too well. We had security around us that backed everybody off.

I was assigned to Letterman Hospital, and when I got there I was restricted to the hospital. They sent me to talk to psychiatrists for every day for like two weeks. I had been assigned to the hospital for some reason, and they said, "Well look, you are no worse off than a lot of people who have been over there." So they gave me an off-post pass and turned me loose in San Francisco and told me to check back every couple of days until they found out what to do with me. They wanted me to be evaluated to see if they could turn me loose on the public. They wanted to check me out because of my combat background. After a couple of weeks they called me in and told me that I could have the assignment of my choice. I said, "That's great. Send me back to Vietnam."

ANTHONY GOODRICH
Member of Mike Company, 3rd Battalion, 5th Marines
Toward the end of my tour I felt safer out in the bush. I don't know how to put it. It was slack in the rear – like a static position. We'd have to go stay in bunkers, and these bunkers were prime

targets for RPGs. The grunts would come in, and we wouldn't stay in the bunker. We would move next to the bunkers where we would set our position up. We were afraid that we were going to get taken out by RPGs or mortars. For the most part, I felt safer in the bush with a small unit. Squad size was a great size out in the bush for patrols because we could move faster. We could move quieter. I always thought that we were fighting like them [the North Vietnamese]. If we were fighting like them, we'd have a chance to maybe surprise them instead of the other way around. Another thing is the Vietnamese own the night there. I used to love to go out at night because you always knew they were going to be moving around or doing something.

My last six weeks in country I was at Hill 52 artillery firebase. I used to volunteer my squad for ambushes every night if I could. I used to have the new guys coming from the States call me names, like "Lifer, What are you doing? The war's over." I just shook my head at these guys. I would get us off the hill as much as I could. It was just a target. The hill was a target. If I could get out there in the bush at night, away from the fire support base I knew we could stay alive. I got lots of grief from these new guys. I hope they understand. I wanted to survive, maybe more than they did. They came in with a bad attitude. In April and May of 1970, these new guys came in thinking the war was basically over. They didn't have to worry about getting killed, and I have no idea who and where they were getting that attitude from. It was scary. That scared the hell out of me. I was probably more worried about getting killed the last month I was there than the first month. I used to talk to God and say, "Don't do this to me my last month here. You should have killed me my first month." I think I was probably more paranoid and more hyper-alert my last month than the first month I was there.

[At the very end] I was ready to leave. In fact, I was so ready to leave, I wanted to hide so I wouldn't have to do anything dangerous. You know it's funny, I remember getting on that chopper and seeing my buddies cheering me as I took off. I was so glad to leave. They were glad to see me leave, but I felt guilty about leaving those guys there. It was really hard. I wanted to leave, and I didn't want to leave. I felt responsible for them. I remember them saying, "Just get back home. We all just want to get out of here and go home. Don't worry about us. We know what's going on." It was tough. It was really tough for me to leave those guys behind. They were like my family. I mean closer than that. Something that I guess I still feel kind of guilty about.

The thing I remember, the amusing thing was when we go to Da Nang, before we could get on the chopper we had to go to a little tent. They had military policemen come in with dogs – drug-sniffing dogs, which I thought was amusing. They had a dummy up on the stage. They took a little pack of marijuana, and they stuck it down in the dummy's crotch and let the dog tear the crotch out of the dummy. So they told us they had these amnesty booths. You could walk into this little booth and they had little slots. Any paraphernalia or any contraband you had, you could drop into the slot. They were saying you have one last chance to drop off your contraband. If we catch you with anything you'll have to stay here. They went through our sea bags, I guess to make sure we weren't bringing home ordnance like claymores or frags. The only thing I got was an AK47 bullet. One round. It was in my pocket. I have no idea how I got through everything. I brought it back with me.

We left the ground and the whole airplane exploded into cheers. We cursed. Cheering and cursing – cursing Vietnam. Looking out that window and seeing Da Nang airbase fade away. I was exhilarated. It was a terrific feeling. Everybody in the aircraft felt exactly the same way. It was like a huge burden was lifted off of us. I can't describe it. It was orgasmic almost leaving Vietnam. The Marines flew us to Okinawa just like we flew over, where we had to take off all of our jungle clothes. Everything that we wore we had to take off and throw into a bin. We got to put our new uniforms on in Okinawa. That's where we got all of our ribbons and medals. We were issued all that stuff there. I had to stay there a week. I got bumped off four days' worth of flights before I could get home. I had fun. I went out and got drunk, got laid. Basically slept in. They were pretty slack on us not really doing anything while we were there. I got a haircut.

Got all cleaned up to come home. I knew I was getting out when I came home.

We flew straight from Okinawa to Travis Air Force Base. Then we got in two busses. From there, we were bussed down to Marine Corps Recruit Depot in San Diego where we went to Separations Company. We stayed there for five days processing out basically. We got to eat in the same mess halls. Getting out of the Marines the same place I went to boot camp was very odd also. We ate in the same mess hall as the recruits. They were on one side; we were on the other. We used to catcall them: "You guys don't know what you're getting into." The drill instructor would yell at us and we'd laugh at him. There were probably a hundred of us who spent five days in San Diego getting ready to get out. They told us about our GI bill benefits. They told us about us being in inactive reserve status. They asked us if we wanted to reenlist. They made sure everything was in order. Got our last medical check up, dental check up. On the fifth day, we left and everybody went their own ways. I flew from San Diego to L.A., then from L.A. back to Albuquerque. I really remember sitting in the L.A. airport waiting to come home in my uniform. Everybody wanted to ignore us; nobody wanted to sit next to us. We sat in the airport waiting to leave and it was just like we weren't there. I just felt like I was an outcast. It was just this odd, strange feeling. Maybe I'd seen too many World War II movies where people have done things like, "Can I buy you a beer or something?" It was like we were invisible. I was surprised by that. People gave us the strangest looks, the ones that did look at us. I thought that was kind of weird. Flew back to Albuquerque. My mom was there, my brother, my aunt and uncle. My father was in Korea at the time. He was still in the Air Force. My best friend was there. He met me there. That was June, middle of June 1970. It took me a while to readjust. I don't think I've ever readjusted completely.

10 LIFE AFTER NAM

As with so much of the Vietnam War and its era, there exists a generalized, and sensationalized, public image of the Vietnam veteran, an image informed less by reality and more by movie portrayals including Robert De Niro's magisterial performance of the unhinged veteran Travis Bickle in *Taxi Driver*. The result has been a mythologized common vision of the American veteran experience. Everyone knows the stereotypes: the veteran who joined Vietnam Veterans against the War and tossed his medals on the steps of the Capitol, the veteran loner, the veteran ready to go off any minute, the homeless veteran.

Like the war in which they fought, the truth concerning the postwar lives of Vietnam veterans is much more nuanced and complex. The veteran experiences of reintegration to society, raising families, working – the simple but infinitely difficult task of living – were intensely individualistic and tended to confound generalizations. Many members of the Vietnam generation locked the war away in dusty corners of their attics – a war of which they would rarely speak. Others spoke of Vietnam as often as they could, trying desperately to do honor to their fallen comrades and to keep the historical memory of their generation alive in a nation that seemed determined to forget them and their war. The war haunted others for the remainder of their days, dogging their every step, leaving them locked in their own personal world of fear. Many veterans crafted marriages of intimacy and love, while others lashed out at their families or tried to drown their feelings in a sea of alcohol. There is no dominant veteran narrative of the war.

Even amid the uniqueness at the center of the Vietnam veteran experience, there exist important commonalities. Over three million Americans returned home from service in the war zone that was Vietnam; of that number, though, only slightly over one million were combat veterans. The veterans as a group stood out, making up only roughly 10 percent of their generation, but combat veterans were almost unique, accounting for only roughly 3.3 percent of their generation. While their generational compatriots had gone to college, begun families, landed jobs, and moved forward in the "real world," combat veterans had watched their friends die and meted out death to others. They had lived on the razor's edge where even a misplaced step could mean going home in a body bag. Whether a combat veteran's old friends or even his family tried to understand or not, they just couldn't. They hadn't been there, and there was no way they would ever know what it was like. For some combat veterans the lack of true societal empathy just became a simple fact of life; for others it became an ever-broadening chasm, isolating them ever more. Veterans were perpetually alone in the crowd.

The Vietnam War lacked a cathartic end. There was no capitulation of the enemy capital; there was no special edition of the local paper with the word "Victory!" in bold type. There was instead an all-too-meek American withdrawal from the conflict and the fall of Saigon. There had been no real end to the conflict, no victory, no cheering crowds to absolve Vietnam veterans of the burden of war. America loves winners, champions. But the veterans of Vietnam had returned home as something less. They had returned home to a deafening silence. As veterans began to grapple with their new peacetime realities, the US, as it so often does, barreled forward into the future, anxious to put the memories of the unsuccessful war in Vietnam and the turbulent 1960s into the past. The unseemly rush to forget Vietnam all too often left the war's veterans alone to carry the memory and burden of war. For some that burden became a crushing weight.

In spite of their experience of war the vast majority of Vietnam-era combat veterans returned home to take their rightful place as members of one of the most distinguished and successful generations in American history. Some veterans became filmmakers (Oliver Stone), scions of industry (Frederick W. Smith, founder of Federal Express), leading political figures (John Kerry, John McCain), and renowned writers (Tim O'Brien), while many, many others forged wonderfully successful lives in their own right as laborers, teachers, parents, police officers, college professors, stock analysts, farmers, and Americans. Indeed, Vietnam veterans are less likely to have suffered from unemployment in their lives and are financially better off than the others of their generation. The hard hand of war had fostered a maturity and industriousness on the part of veterans, a seriousness and work ethic that served them well.

But for many, even while achieving business and family success, the scars born of war endured. Published in 1990, the massive *National Vietnam Veterans Readjustment Study* found that over 800,000 Vietnam veterans suffer from some level of post-traumatic stress disorder (PTSD). Surrounded by its own mythology, PTSD is most often badly misunderstood. Combat is traumatic – a world of death and horror that it outside the norms of human behavior – and the nearly unimaginable rigors of battle put extreme stress on the psyche. As Victor Frankl, a concentration camp survivor, stated, "An abnormal reaction to an abnormal situation is normal." There is no less normal situation than combat, and soldiers often emerge from combat irrevocably changed. All too often alone in society, swept under the cultural carpet, too many Vietnam veterans were unable adequately to heal from their experience of combat. That experience, the death and suffering, became an integral part of them; Vietnam would always be a major presence in their lives. That enduring presence is PTSD. At its furthest limits PTSD is crippling – a world of flashbacks, depression, and alcoholism. But for many more combat veterans PTSD is something to be lived with – an inability to trust, the need to control hyperalertness, quickness to anger, emotional distance. For most veterans who suffer from PTSD, Vietnam remains part of their life but does not dominate their life.

In 2013 the 18-year-olds drafted in 1965 will turn 66 years of age. Vietnam veterans are part of every segment of American society and are often so thoroughly integrated into society that many are not even aware of their veteran status. Frank is a pilot; John is a photographer; George is Emily's father. They are all just Americans, but they are something more. They are men who spent a single year of their life's span engaged in brutal, small-unit combat in a distant land. They are men who once made life and death decisions in the blink of an eye. They are men who fought in a war that so many of their countrymen tried to forget. They are Vietnam veterans.

PAULINE LAURENT
Wife of Howard Querry

[A few weeks after her husband Howard Querry's death, Pauline gave birth to their child.] You know, for the first child, it was pretty smooth. I was only really in intense labor for like two hours. And my daughter was born, and you know, at the time I thought, "God, I hope she's normal because she's been through this trial with me." And I thought, you know, I thought she would be normal because she looked normal. I didn't realize the emotional impact it had on her, but she had ten fingers and ten toes and a head and all the things that a baby was supposed to have. Howard and I picked her name before I had her. It was Michelle and then the middle name was Howard's grandmother's name. He was really close to his maternal grandmother. And so Marie was her middle name. We named her after his maternal grandmother.

[After having the child I still couldn't bear to look at Howard's belongings from Vietnam.] And I left them in the closet until I would move, and I moved frequently. I kept moving, trying to get away from the pain that would well up inside of me. You know, when you moved, your whole life gets torn apart; you have to start all over again. So I kept starting all over again, and that kept me busy, so I didn't have to open those boxes and look at them. And every time the topic of Vietnam would come up, I would disappear, get silent, go run away and hide, not talk about it. People asked me where my husband was. I would try to avoid answering because when I did answer and say, "He died in Vietnam," it would be like dropping a grenade in the middle of a conversation. People were just stunned. They did not know how to respond, and I learned really early in my life to have everybody else be more important than me. So everybody else's feelings were more important than mine. So I denied my feelings, and I kept shut about Vietnam. I kept quiet about Vietnam, the fact that I was a widow. I carried it all in myself. And this went on from 1968 until 1990. In 1990 I quit a job that was really important to me, and I ended a relationship with a man that was really important, and I didn't know what happened to me, but I actually stopped bathing, stopped brushing my teeth, couldn't get out of bed, and became suicidal. I didn't know what was wrong with me, but there was something in me that told me to go to an Army base and to see a psychiatrist.

By this time, I was living in California. I found my way to Letterman Army Hospital in San Francisco and I went to see a psychiatrist. He was dressed in full Army uniform. I remember walking in the room and looking at his uniform and just freaking out and telling him, "I want to die. I want to kill myself and I don't know why." And it was then that he asked me a bunch of questions and told me that I was clinically depressed and that if I took these pills, I would get better. So I went home and I took the pills, and three months later I was still suicidal, and I was seeing him like once a week, and he kept waiting for me to change my mood, and it didn't change. So after three months he weaned me off of those pills and started me on new pills, and about six months after that I started to see a ray of hope in my life again, and it was then that I started to want to live and changed my mind that maybe I didn't want to die.

[What had kept me going] was my daughter. I knew that it wasn't just me, and if it weren't for my daughter, I probably would've committed suicide. I'm sure of it, but I knew that my daughter already had no father, and that if I committed suicide, I would take away the only parent she had, and I knew I couldn't do that. So, you know, I would drive down to San Francisco through the traffic and go to these appointments. It was really her that kept me going. And, you know, I'd been committing suicide slowly for all those years, but I did it through my addictions. Addictions are like a slow suicide, but when I got to 1990, it was like I wasn't on the slow path to suicide anymore; I was on a fast track. I was going to do it quick, and I had it all planned and how I was going to do it. I think the pivotal thing that happened was one day, I used to call my daughter and tell her how much pain I was in. She was really the only person I would talk to anymore, and one day she said to me, "You know, mom, I can't stop you from committing suicide. That's your decision. I really can't intervene; I can't do anything about it. I can't watch you 24 hours a day." But she said, "I'll tell you one thing, suicide is not something you can change your mind about, and, if you do it, you'll miss my wedding and you'll miss knowing my children."

And I think that deeply affected me, and that's when I realized that it wasn't just me and my pain, that I had to find a way to release this pain, to get through it because I could not do that to my daughter. And so I took the medication, and I got into therapy, and I started for the first time talking to a therapist. She would just let me come one hour a week and I would talk about Howard and I would cry. It was the first time anybody let me cry. It was the first time anybody asked me questions about Howard. It was the first time anybody wanted to know what it was like for me. [Later I met a marriage and family counselor in Santa Rosa.] She was giving a talk somewhere and I went to hear her speak, and I just knew intuitively that, you know, I wanted to work with her. She had shared some of her life experience and traumatic things that had happened to her, and I knew because of her trauma that she would be able to hear my trauma. And she was someone I wanted to become. I looked at her and I thought, "I want to become that woman. I want to become who she is." She was self-confident, she was compassionate, she was gentle and sweet and soft. At the time, I was very hard, frozen and solid. She was everything I wanted to be and she had spoke about surviving her own trauma.

Pauline succeeded in her goal, and transformed her life. She has written about her experiences in Grief Denied: A Vietnam Widow's Story *and now serves as a life coach to help others who are in need. Michelle's daughter, Alexis Monhoff, is presently a Rotary Youth Ambassador in Italy.*

DON TRCKA
Member of 3rd Platoon of Charlie Company

[After my long stint of recovery in the hospital] I went on R&R for 30 days; rest and recreation for 30 days. Went home; did nothing. I was down to only 143 pounds, but now the colostomy bag was gone. All my plumbing was back together. It sure was a big relief. I did eat a lot on that R&R. Course you had good home cooking always there.

Then I got my orders to go to Fort Hood. That's where all the returning Vietnam veterans went, the majority of them from Texas, just biding their time. They put me in charge of the postal mail. Boy, that was a great job. I'd get the mail in, and I'd put it in the slots of the guys. And then, they would send me to like projectionist school where I was able to show movies to the guys.

And then I recall that that the unit had to go to Chicago because of a riot that they were having, but I didn't have to go. The first sergeant said, "Don, you don't have to go. You stay back here." I said, "Okay, First Sergeant." So, I stayed back while they went. And they were probably gone a week, maybe a week and a half. But I still did my morning reports and did what have you because I was a lot better. And I was still running, you know, because I loved to run and stay in shape.

And then one day – it was about, I guess, 60 days before I got out – the first sergeant said, "Don." He said, "Would you consider to go to OCS, Officer Candidate School?" And I said, "First Sergeant, I just wanna get out." He said, "Don, you would be a good candidate. Would you just think about it?" I said, "Yeah, First Sergeant." But of course, I'd done made my mind up; getting outta here. So, on May 12, that was it. I'd served my country, and my tour was over.

I went back to League City. And, of course I had a job before I even got out of the service. I had applied at a finance company. And I got out on May 12. I started work on May 14. I got married on May 18. So, I jumped from the frying pan into the fire. I stayed at that job about three years. Eventually I ran over a million-dollar office, but I got tired of that. So, I decided to go sell cars, because at the time the car business was good, and I could always talk a good talk. So, that's what I did. I went to a Ford company called Charlie Thomas Ford.

Bev [my wife] and I lived in Houston, in an apartment, at that time. So, that's where I started my career. And I was with them for a total of 34 years. I retired in 2006, never changed again. Charlie Thomas Ford, it's called Auto Nations now. It's the biggest company of its kind in the United States. They own 300-something new car dealerships. Anyway, I was a director. I had nine people under me.

We have three boys and three girls. They all have degrees. Where Bev and I didn't have a degree, they all have degrees. Their ages now are 30 is the youngest, and the oldest is 40. We have now 11 grandkids. We're fixin' to go to a family reunion that we have every year, and this is our 75th year. We have over 200 and something people coming this year. They last a whole day, but it's a lot of good food. They even make that homemade noodle soup.

[As the war was winding down] I was watching it on the news and people demonstrating, and I said to myself, "Why aren't your asses over there?" I said, "No, because you're draft dodging everything." Because those were the ones that were protesting the war. All we did was do a job to protect this country. And some of them blamed us because we were over there. We weren't over there by choice. The war's ending made me feel like, "Why were we there if we didn't win the war? Why were we there?"

We lived in Houston a long time, and when I retired we came up here to a little town called Nolanville, population 1,900. It's about 3 miles from Fort Hood. So, I have my next-door neighbors, they are Army personnel, and some of them been there three, four tours in Iraq or Afghanistan already. I know exactly what our current service men go through.

My wife tells me that I've had dreams about the last two years, said I cry. That's what she tells me, course I don't remember, but she says I'm crying. And course you know, because I was wounded in Vietnam, I did get 100 percent disability, and I go to the VA hospital. Talk about a hospital that takes care of veterans – that hospital is the best one I've ever seen. I mean this hospital takes care of their veterans. The hospital is so big, but they take care of the vets.

But I'm 66 years old now, and I try to keep myself busy because I do have six kids and 11 grandkids. They're all coaches and teachers. They graduated from New Mexico State, to Houston, to Texas Tech, to Sam Houston, and the last one went to A&M. I keep busy. I have a daughter that's head coach at University of Mary Hardin Baylor, softball coach. And then I have a son up here, he's at Belton, which is about 5 miles from me. And then I have a son that coaches baseball, high school, at Cliff High School which is about 4 miles from me. So, in the summertime, or starting in February, I'm always busy watching them. And then of course I go to Dallas to see my other grandkids play soccer, basketball, football. So, we're busy. I'm very proud. They've accomplished a lot. They're good kids.

I haven't even mentioned Vietnam to them. They've never asked me. They've seen the scars on me, and I'll them, "Yeah I got that in Vietnam." That's all. And I tell them I had the colostomy. They know what that is. But now I've got my grandkids, when I had my shirt off, and they'll say, "Papa, where'd you get them scars from?" Of course, I tell them.

JEANNIE HARTMAN
Wife of Ernie Hartman who served in 1st Platoon of Charlie Company

[After my husband Ernie came home from Vietnam] mostly I just prayed a lot. There wasn't a whole lot I could do. He would not mention it [Vietnam]. He would not talk about it whatsoever to me or to anyone. He held it inside for years. He came home from Vietnam an alcoholic. He came home a genuine alcoholic. I'm very old fashioned when it comes to dope. And I will never forget he brought some marijuana home. I was cleaning my car one day, and I found it under my seat. And I thought I would kill him. And I made him get rid of it and told him right then, "I won't tolerate it. You either decide you're not going to do it, or I'm not living with you." He would have nightmares. If the fire station siren went off, he would start yelling and screaming and on the floor and crawling. Several nightmares were just terrible for him. He would either punch me or pick me up, not realizing it, thinking he was in Vietnam. Before the war he wasn't an alcoholic, and he wasn't violent. He had a wonderful, wonderful sense of humor, just a wonderful all-around guy.

Ernie quit believing in God when he was in Vietnam. He does not believe in God, so that has become very difficult for me. I used to go to church every week, and I quit going to church because every time I went to church, he went to a club and drank. So, I'm still very religious, but I don't go to church because of that. And he no longer believes in God because he saw too many of his buddies killed, and he saw one on each side of him killed every time he was wounded. And he said he has bad guilt, remorse.

[Ernie worked the same job for 37 years] and hoped to retire from there. We never had children, so we adopted a child. Ernie worked nights for 25 years, and so I basically raised our son. And so they've never, ever been close. Our grandson, Dylan, idolizes Ernie and is a big part of our lives.

He lost his job after 37 years. It went to China, and he lost his job. And we could not live on my income. It had triggered Vietnam in him big time; everything just started coming back to him. I mean he had problems all through the years, but it got worse at the time that he lost his job. He did go and apply finally with my prodding to get some disability help with the VA, which took us probably over two years to get. And he had several hearing evaluations and all this stuff. He finally was granted a certain percentage of disability at that time. And that's when he finally started talking to some counselors about Vietnam, and they had told him he needed to be talking to me. And he told them he didn't want talk to me, because it was such a bad time in his life he didn't think that I needed to know it or worry about it. He didn't want to drag me into it. And I kept telling him he really needed to confide in me because I was married to him and stuck by him all this time that I needed to know something. Then he did start opening up a little bit to me.

And then at some point, his counselor called me in with him and said that she wanted a session where I could ask him anything I wanted to, and he had to answer it. But she was there in case there was a problem to mediate. And I asked him right out why he never told me about Vietnam. And I wanted to know something about it, and he'd start talking about it. And I thought I had a right to know. And that's when he did tell me certain things that he would lay in a hole covered in leeches, and he couldn't say a word or do anything because the enemy would know where they were and kill them. And he had tied himself in a tree before, and had to be up there and tried to lie there to sleep a little bit. And there again, he couldn't say or do anything. Then he started to come out with all sorts of stuff like this.

Then he became a little more open. But then he kind of shut up again, and about the only time he will talk to me is when he's drunk. But he has started talking to me, the last five years. I helped him get some help. He had a real hard time accepting that help. He deserves it. I mean, he definitely has PTSD, definitely. Hearing about Vietnam from him has definitely helped. He doesn't think I should need to know, and I think yes. It does help me understand why that's the way he does sometimes and thinks the way he does.

I have had a lot of people ask me why I haven't left him. And I guess, when we got married it was like, you get married, you're on your own. Don't come running back home, although I know they would have taken me. And I really do love him, and he's a wonderful person. And when he isn't like this, he is wonderful. And I keep trying to remember that. I keep trying to remember he is a good person. And he can be a wonderful husband. And my grandson idolizes him. Sometimes, I'm not sure how to stay sane. Right now Ernie is probably worse than I have seen him, depression-wise. And I asked for some counseling, but my insurance won't pay it. So, I have nobody to talk to, no one. My mother had a stroke four years ago, so I don't have her to talk to anymore. And I can't afford to pay for counseling. So, I don't really have anyone to vent to, so I do a lot of praying.

JAMES NALL
Member of 1st Platoon of Charlie Company

I got married to Lilly in 1978. I was just a regular laborer. I worked inside the post office. I'd go in the trucks and take out crates of mail. I had problems with forgetting Vietnam, especially when I first came back out and I went to Alabama – I would wake up screaming and hollering. You can ask my wife. I used to jump up out of the bed and just start running through the house. She don't really like me to watch any war movies. She'll say, "Oh boy, you're going to be over here with that Vietnam stuff."

When I came back to L.A. they began using helicopters. The L.A. police started running helicopters over your neighborhoods and in the city. Every time they use helicopters, Vietnam pops into my mind. Celebrations like New Year's and Fourth of July bother me. All those fireworks. I hit the floor when I hear a loud sound go off, because it sounds like somebody's shooting. I'm not a fireworks person, because it reminds me of Vietnam. A lot of times I like to go out of town [for those holidays] and go somewhere, in a hotel or something, where I won't hear the fireworks.

I never did drink. People never could understand why I didn't drink. I was hurting, but I never did drink. When I retired God told me I was in denial. I said, "Ain't nothin' wrong with me."

But I went to the VA in 2000. I had just retired. I think a lot of the veterans are in denial. I went to the VA, and I got to talking to them and seeing a counselor. And I saw a psychiatrist, and I talked to him. He just set me down and just told me to open up. I would sometimes cry, just some things really affected me, even doing my job and my marriage. A lot of things happened. That's why a lot of guys get divorced.

I see young people, and I say you know what, they need to go to the war. They think they are tough, but in war they'll really find out what fear is all about. That is when I really found out what fear was all about, when I went to serve in the war. After training they said you are combat ready, and I said, "Well we're gonna go over there and kick Charlie. We are gonna destroy him." But you know what, when I first saw Peterson and all those guys get killed, my whole life changed in Vietnam. It's like, "What if the rabbit has the gun?" What is the rabbit? What is the deer? The whole thing would have too many hunters. That's the way I pictured the war. I was firing at a target, but when the target's firing back at you, that's the rabbit. That's the deer.

TERRY MCBRIDE
Member of 3rd Platoon of Charlie Company

In '72, I loaded up, got the hell out of L.A. and went to Alaska. I had a pocketful of money and just decided to do something totally different. I met a nice lady the first night I was up here and stayed with her for almost 20 years. We were married for like 17 of that.

I went in the Guard from '75 to '83, and I worked in a topless bar. I did that for pretty much the whole time I was up here, just the security doorman, and I did some bodyguard stuff, just a bunch of stuff like that. But I made pretty good money. I've pretty much seen it all. I'd take guns away from people and knives away from people, kinda part of the territory.

Alaska is like 70 percent of the dudes that are up here are vets trying to get away from everything. I had lot of problems with Vietnam. It kinda dumped on me pretty heavy. A lot of sleepless nights. I first saw doctors after when I went into the Guard, because the Guard kind of brought a lot of things back that I hadn't thought about in a long time. That smell, being back in that green uniform – stuff that I wouldn't have thought would have bothered me but did. My wife, who died in 1990, worked for the VA and got me involved in a couple programs for PTSD to put my shit back together. I get a lot of nightmares; a lot of nights I don't sleep. Wintertime everything's all white, so it kind of diffuses some of it, but the summertime up here – when everything's all green again – get you fired back up. I'm looking for that sniper in the trees and a gun emplacement in the weeds. Vietnam never did go away. It's always been there. It's always been right in my back pocket.

[My wife's name was] Mardy. Actually, really it was Marlene, but she went by Mardy. She was the one who brought the subject up and had done some research on the stuff. I ended up getting into a program before the program was even actually started by the VA. So, it was probably some of the first years that it started. It helps somewhat. It kicks it back a little bit. I've got a list of phone numbers I can get on if it starts to get under my skin.

[After Mardi died] it was sporadic for me instead of a full-time thing. Then I met Patti. We were married together for seven years, something like that, before we got divorced.

I'm single now, and I'm pretty much retired. Kicking it at home; I get 100 percent from the VA. I got my rating the day that Saddam Hussein jumped off into Kuwait, August 2, 1990. So, I got my war money at the start of another war. It's both physical and PTSD. I've been having some problems with liver flukes, a water-borne parasite that is in the water over there in Vietnam. It becomes a lifetime infection. They said it doesn't really come on until your 50s or 60s or so. What it does is it gets into your intestines, and then it gets into the little lead that goes up into your liver. And then it gets into your liver, and then it ends up eating up from the liver into your pancreas.

I went to my first company reunion in 2005. It's like we were never really apart. Everybody seems like they're pretty much the same person, still into the same stuff they were into then. For me it's really a saving grace I think in a lot of ways, just being able to tap in.

I was pretty much floored when I first saw the guys in 2005. It took me a while to recognize them, plus I guess for them to recognize me too. They started out as a bunch of youngsters, skinny with no hair on their face. And after that, everybody's just a bunch of old turds.

I'd go through it all again if I had to if they turned back the clock. I'm very adamant about that too. If you weren't there you don't know, and if you were there you do know. To me it's just important to pass it on so other people get it.

MIKE LETHCOE
Member of 2nd Platoon of Alpha Company

[After coming home] I paid attention to everything that happened over there [Vietnam], and I was highly pissed. Everything we went through, all my friends that were killed, all the people that I killed was for nothing. And I live with that. I'm highly pissed about all of it. The way we were treated when we got back, it was dogs and soldiers keep off the grass. I felt slighted by the government. I felt slighted by the country. I was proud to be a soldier. I was proud to be in Vietnam. I was proud to be a good soldier. A soldier used to be a respected profession, and I expected that when I got back. And it just wasn't that way. Everybody looked down on you because you were there. Everybody looked down on you because you'd been through what you'd been through. I resented the hell out of it.

Vietnam is still with me. I still have bad dreams, not near as bad as I did. Because when I first got back from Vietnam, almost nightly I'd wake up in cold sweats and in terror. Things I went through there that didn't bother me at all in dreams would terrify me. I still have dreams occasionally about it. It's with me daily. It's with me constantly. It's what I live with. I haven't received treatment for PTSD. I haven't asked the VA or the Army for anything since I got out because there are guys that needed it [treatment] a lot more than I did. I went down a few times for physicals. It's just a mess. When you go into the VA, you take a book with you 'cause you're gonna be in there all day. For the simplest things, you might have to make three or four trips back. So I just didn't do it.

I bummed around for a couple of years, trying to find myself and trying to find America, and I still had the adrenaline addiction. I lived off the back of a motorcycle for two, three years. I'd sleep by my bike or wherever I could crash. It was just party time, and let's go out looking for America. I started messing around with a rough crowd. And one day I snapped and said these guys are sorry pieces of shit, and if I keep messing around with 'em I'll wind up the same way. And I met a good woman. And I changed my life. I stopped messing around with the people I was seeing.

I got a job driving a truck. But then I saw an advertisement on television: "travel adventure, high pay, be a deep-sea diver, approved for veterans." That was on Saturday night. The next Monday I was down there and signed up for commercial diving school on the GI Bill. I went to work the day after I graduated from diving school and never looked back. It answered that need for the excitement. It kept me out of jail and kept me alive, actually. And I was a diver for years. And now I'm a diving consultant. My last job out was a diving consultant for Chevron, cleaning up after the hurricane tore up the oil field off of Louisiana.

I met a little girl from Georgia, one of the finest human beings I've ever met in my life. Her name is Katherine. We met in '75. The more I saw her, the more I liked her. When I really actually got to know her, I really liked her. We've been married over 33 years now. No kids. I talk to her about Vietnam. I talk to anybody about it. I've found it's better to talk about it. I didn't talk about it for a long time, but I found out it is better to talk about it. Get it out there, and you're not just carrying it bottled in. And I talk to her about it quite a bit.

ANTHONY GOODRICH
Member of Mike Company, 3rd Battalion, 5th Marines

My sleep habits for the first ten years I'd say were like in Nam. I still wake up at three o'clock in the morning 32 years after the war. I came back and I drank heavily the first two years, and I smoked lots of pot. The reason I did those two drugs especially is because I didn't dream. I could actually pass out. Not really sleep. No dreaming. I hated the dreams I had about Vietnam. I did that until about 1980. It got a little bit better after '80, but not too much. I worked in bars. I had several jobs doing everything from cab driving, to janitor, to bartending, to dealing marijuana. I probably would last a year or two with a job, then I would quit the job or get fired, one or the other until 1980. The first ten years after the war are kind of a blur to me also. I don't remember too much. I bought a motorcycle. I used to like to go to bars and get into fights. I was confused, to say the least. I know that we weren't well liked. My first year back I went back to the University of New Mexico, took a couple of classes. We were told in our classes that we were baby killers and rapists.

The mainstream veterans' organizations, the VFW and the American Legion, I tried to go down and join those. We were told there that we were losers and drug addicts. They basically told us you guys' war wasn't a real war. We don't think that you are deserving of us. That was fine with me. I just walked out of those places. That was fine. We were ostracized from society. I felt like I had done something wrong. I was told that I should feel guilty, that I should feel ashamed. I guess I bought into that. I grew my hair out. I didn't let anybody know I was a vet. It was sad, I guess. I look back and I was so goddamn angry. I was so angry at the way the war was. There were too many of my friends that were dead, and there were too many of them wounded. There were too many of them still there, and that angered me. My own peers made me angry, too, because they didn't want to listen to anything I had to say about the war. The ones that really angered me was the treatment of me and my vet friends by the World War II guys, specifically in the American Legion and the VFW. They thought that we were less than them. That really hurt. That really, really hurt me. I got really angry at them.

It was that whole sense that we were outcasts. We were not welcome. We had done something wrong. I had a huge problem with that because I know I didn't do anything wrong. I bought into it. Like I said, after a couple of years I wouldn't tell anybody I was in Vietnam. Whenever I applied for a job, I wouldn't tell them I was a Vietnam vet. I just didn't want anybody to know, even though I wanted to say something so bad. I wanted to tell them. I wanted to tell them what Vietnam was about. I joined Vietnam Vets Against the War, but in name only. I still had misgivings. My friends are still there. They're still getting blown up. They're out there doing their job. I can't get out there and say Ho Chi Minh is going to win. There was a huge tug there, too.

I went back to the university for two semesters. I dropped out, because once people found out I was a vet, then I was a target. I was confused. Let's put it that way. I was very confused. I wanted the war to end so my friends could come home, but I couldn't get out there and spout the antiwar shit that I heard. I know they had no respect for me as a vet. I remember going to an antiwar rally one time on campus. This was probably in late summer or early fall. It must have been late fall because it was the first semester I was back. I wanted to speak. You could get in line to go up to speak. They asked me who I was, and I said I was a vet. The guy told me I couldn't speak because I was a veteran; I was a baby killer. This guy said, "You're a baby killer. You should have gone to Canada. We're not going to let you speak." I turned around and walked away. I should have punched the guy, but I didn't. I figured "Goddamn, they didn't even want to listen to me. I'm on your side; I want to end the war." I didn't understand why we were looked at with such disdain. There was the apathy towards it too. People didn't care. They wanted to forget about the war and about us. That hurt. I used to go to bars and we'd find each other. Veterans would find each other. We'd sit there and get drunk. I'm sure people looked at us weird then. Basically we would get mindless together. We'd get drunk or get high. Didn't talk about the war very much. We'd sit there and talk about what we were seeing in the country and how we were being treated, what was going on. Why can't we express our feelings about our friends that are still there? It was just a big confusing time for me. I was only 20 when I got out.

[Not even my family] wanted to talk about it. My father, like I said, was in Korea. I showed my mom my slides, I remember, and she didn't ever talk to me about it. It was just something that everybody wanted to shove under the rug. Nobody wanted to listen to anything I had to say or we had to say. It was just like I had gone away on a camping trip or something. Even my best friends from high school didn't want to hear anything about Vietnam from me. It was a disappointment. I thought I had to something to say.

My mom aged a lot while I was gone. I came home, and that was the first thing I noticed about my mom; she had gray hair. She never had gray hairs before. Her face had lines on it I had never seen before. I didn't realize how much I affected her during my tour there. She saved all my letters I sent her. I've read those letters since then. I'm amazed. I thought I didn't tell her anything, but some of the things – good Lord, I'm telling my mom this? That this ambush happened; I sent her articles out of the *Stars and Stripes* about us getting overrun. I always thought I'm going to protect her. I got home and I remember talking to my brother and my dad about how much mom would worry. She watched the news every night, any time the Marines were mentioned. Any time that I Corps or An Hoa was mentioned she was always wondering, that's where Tony is, isn't it? I aged her. I feel bad about that to this day. I know that she prayed for me, and I know that she was prematurely gray because of my tour there. I don't think she wanted to hear what I had done, what I had witnessed. Even though since then we have talked about it. About 25 years after the war, I think I finally got around to talking to them.

The whole Paris Peace thing, the whole "Secret Plan" that Kissinger and Nixon had in '72. All those events angered me, more than anything else. I knew the war could be ended; all they had to do was just end the damn thing. I just thought it was just a way for us to save face in some way or another. I don't think I voted for anybody only because I didn't think there was anybody to vote for. I saw the government as the enemy. I think to this day, I probably still think of them that way. I lost faith in the government. I lost faith in the country. I lost faith in God, all kinds of things I had believed in as a young man. That was gone. It still affects me today, I guess. I'm not real trustful the government tells me the truth. I just lost a lot of faith. I lost faith in everything that I believed in before I went to Vietnam.

VIETNAM

I remember '75 when we pulled out of Saigon. I remember that being on live TV. I remember how sad I was. I wasn't angry anymore. I was saddened by the whole bug out we did. I thought about all the Vietnamese we left there that we said we could get out, and we left them there. That was so damn sad. To this day I can see those Marines on top of the embassy getting into that chopper. I can see them punching people in the face, knocking them away from the chopper. I can see the aircraft carriers dumping helicopters overboard. I can see the Vietnamese flying out. They're jumping out of their aircraft over the water. Just abandoning those people. That has always stuck in my craw – that we abandoned these people after telling them that we were going to help them. When the tanks rolled into the presidential grounds, I remember that too. I was thinking, "What the hell was this about? Was this for nothing? Did my friends die for nothing? Did I go through this for absolutely nothing?" I think I shut down my Vietnam side for about 20 years after that whole debacle. I didn't want to see, hear, or read anything about Vietnam.

When I got married in 1990, I finally found a woman who didn't give a shit that I was a Vietnam vet. Her father was career Navy. I knew her for ten years before I could trust her and myself enough to ask her to marry me. I went through probably 50 relationships with women. Especially early on, they'd find out I was a vet and they would drop me, which hurt. I met Judy and she basically pulled me out. I was wallowing, pretty much, in my pity and my depressions and my anger and everything. I had gotten into a couple of motorcycle accidents, and I had done some real stupid things. Just doing stupid, stupid things. Going to bars and trying to get in fights. Trying to punch out police officers and just being a complete reprobate. Then I met Judy. We got married in 1990. I went back to school at the university and got my bachelor's degree. There was a professor there that I met who was also a Vietnam vet: 23 years in the Marines. He was the first vet that actually sat down with me and talked about how we felt: our emotions; what it was like in combat; what that first firefight was like; the first time I sat down and talked to somebody one on one like that. That kind of brought me out of my denial.

LIFE AFTER NAM

In 1995, when I was in graduate school, three hours short of getting my master's degree, getting ready for my oral comps, I lost it. I started dreaming about Vietnam again, which I hadn't done. I started drinking heavily again. For some reason Vietnam just came smacking me right in the face. I woke up one day after a real three-day drunk. My wife said, "You need to get some help. You need to go out to the VA." I was reluctant to do that. I didn't think there was anything they could do. I went out there for her, not for me. I got out there and met some great counselors there. They told me first, I had to go to substance abuse because I was just tearing up my body from the alcohol I was doing. After that substance abuse program, they did a PTSD assessment, and they said that they wanted me to go through a program out there. I thought about it for about three months and then decided, "Okay, I'm going to do this." I went to the program; it was terrific. It made me understand why I had lived my life the way I had been living it. I tried to understand my emotions better. They gave me coping mechanisms that I could use. It was a godsend and a lifesaver. It saved my marriage and probably saved my life. I'm sure that I wouldn't be alive today if it wasn't for the VA.

I go to the vet center now, once a week. I've been doing that since 1995. Being around other veterans who feel the same way I do has helped me just tremendously. I guess my feeling of loneliness in this whole thing after I came home, that I was the only one who was feeling this, and I was the only one who had gone through these things after the war. Then I met other people that had been doing it. There was nothing wrong with it. I mean, we're not evil people. The VA has done a great job. The vet center I go to is one of the best things I've done. It's not necessarily a struggle every day, but it's something I have to be aware of constantly. They taught me that there are certain emotions, certain anniversary dates that are going to make me feel a certain way. Now, I can see them coming and I can cope with them much better. I have people to talk to. I think that's a big thing with me. I just feel lucky as hell that I have a wonderful wife that loves me. Also I have other vet friends who can understand and give me their opinion and their coping mechanisms they use and I just feel very lucky.

VIETNAM

[Before I started treatment] I always felt ashamed. I felt that I had done something wrong. The whole guilt thing about "why did I survive?" So many good men I knew didn't make it. The best people I knew in Vietnam died. Why did I survive? I'm not this great, good person. I came to realize after talking to my therapist out there and going through the PTSD group out there, I must have done something right because I'm here. I've come to realize that I'm here for a purpose. I'm not sure what it is yet, but I survived. I have to keep the memory of the men that I loved in Vietnam; I have to keep their memory alive. I have to try to live my life as good and as honorable and as peaceful and with as much integrity and dignity as these men would have lived their lives. My guilt isn't about survival anymore. My guilt, which is not as severe, is about me not doing certain things. I'm not guilty about anything I did in Vietnam. It's more about if I had been a little bit quicker, a little bit more aware. But that guilt has been fairly well coped with. I feel that my service to my country, but especially to the men I served with, was well worth it. I would do it again in a millisecond if I could serve with the same men I did. For a long time, I never thought that.

The good thing that came out of Vietnam for me was the people I served with. We were the best. These men were the best people I've ever known. I tried to explain that to my wife, my wife and my friends, and it's hard. I love my friends. I love my wife. These guys, we went through something that I can't describe. I've always been loyal to them. If they ever wanted me to do anything now, I would be right there next to them. That, to me, is the best thing that's come out of Vietnam. Just that feeling that we did something that most people haven't done. We did it with honor and integrity. We weren't the horrible things that we were told when we came home, that I bought into. I lost the faith, but I've gotten it back now. *Semper Fidelis* is that term that the Marine Corps uses as our motto. I wasn't always faithful, even though I should have been. I've gained that faith back, I think. I have to honor the men who did not come back with the ones who came back or were seriously wounded.

LIFE AFTER NAM

STEVE HUNTSMAN
Member of 1st Platoon of Charlie Company

I got out of the Army there at Fort Knox. I was there about a year and a half, I guess. I don't know exactly how long it was. I moved to St George, Utah and started school again at St George. I was going to school on the GI Bill. I only went about a year and a half, and then I dropped out. My daughter had to have her tonsils out, and I didn't have the money to pay for it so I dropped out of school, tried to find work, pay my bills, and then go back to school. But I never made it back to school.

After I dropped out of school, I went to work as a truck driver for a trucking company. And that's what I did for 27 years. I retired from that. And that's when I went through most of my problems, during those 27 years. Actually, it turned out to be 32 or 33 years without any help for my problems. My kids didn't even know I had been in Vietnam. I didn't talk to anybody, my first wife, nobody.

I'm on my fifth marriage now, and she understands because she has gone through my learning I had problems, my PTSD, with me. We've been married about five years, and she is really, really good. She's listened to me and helped me out. She's a nurse, so she's a caregiver anyway. But she is really, really good to try to understand what I'm going through. Some of the others, well they weren't so understanding. They didn't care at all. Most of 'em didn't know what I was doing because I didn't. They give you that list of PTSD symptoms, and I had probably 85 percent of them. I stayed in an alcohol-induced stupor all the times I wasn't working. And obviously that's not good for family or friends or anybody else.

The only thing that got me to the VA in the first place was living in Vegas. And just about the time I had this meltdown, my uncle, he was in Korea, he had been trying to get me to go see somebody at the VA, and I just wouldn't go for it. Finally I had a meltdown. I was watching a basketball game on TV. The TV camera panned around this referee just as he blew his whistle, and it just brought everything screaming back. There was a flashback, and I felt like my whole inside, guts and organs, were flowing out from the bottom of my feet. I just went into a deep panic like something's happening. That's the best way I can describe it. It just felt like everything was sinking out from my body through the ends of my feet. Pat [my present wife] wasn't there when it happened. And when she got home, I was lying on the bed crying. And she had no clue what it was about. And I was just in real bad panic mode, just thinking man there's something wrong here.

I was still drinking at the time. Every day I'd get home from work and either get a beer or something else. I'd sit down and watch TV. She didn't come home until three or four hours after I did. I worked earlier. She just tried to talk to me, and I tried to explain to her what happened. It was getting later in the evening, and I just told her that I had to find some help. And she said, well why don't you go to the VA? So, I told her I was gonna go, and the next morning I did.

I didn't have an appointment, but they said if I sit down there, they'd take me if I waited until an opening came up. So I did. And when I walked in the office, a doctor asked me what he could do to help me, and I said, "I don't know. I don't know what's wrong." He said, "Well, tell me the feelings you had," and I start telling him. And he just stopped me right there. He said, "I know what's wrong with you; you don't have to go any farther. You've got PTSD." And I said, "What the hell's that?" I'd never even heard of it before that. And so he prescribed some medication, and he said, "If you can't fill them [the prescriptions], I'll have to put you in a hospital." I said, "Okay, I'll try." I managed through that.

With this guy I was going to see, I really developed a bond with him. He helped me learn how to deal with the symptoms and the triggers and stuff like that. He'd point them out to me, and I think I'm doing fairly well on that now because when I get some of these feelings now I can stop, think where they're coming from and what to do about them. He did a great job for me.

I've asked my sister if I had changed after the war, and she said, "Yeah, you weren't even the same person when you came back." And I didn't see it. I never did see it. She's told me here within the last month that I was not the same person after I got back. Today I don't want to see things that remind me of Vietnam. I just want to be normal.

LIFE AFTER NAM

BARBARA JOHNS
Wife of Jack Geoghegan

[After the death of Jack] I had Cammie, and I didn't want to seek employment somewhere and leave her. I promised her I would be both parents to her, and I didn't want to leave her upbringing to a babysitter. Of course, Jack's parents were right there, but I would not have wanted them to feel that they had full-time care of her. So I didn't seek employment but joined the League of Women Voters, I did a lot of writing, I gave talks to schools and church groups about our time in Africa. I filled my time with a lot of that.

I'd go out on dates, but I never met anybody that I could be serious about. And that didn't bother me because I really didn't think I would marry again. I was very content with my memories of Jack, and that would sustain me my whole life, I thought, at age 23. Of course, let's see now. That would have been a couple of years later, so it was 1968 when I met John Johns. And I liked John. As soon as I met him I liked him very much, but I didn't think I would be serious about him. I just liked him very much. He called me a couple of weeks later. He went to Alabama, where he's from, for Christmas. When he came back to West Point, he called me. He's almost 14 years older than I am, and I had never dated anybody more than two or three years older. So that was something. So he was 40 and I was 26. But then I did go out with him and I liked him very, very much, and I realized that people my own age or even a couple of years older seemed so immature to me after what I had been through, that my life had taken such a dramatic turn and it aged me quite a bit. So the age difference really didn't matter to me. We didn't know each other terribly long before we got married. We met in December of '68 and were married on April 5, 1969, then we moved to West Point – or I moved to West Point.

Of course, being a military man himself, he was aware of that battle and all of it. It just saddened him tremendously, too, to have – I guess meeting somebody like me who had been through this really brought it home to him again. He had also had friends who were killed in Vietnam. But it was very important to John to carry on Jack's memory. I don't mean on a day-by-day basis. He didn't close the door when we were married and that's the end of that – not anything like that. In fact, when we were married, Jack's parents came to our wedding. We just had a small wedding ceremony and then a small luncheon, and they didn't want to come to it at first because they felt they were casting a shadow on a happy event just by being there, and he insisted that they be there, that it just wouldn't be right for them not to be. So they did come there and to the wedding reception, and I was very glad they did. And I felt very good about the fact that they were there, the fact that they were part of the transition to a new life, and it was very, very important for them to be there. I couldn't imagine my life continuing without them being in it. That was something else that was important to John, that we spend time with them, and when we were still living at West Point, we would visit Connecticut. It was also important for Cammie to spend time with her grandparents.

Cammie adored John because he was very good with children. She was very, very fond of him, and he was very good to her. He was a wonderful father to her. And one thing that Jack's mother requested of John was that he not change her name because she felt that if John adopted Cammie and changed her name it would be that Jack would lose his daughter, is the way they felt about it. And John had no problem with that at all. It didn't make any difference to him in how he could be a father to Cammie. She always remained Camille Geoghegan.

[In 1997] Cammie and I and John and our other two children went to the Vietnam Memorial where General Hal Moore [Jack's commander during the battle of the Ia Drang Valley] presented the Silver Star to Cammie at the Vietnam Wall. That wall is like a shrine. It's incredible what it has done for people. I always felt that it actually had to be in place before people could appreciate it. It must be very hard to imagine what somebody said what it was going to be, and it would be very hard to picture the impact it would have on people, to actually have this wall with fifty-eight thousand names on it. It really makes you realize the tremendous sacrifice those men made in all wars, but it's the first time I guess they ever had a wall with names on it.

[Jack's death] was a subject that was always open to Cammie to talk about if she wanted to, and if there was ever a time that I might try to prompt her to ask about it, she shied away from it a lot throughout her teenage years. She always knew that her father was killed in Vietnam, but we didn't dwell on it or talk about it a great deal. She was just aware of it, and we were open to any questions she might have. But it wasn't until much later, even when Joe Galloway was writing – Joe and General Moore were writing the book [*We Were Soldiers Once ... and Young*] – Joe asked me if I would be willing to write part of the chapter on the families left behind, and he wanted Cammie to, also. But she never could do it. She just couldn't. She was still pushing that aside. I think she was fearful of the emotions that it would bring out in her. I'm not sure she knows why she tended to shy away from it. So it wasn't until later and it wasn't until she was married and had children, her first child, I think she realized. She looked at Stephanie and realized that Stephanie wouldn't be there if her father hadn't been there and the ongoing generations, the fact that he lives on, not just in her but in his granddaughters. And I think that really had a profound effect on her. That in itself, and then she was older and more mature and more able to deal with the emotions of it. And she can get very, very, very emotional about it. And then when the book and later, the movie, and all the people she has met because of the movie [*We Were Soldiers*]. We went up to what was Pennsylvania Military College, now Widener University, and they had a special screening of the movie the year that it came out, 2002.

We went there because they had a special showing of it and many of Jack's classmates were there, and they were so startled, many of them, when they saw Cammie because a couple of them said, "She looks exactly like him." She does. "She's a female Jack," they would say. And she does. She has always looked like him and that's always been wonderful. She doesn't have the red hair and freckles but she has his features. Stephanie, her daughter, has the freckles.

CARL CORTRIGHT

Member of 1st Platoon of Charlie Company

I felt kind of sorry for myself for a while. Then a couple of months went by in the hospital recuperating, and I realized that half the guys in my situation were quadriplegics; some couldn't even use their hands. I had full use of my hands. You haven't lived until you try to get your clothes off when you are paralyzed. That was frustrating for a few weeks. But then I realized that those other guys can't even move out of their beds; they have to have help to do almost everything. One guy was cheering me on, and he only had partial use of one arm. I thought that was something. So I stopped feeling so damn sorry for myself after that. I could get in my chair and leave; get in my car and go. They retired me in the hospital. I had been in military service exactly one year.

When I got out of the hospital for good I went to live with my parents. The VA got me a wheelchair. In 1970 I bought a home in Oxnard [California] that a government grant helped pay for. I was on 100 percent disability, so there was no problem there. Getting back to life was a slow process. I did a lot of traveling with my parents. We had a mobile home. One year we went all the way to Maine. It was hard getting around in a wheelchair at first. In those days wheelchairs were heavy. But when you are 21 you can overcome almost anything. It didn't take me long to get used to it. I went to a few parties and tried to forget about my troubles for a little while. I went out to movies and started dating. I bought a car with hand controls. Went cruisin'. People are still surprised to this day that I drive. There was no such thing as handicapped access back then. You had to look to park by a curb to get your wheelchair out. Handicapped parking started because of Vietnam. Us Vietnam vets were coming back, and we needed a spot where we could open up our doors wide. These guys would park next to you and you couldn't get in or out. In the early days my dad would ride with me and get my chair out of the back seat. When I started dating, though, that wouldn't work. So I would fold up the chair by myself and put it behind the front seat. It was complicated getting in and out, but I did it.

LIFE AFTER NAM

I used to have nightmares at first for a few years. Everything was slow motion; I couldn't get away. But I don't have those anymore. It bothers me a little bit, but it's nothing I can't handle. I belong to a veterans' group. It doesn't do any good to be bitter. It happened. Sometimes I'm bitter when I think about Johnson or McNamara and the farce over there. But life goes on. The protests irked me at first. We weren't treated very good when we first got back. The media portrayed us as cold-hearted gun slingers who were always shooting women or children. When I saw Saigon fall, I thought of the guys who were wounded or killed and wondered if it was all for nothing. What was it for? I met a woman in 1979, and we were married in 1981. I had a stepchild, and we divorced in 1989. At first I wasn't working, but I went to college and got a certificate in photography. That was kind of fun. Then I got into working with stained glass. I also did some work with photo imaging. I also do a lot of traveling. Every year I go to the largest veterans' wheelchair games in the world: the National Veterans Wheelchair Games. They have 15 or 20 events. Now I compete in trap shooting. I got a gold in trap shooting; I can't believe it. There are usually about 600 of us. You can do up to five sports, and I chose four. I compete in bowling, airgun, table tennis, and trap shooting. Years ago there was a social worker at the VA who kept asking me to go. For years she kept asking me, "When are you going to come with us?" I always said, "Well, I'll think about it." Next year she would ask again. Finally, it was in 1995, I thought, "Why not just go?" So I told her, "You know what? I think I'm going to go this year." My first one was in Atlanta. It is very similar to the Olympics. In fact the Olympics [in Atlanta] were the next year. They had hundreds of veterans in this big, huge hotel. What it was was a dry run for the Olympics. What is great about it is that you get to connect with other folks like yourself. Normally when you go out you are around very few other people in wheelchairs. But now you get to see hundreds of people who are just like you. For just a short while, like one week, it is like we are the norm.

BIBLIOGRAPHY

ORAL INTERVIEWS

Extensive oral interviews with Vietnam veterans and their family members form the bedrock source for this work. Several of the interviews are taken from the extensive collection of the Oral History Collection of the Vietnam Center and Archive at Texas Tech University. Interviews with veterans and family members of Charlie Company, 4th of the 47th are part of the author's collection and are housed in the Center for Oral History and Cultural Heritage at the University of Southern Mississippi.

Vietnam Center and Archive Interviews
Gary Franklin; Anthony Goodrich; Barbara Johns; Pauline Laurent; Frank Linster; James Moran; Darryl Nelson

Charlie Company Collection Interviews
Carl Cortright; Bernice Geier; James Geier; Ernie Hartman; Jeannie Hartman; Barbara Hill; Steve Hopper; Steve Huntsman; Mike Lethcoe; Larry Lukes; Terry McBride; James Nall; Walter Radowenchuk; Alan Richards; Richard Rubio; Frank Schwan; Kirby Spain; Elijah Taylor; Don Trcka; Ron Vidovic; John Young

SECONDARY SOURCES
9th Infantry Division: "Old Reliables," (Paducah, KY: Turner Publishing, 2000).

VIETNAM

Appy, Christian, *Vietnam: The Definitive Oral History Told from All Sides* (New York: Ebury Press, 2003).

Appy, Christian, *Working-Class War: American Combat Soldiers and Vietnam* (Chapel Hill: University of North Carolina Press, 1993).

Atkinson, Rick, *The Long Gray Line: The American Journey of West Point's Class of 1966* (Boston: Houghton Mifflin Company, 1989).

Clarke Jeffrey J., *Advice and Support: The Final Years* (Washington: Center of Military History, 1988).

Croizat, Victor, *The Brown Water Navy: The River and Coastal War in Indo-China and Vietnam, 1948–1972* (Poole, UK: Blandford Press, 1984).

Cutler, Thomas, *Brown Water, Black Berets: Coastal and Riverine Warfare in Vietnam* (Annapolis: Naval Institute Press, 1988).

Dunnavent, R. Blake, *Brown Water Warfare: The U.S. Navy in Riverine Warfare and the Emergence of a Tactical Doctrine, 1775–1970* (Gainesville: University Press of Florida, 2003).

Edelman, Bernard, *Dear America: Letters Home from Vietnam* (New York: Pocket Books, 1985).

Fawcett, Bill, *Hunters & Shooters: An Oral History of the U. S. Navy Seals in Vietnam* (New York: Harper, 1995).

Fitzgerald, Frances, *Fire in the Lake: The Vietnamese and the Americans in Vietnam* (New York: Random House, 1972).

Forbes, John and Robert Williams, *The Illustrated History of the Vietnam War: Riverine Force* (New York: Bantam, 1987).

Fulton, Major General William, *Vietnam Studies: Riverine Operations, 1966–1969* (Washington, D.C.: Department of the Army, 1985).

Gregory, Barry, *Vietnam Coastal and Riverine Forces* (Wellingborough, UK: Patrick Stevens, 1988).

Hunt, Major General Ira, *The 9th Infantry Division in Vietnam: Unparalleled and Unequaled* (Lexington: University Press of Kentucky, 2010).

Karnow, Stanley, *Vietnam: A History* (New York: Viking, 1983).

Krepinevich, Andrew Jr., *The Army in Vietnam* (Baltimore: Johns Hopkins University Press, 1986).

Lehrack, Otto, *No Shining Armor: The Marines at War in Vietnam: An Oral History* (Lawrence: University Press of Kansas, 1992).

Maraniss, David, *They Marched Into Sunlight: War and Peace, Vietnam and America, October 1967* (New York: Simon & Schuster, 2003).

Maurer, Harry, *Strange Ground: An Oral History of Americans in Vietnam, 1945–1975* (New York: De Capo, 1998).

McAbee, Ronald, *River Rats: Brown Water Navy, U.S. Naval Mobile Riverine Operations, Vietnam* (Honoribus Press, 2001).

MacGarrigle, George, *Combat Operations. Taking the Offensive: October 1966 to October 1967* (Washington, D.C.: Center of Military History, 1998).

BIBLIOGRAPHY

Marolda, Edward and Oscar Fitzgerald, *The United States Navy and the Vietnam Conflict, Vol. 2, From Military Assistance to Combat, 1959–1965* (Washington: Naval Historical Center, 1986).

Mobile Riverine Force. America's Mobile Riverine Force in Vietnam (Paducah, KY: Turner Publishing, 2005).

Moore, Harold and Joseph Galloway, *We Were Soldiers Once ... And Young: Ia Drang, the Battle that Changed the War in Vietnam* (New York: Random House, 1992).

Moyar, Mark, *Triumph Forsaken: The Vietnam War, 1954–1965* (New York: Cambridge University Press, 2006).

Prados, John, *Vietnam: The History of an Unwinnable War, 1945–1975* (Lawrence: University Press of Kansas, 2009).

Race, Jeffrey, *War Comes to Long An* (Berkeley: University of California Press, 1972).

Santoli, Al, *Everything We Had: An Oral History of the Vietnam War by Thirty-Three American Soldiers Who Fought It* (New York: Ballantine, 1981).

Sheehan, Neil, *A Bright Shining Lie: John Paul Vann and America in Vietnam* (New York: Random House, 1988).

Sorley, Lewis, *The Vietnam War: An Assessment by South Vietnam's Generals* (Lubbock: Texas Tech University Press, 2010).

Terry, Wallace, *Bloods: Black Veterans in the Vietnam War: An Oral History* (New York: Ballantine, 1985).

Tucker, Spencer, *Encyclopedia of the Vietnam War: A Political, Social, and Military History* (Oxford: Oxford University Press, 2001).

Uhlig, Frank ed., *Vietnam: The Naval Story* (Annapolis, MD: Naval Institute Press, 1986).

Westmoreland, William, *A Soldier Reports* (New York: Doubleday, 1976).

Wiest, Andrew, *The Vietnam War, 1956–1975* (Oxford: Osprey, 2002).

Wiest, Andrew, *Vietnam's Forgotten Army: Heroism and Betrayal in the ARVN* (New York: NYU Press, 2008).

Willbanks, James, *Vietnam War Almanac* (New York: Checkmark Books, 2010).

ACKNOWLEDGEMENTS

As in any work of scholarship, I have accumulated debts both large and small in the course of working on this project. I would like to thank the wonderful staff at Osprey Publishing, especially Kate Moore and Marcus Cowper (publishers) Emily Holmes (project editor), Julie Frederick (copyeditor) and John Tintera for first helping to dream up this project and then for shepherding it along its path to fruition.

I owe many thanks to my wonderful colleagues at the University of Southern Mississippi, especially those who work with me in the Center for the Study of War and Society – Susannah Ural, Kyle Zelner, Heather Stur, Kenneth Swope, Allison Abra, and Mao Lin. You are wonderful friends who push me forward and make it fun to come to work every day. Special thanks goes out to our History Department Chair, Phyllis Jestice, who read my manuscript and helped in so many ways to make it better.

During my time working on this project, I have been the fortunate recipient of funding from the University of Southern Mississippi without which this book would not have been possible. In 2008 I received an Aubrey and Ella Ginn Lucas Endowment for Faculty Excellence research award and in 2009 I was named Charles W. Moorman Distinguished Alumni Professor.

The funding associated with these two important honors was central to my success in this project.

My thanks also goes out to Steve Maxner and his staff at the Vietnam Center and Vietnam Archive at Texas Tech for their work in collecting and then transcribing many of the interviews utilized in this study. Closer to home, Ruth White and Jeremy George – two of our top graduate students – provided me with tremendous aid in transcribing many of the interviews in my own collection. Special thanks go out to Robert Thompson, another of our graduate students and a Vietnam scholar in his own right, who both did the transcriptions for and wrote the introductions to chapters 3, 7, and 9. I also owe a debt of gratitude to Corrina Thompson for cheerfully allowing Robert time away from a very busy schedule to work on this book with me.

My greatest thanks, though, go out to the veterans and their families whose stories appear in these pages. They not only served their nation with honor but also they sat down and were interviewed for hours, often covering some of the most difficult experiences of their lives with relative strangers, to help ensure that the true story of their experiences the Vietnam War was never forgotten. Finally, I offer my profound thanks to my wonderful family – my wife Jill and my children Abigail, Luke, and Wyatt. They make every day joyously fun and don't seem to mind when I disappear to write.

If you enjoyed this book you should read Andrew Wiest's recent book The Boys of 67: Charlie Company's War in Vietnam. *This is an exclusive extract from the book, which is available now from all good bookstores and is widely available as an eBook from all online sellers and from www.ospreypublishing.com*

THE BOYS OF '67: CHARLIE COMPANY'S WAR IN VIETNAM

BY ANDREW WIEST

PRELUDE: LOSING THE BEST WE HAD

May 18
1 Year and 1 Day [since being drafted]

Dear Mom, Dad and Fran,

I shouldn't tell you this, but you'll worry anyway, so I'll tell you. We ran into a battalion of 300 VC ... and they pinned us down... It started about 11 A.M. and we were still there at 6:30 that evening! I always thought I'd be scared to death in a situation like that, but you don't have time. When you hear a bullet go by (and you can hear it!) you just look around and say "you dirty son of a _____" and fire back. You are so excited that you don't even think, you don't have to, you react. You're laying there,

40 guys, knowing that there is a hell of a lot of Charlies out there and all of a sudden the jets start bombing and strafing, artillery zeroes in, and the helicopter gunships start their destruction. And then you feel like you just won the Irish Sweepstakes! Your wife had a baby! Or the Cubs won the World Series! Probably all 3 rolled into one. Charlie started out with 300 guys that day, and left 150 lying in the field when he pulled out at nightfall. It is not good to kill, but it also is worse to be killed and I can't say that I have a guilty fiber in my body.

Love,
Jim [Dennison]

On the evening of May 15, 1967, the bone-weary draftees of Charlie Company settled down into their night defensive positions, but few of the exhausted men could sleep. Some tossed and turned in the mud, while others gathered in small groups and discussed in hushed tones the adrenalized yet devastating events of the day.

It had been a day like any other, more notable for boredom and exhaustion than imminent death. With uniforms soaked to the skin in the 110-degree heat and unable to walk along the dikes, which were likely to be mined or booby trapped, the men had humped M16s, LAWs (Light Anti-Armor Weapons), M60 machine guns, spare ammo, spare barrels, and radios through the sucking, leech-infested paddy mud. Dug into invisible bunkers amid the dense foliage, a reinforced company of Viet Cong had waited until 1st Platoon had reached the middle of a wide paddy, where there was no cover, before springing a well-laid ambush, raking the Americans with small arms and automatic weapons fire. Amid the sudden fury a few GIs froze, one even lost control of his bowels, but the vast majority of the Charlie Company draftees reacted as their months of training had dictated. While the 2nd and 3rd Platoons laid down a covering fire, the 1st and 3rd squads of 1st Platoon were able to scramble to cover behind nearby rice paddy dikes. The men of 2nd Squad, though, had been caught too far out in the open and fell where they had stood.

The battle had raged for most of the day; Charlie Company had attempted both to flank the well-concealed enemy positions and to rescue its fallen even as air and artillery strikes turned the tide against the Viet Cong. Finally, as evening neared, facing certain death at the hands of overwhelming American firepower, the surviving VC had burst into the open in a desperate bid to flee their crumbling bunkers. It had been a powerfully cathartic moment for the men of Charlie Company. After months of taking losses to unseen enemy snipers or booby traps and a day of battle against invisible foes in bunkers, there they were – live VC. Mud spattered, black pajama-clad Victor Charles. Fire rang out from M16s, M60s, LAWs, and grenade launchers, and the killing was prodigious. With dead VC littering the landscape as night fell, by any accounts Charlie Company's battle had been a victory.

It was neither their victory nor the killing that were the main topics of quiet conversation that night. The firefight had been Charlie Company's first major engagement – its baptism by fire – and, amazingly, it had taken place exactly one year to the day after most of the men in the company had opened their mailboxes to find their draft notices. In the eerie calm that follows battle and as the heat slowly dissipated in the tropic night, the men of Charlie Company spoke of loss – the abrupt and brutal loss of friends with whom they had trained, sweated, and toiled for a year of military life; the loss of their brothers.

Fourteen men had been wounded that day. While some of their wounds had been slight, others had been ghastly. Charlie Nelson, a Navajo Indian of whom the men of Charlie Company had become quite protective because of his diminutive stature, had been shot through the neck while attempting to help a buddy and had later received a second wound when a Viet Cong bullet sliced through his knee. Dave Jarczewski, who had stooped to help the fallen Nelson, had been shot through the shoulder. The bullet had exited through his back resulting in internal injuries that had left Jarczewski gasping for breath and turning blue as he hovered near death. Steve Huntsman had been hit in the arm, severing an artery that spewed a fountain of blood each time his heart beat. James "Smitty" Smith had hit the ground and held his arms in front of his head; the bullet that struck his forearm otherwise would have hit him square in the face. Tony Caliari had a bullet pass through his lower leg, shattering the bones and leaving his foot flopping uselessly. The explosion of a rifle grenade had left Don Trcka with wounds to his stomach and jaw, and he had also been shot through the arm. Worst, perhaps, was Carl Cortright, a recent replacement who was on one of his first operations with Charlie Company. Caught with those unlucky few who were furthest from cover, Cortright had been shot below the breastbone, and the bullet had exited through his spine, leaving him paralyzed. After lying helplessly for hours, Cortright had finally been rescued but had to be manhandled over the protective rice paddy dike, resulting in excruciating agony.

Emergency medevac helicopters had rushed to the scene to retrieve the most badly wounded. There had been no time for niceties, for speed was critical to saving lives. As the battle continued to rage, those who were still sound had wrestled the shattered bodies of their brothers onto the choppers, which had then sped them to hospitals at Dong Tam and Bien Hoa. For those who remained behind on the battlefield that night, dealing with the wounded had been jarring and unsettling. These men with whom they had trained, whose letters from home they had shared, were simply gone. One minute they were there like always, the next they were covered in their own blood, the tips of broken bones protruding from their wounds. Then they were simply and abruptly gone.

Whether silently wrapped in personal remembrance or in quiet commiseration with others, on the night of May 15 the thoughts of everyone in Charlie Company centered on the death Don Peterson. "Pete," as he was known to many, had been a strapping kid from California. Good looking, and with an easy sense of humor, Peterson was respected and universally liked. In a group made up almost wholly of young men aged 19–21, Pete stood out from the crowd as one of the few who were married. While at Fort Riley, Pete and his wife Jacque had shared a cramped, off-base apartment with two of the other married couples from the unit, Don and Sue Deedrick and Steve and Karen Huntsman. Even the most convinced bachelors of Charlie Company felt an affinity for those few in their midst who had chosen to take on the responsibility of marriage amid the uncertainty of training for war and respected the difficulties the young couples faced. For Pete, though, the bonds of friendship with the men of Charlie Company had run even deeper. Just before his departure for Vietnam, Jacque had given birth to the couple's first child, Jimmy. Having spent only a few moments with his son before departing, Pete had carried a single picture of the child to Vietnam – a picture that everyone in Charlie Company knew well. Pete had never tired of showing that picture off – to audiences from sweaty base camps to muddy foxholes – always ready to talk about the future that he planned to share with his son. Although half a world away, through quiet conversations with a proud father amid the crucible of war, the men of Charlie Company had become Jimmy Peterson's surrogate uncles and cousins.

Pete had been hit in the chest by a burst of Viet Cong fire as he had tried to cover 2nd Squad's retreat from the kill zone, but it was near dusk before two members of 1st Platoon, Doug Wilson and John Bauler, had been able to retrieve Pete's body from the battlefield. Heavy enemy fire, the need to evacuate the badly wounded who still had a chance to survive, the rush to resupply dwindling ammo reserves, and the need to keep down during incoming friendly artillery fire and jet strikes – the symphonic chaos of battle – had all taken precedence. As darkness fell First Sergeant Lynn Crockett, a hard-bitten farm boy from Kentucky who had turned career soldier, knew the difficult truth. There would be no more evac flights; Pete would spend one more night with Charlie Company. Standing 6 feet 5 inches tall, features chiseled by a lifetime of hard work, Crockett was the looming figure who had met the bewildered Charlie Company recruits as they had arrived at Fort Riley. While he had been a feared and respected presence during training, making liberal use of his booming voice and the colorful lexicon of a drill sergeant, over the past year Crockett had become quite close to his men and knew that the difficult night ahead was going to be a formative moment for the company. Their year of training and war had been invaluable in that it had given Charlie Company a sharp edge, but Crockett also knew that his men had become brothers in the process, brothers who now had to wrestle with the loss of one of their own.

Determined to do what he could to help, Crockett began to make the rounds to speak to his men. The first man Crockett met was Ben Acevedo. Of Hispanic descent, "Ace," as he was known to all in Charlie Company, was the son of rural farm laborers in the Yakima Valley, Washington, and had taken an instant liking to Don Peterson in training. Ace struggled to understand the value of Pete's sacrifice. In tears, Ace asked Crockett, "First Sergeant, what the hell are we doing over here?" With a pat on the shoulder Crockett replied, "Son, we are over here because our country sent us over here. We are here to do our job."

As Crockett walked further he came to a small knot of silent men gathered around Pete's body. In that group was John Young, a short, wiry Minnesotan. Unlike most of Charlie Company, Young was not a draftee but instead had actively sought service in Vietnam. With a keen sense of duty, and afraid that the war would end before he could play his part, Young had dropped out of the University of Minnesota to enlist. A gung-ho true believer, Young found it jarring to deal with the loss of someone so close and with so much to live for, killed before his very eyes. When Crockett appeared, through his tears Young released a burden of regret that was common to the men of Charlie Company: "First Sergeant, we just couldn't find him out there; we just couldn't find him." Young had been part of a group of volunteers that had searched the battlefield under heavy enemy fire to retrieve the wounded – a group that had not been able to save Pete. Now Young and the others lived with that guilt – could they have saved him? Should they have saved him? Crockett did what he could to console the men. It had not been their fault. He stressed the brutal reality of combat; young men die – good young men, young men with everything to live for – and there was nothing that other young men, no matter how devoted and able, could do to change that.

All across their night defensive positions, the men of Charlie Company dealt with the losses of the day. Jim Dennison, a hardscrabble city kid whose father owned an Irish pub in Chicago, could not bring himself to look in the direction of Pete's body, feeling that if he didn't look it would not be real. But it was real, and had a transformative effect on the young Cubs fan. Before May 15 Dennison believed in the war, but after the loss of Peterson and the maiming of so many others he felt that his emotional spinal cord had been severed. As he sat there that night the same refrain ran through his mind over and over: "The war ain't fuckin' worth it. It ain't fuckin' worth it." Even as he wrestled with the eternal question of the value of war against the price of losing friends, Dennison's mind shifted to a common course for young men in combat – a course that eventually exacted a heavy price of guilt. He had loved Pete, and grieved for his young family – but after the intensity of battle Dennison was still alive, his dreams intact. Even though Pete was his hero and he had so much to live for, Dennison couldn't help thinking, "Thank God it was him and not me."

James Nall had developed a special relationship with Don Peterson. A poor black kid from the streets of Fairfield, Alabama, Nall had grown up with the harsh reality of segregation. Only permitted to drink from "colored" water fountains, Nall had never even tasted "white water" until he arrived at Fort Riley. Initially Nall had been very unsure about what his relationship with white soldiers would be like – until he met Pete. The happy-go-lucky Californian had only limited interaction with blacks before joining the military, but his easy demeanor immediately impressed Nall, and the two had become fast friends, with Nall being one of the first to learn of the birth of Pete's son. Crouched in a foxhole within sight of Pete's body, Nall realized that his whole life had been changed. It had taken a while for it to set in, but Pete was gone – this war was for keeps. Nall had lost a friend, one who had introduced him to a new way to look at the world, but his thoughts that night ran deeper and were more visceral. Before May 15, Nall, with the sure invulnerability of youth, had believed that he could not die in Vietnam. But there was Pete, lying close by – a body, beginning to smell after a day in the tropic sun – death had become real. Shaking both from the residual fear of the day and the onset of the relative cool of the night, Nall realized that anyone could die at any time in Vietnam. There was no such thing as invulnerability; there was only death.

Manning a defensive position in a nearby tree line, Doug Wilson, who had helped to carry Pete's body from the battlefield, had an eerie feeling as he heard quiet sobbing around him break the silence that night. Wilson was a kid from California, like Pete, who had been too interested in surfing to keep up his college grades, which had resulted in a surprise draft notice from Uncle Sam. Like everyone else, Wilson wept for Pete and for his wife and child, but as the night went on his thoughts drifted to the juxtaposition of the banality of war set alongside the human emotional shock of battle and loss. Pete was dead, and the wounded were struggling for their lives, but the war went on. Night defensive positions had to be dug and manned, supplies gathered, and tomorrow would be just another day of slogging through rice paddies looking for Viet Cong. The war didn't care about Pete, or Cortright, or Jarczewski, or the hundreds of enemy dead, or the strained nerves of the survivors – the war went on. To Wilson what had started as a job or perhaps even a needed crusade now seemed a slow march toward a distant goal. Reality became clear – it didn't matter how good or bad the next day was, the war was going to go on for another eight months or until the enemy got him too. And if he died, the men of Charlie Company would throw him onto a helicopter and continue their lives as their war marched on.

The next morning, as the men of Charlie Company gathered their gear and made ready to move out, a single helicopter arrived to take away the body of Don Peterson. The only other passenger on that chopper was Bill Reynolds, who was being sent to the rear to receive treatment for a painful cyst. Raised outside Los Angeles, Reynolds had been crazy about cars and loved the cruising and drag racing scene. Reynolds, like so many others, had looked up to Pete as a larger than life, heroic figure. As he squatted beside Pete and the chopper took off for the short ride back to the divisional base area at Dong Tam, the wash of the rotor blades blew the poncho off of Pete's body. For the remainder of the flight, Reynolds could not take his eyes off Pete. With tears running down his face, he thought, "Oh my God, if they can get Pete, we're all in big trouble."

INDEX

INDEX

INDEX

Anne Arundel County
Public Library
Severn
410-222-6280

Library name: PRO
Title: Vietnam : a view
from the front lines
Item ID:
31997082938150
Date due: 8/15/2018,23:
59

To renew your materials:
Go to the Library's
Website at www.aacpl.net

or call any branch.